New York and
the Literary Imagination

New York and the Literary Imagination

The City in Twentieth Century Fiction and Drama

EDWARD MARGOLIES

McFarland & Company, Inc., Publishers
Jefferson, North Carolina, and London

LIBRARY OF CONGRESS CATALOGUING-IN-PUBLICATION DATA

Margolies, Edward.
  New York and the literary imagination : the city in twentieth
century fiction and drama / by Edward Margolies.
    p.   cm.
  Includes bibliographical references and index.

  ISBN-13: 978-0-7864-3071-0
  softcover : 50# alkaline paper ∞

  1. American fiction — New York (State) — New York — History
and criticism.   2. American literature — 20th century — History
and criticism.   3. Literature and society — New York (State) — New
York — History — 20th century.   4. New York (N.Y.) — Intellectual
life — 20th century.   5. New York (N.Y.) — In literature.   I. Title.
PS374.N43M37   2008
813'.009327471 — dc22   2007036060

British Library cataloguing data are available

Cover images ©2008 Shutterstock

Manufactured in the United States of America

*McFarland & Company, Inc., Publishers
  Box 611, Jefferson, North Carolina 28640
  www.mcfarlandpub.com*

For Claire, as always

There now is your insular city of the Manhattoes, belted around by wharves as Indian isles by coral reefs — commerce surrounds it with her surf.

— Herman Melville

I'll make a brand-new start of it in old New York.

— Fred Ebb

The basis of ethics is man's right to play the game of his choice. I will not trample on your toys and you will not trample on mine; I won't spit on your idol and you will not spit on mine. There is no reason why hedonism, the cabala, polygamy, asceticism ... [a] blend of eroticism and Hasidism could not exist in a play-city or play-world, a sort of universal Coney Island....

— Isaac Bashevis Singer

And is New York the most beautiful city in the world? It is not far from it. No urban nights are like the nights there. I have looked down across the city from high windows. It is then that the great buildings lose reality and take on magical powers.... Squares and squares of flame set and cut into the ether. Here is our poetry, for we have pulled down the stars to our will.

— Ezra Pound

I see great forces at work; great movements; the large and small buildings, the warring of the great and small.... While these powers are at work ... I can hear the sound of their strife and there is great music being played. And so I try to explain graphically what a great city is doing.

— John Marin

In New York, who needs an atom bomb? If you walked away from a place, they tore it down.

— Bernard Malamud

... in the murky water of fetid tenements, a city of black people ... are convulsed in desperate living, like the voracious churning of millions of hungry cannibal fish. Blind mouths eating their own guts. Stick in a hand and draw back a nub.
   That is Harlem.

— Chester Himes

Is it the Lido I see or only Asbury Park?

— Cole Porter

New York is striped with parallel, incommunicable meanings.

— Jean-Paul Sartre

Fear not — submit to no models but your own O city!

— Walt Whitman

Table of Contents

Table of Contents

Preface

The germ of this book came to me about twenty to twenty-five years ago when I had begun teaching a college course called "The City in Literature." At the start, my students and I drew on how some characters act, react, and interact in their urban environments. It would not be long, however, until we saw that despite different time periods, culture, and geography, certain themes and images emerge and reemerge in very nearly all the works we looked at. So many of the authors, from the Bible's Genesis to Balzac, to Dickens, to Melville, portray their cities as roiling, unhealthy, corrupt, and evil places. It thus became clear to us that the myth of the wicked city had a very long lineage. Yet into these maelstroms, often enough, come heroes (chiefly) and heroines who may or may not survive and conquer. Their victories, however, are often dubious because they themselves become contaminated in the process. But what can we say of the defeated? Why do we mourn their losses when we know that what they sought could never have been attained in wicked surroundings? Perhaps we weep because underneath we also dream of cities as sites of enchantment, fame, power, wealth, and rebirth. Rather than a simplistic outlook, combinations of good and bad, positive and negative constitute a more sophisticated mythology.

Years afterwards it dawned on me to write about these contradictions and ambivalences in the literature of America, a new country whose cities were only recently created. And perhaps just as importantly, America had become a truly urban nation in the twentieth century. What about cities like Chicago, Los Angeles, San Francisco, Philadelphia, Boston? Did I know about these cities, their traditions, their ambience? Perhaps yes and no, but I didn't or hadn't lived in them long enough to feel somehow secure with their myths. Instead then, why not write about my own adopted city, New York, where I have lived for more than fifty years? New York's history and development and constant changes are surely both the same and different from those of other

1

cities. Still, where to start and how to separate the variegated strands of myths that have sprung up about the city? I decided to begin with twentieth-century authors because so many earlier American writings about cities resort to traditional one-dimensional images. I made exceptions for William Dean Howells and Stephen Crane because, it seemed to me, both authors anticipate so much of the complexity and outlook of their successors. And I decided to dwell less on any of the authors' lives than how their lives are expressed in the presentation of the city. Although I have given over more pages to some writers than to others, this should not necessarily be construed as an aesthetic judgment but rather as the way New York City myths have been projected.

I am surely responsible for the conclusions and inferences I have drawn, but I have benefited from some background histories which I believe have given me a better perspective. Among the many works I appreciated are *Mirror for Gotham* by Bayrd Still (1956); *American Moderns: Bohemian New York and the Creation of a New Century* by Christine Stansell (2000); *Gotham: A History of New York City to 1898* by Edwin G. Burrows and Mike Wallace (1999); *Working Class New York* by Joshua B. Freeman (2000); and, of course, the wonderful *Encyclopedia of New York City* edited by Kenneth T. Jackson (1995). And since I've devoted two chapters to the contrasting perceptions of Jews and African-Americans, I found several of the following works most informative: *World of Our Fathers* by Irving Howe (1976); *The Promised City: New York's Jews, 1870–1914* by Moses Rischin (1962); *The Image of the Jew in American Literature* by Louis Harap (1974); *Strangers in the Land: Blacks, Jews, Post-Holocaust America* by Eric J. Sundquist (2005); *Slavery in New York*, both edited and with an introduction by Ira Berlin and Leslie M. Harris (2005); *The Black New Yorkers: 400 Years of African American History*, the Schomburg Center for Research in Black Culture (2000); *Black Manhattan* by James Weldon Johnson (1930); *When Harlem Was in Vogue* by David Levering Lewis (1981); *The Afro-American Novel and Its Tradition* by Bernard W. Bell (1987); and *The Negro Novel in America* by Robert A. Bone (1965). I also found useful some detailed information of New York artistic and literary lore in each of the following: *The Art of the City* by Peter Conrad (1984); *Remarkable, Unspeakable New York: A Literary History* by Shaun O'Connell (1995); *New York Literary Lights* by William Corbett (1998); and *Literary New York* by Susan Edmeston and Linda D. Cirino (1976).

Finally I would like to acknowledge the support I have received in dealing with the computer monster from the following: Hazel Rowley, Walter and George Vranesh, Robert Baker, Robert Kreizel, and Joanne Davidson. I am also enormously grateful to my wife, Claire, who typed and helped me edit this book, to my son William, who also typed some material, to his brother Jacob, who came through with much "googled" research, and to Cyma Horowitz, library director of the American Jewish Committee's Blaustein Library.

Introduction

They all came to New York — authors as far back as Washington Irving at the birth of the Republic and extending to the present day. To name only a few: Edgar Allan Poe, Walt Whitman, Herman Melville, Willa Cather, F. Scott Fitzgerald, Saul Bellow, Thomas Wolfe, Richard Wright, and William Faulkner. Some loved the city's vitality, some feared the anomie; many had mixed feelings and moved away. Each felt intensely. Nor were they so different from the Spanish poet Garcia Lorca or the Dutch artist Piet Mondrian. One trembled at the city's menace, the other projected bright happy complex patterns he called *Broadway Boogie Woogie*.

When in 1889 the magisterial editor-author William Dean Howells gave up his longtime Boston residence to live in New York (having recently assumed the editorship of the relatively upstart *Harper's Magazine*), many among America's elite regarded the move as a distressing shift in cultural geography. Was Brahmin Boston, the cultural capital, losing out to the powerful financial attractions of polyglot New York? Until now the gothic popular fiction of nineteenth-century authors — George Lippard or George Thompson, as examples — painted the city in lurid tones of vice and crime. Even Matthew Hale Smith's celebrated study of contemporary New York (*Sunshine and Shadow in New York*, 1868) depicted considerably more shadow than sunshine. Among major writers, only Whitman imagined democratic possibilities — though even he expressed reservations in post–Civil War years. Herman Melville, meanwhile, envisioned the city's inhabitants as hellishly trapped or imprisoned.

In any case, what Howells' arrival portended, among other things, was a New York that would come under a revised scrutiny from American artists and authors. An "Ashcan" school of painting examining the city's street life would spring up at the start of the new century, although a decade earlier Howells would portray the city in his *A Hazard of New Fortunes* (1890) as almost a character in itself. Others followed suit — the city viewed as something more than a passive setting that alters or defines one's writing but also as an active agent that alters and defines the character of the author. Of course, an author's initial expectations and his responses to his life *in* the city are related to how he *sees* the city. And beyond, by portraying New York to accord with his experiences, the author may alter or redefine the image of the city — the way the world looks at the city, the way the city looks at itself. In this fashion, interminglings of history, personal experience, and dreams produce city myths. And what are these myths but collections of assumptions, ideas, and tales? Granted, they may contain underlying truths, but in the final analysis they are perceptions of a shifting, complicated, evolving, amorphous city. Yet though they may not always be logical or consistent, we cling to them as a means of understanding experience, of anchoring our sense of reality.

Mainly our writers were outsiders whose expectations were swallowed up in a mix of experiences they had not anticipated. Here at last, among the myriad identities the city proffered, they would discover their own. Alternatively, born and bred native New Yorkers who in time departed seldom escaped their city consciousness, and again and again imaginatively reentered the streets and neighborhoods of their childhood. What follows is by no means intended as comprehensive literary history, but rather to suggest varieties of transference between mind and city, city and mind.

To be sure, such exchanges do not occur in a cultural vacuum, and American perceptions of cities are fraught with ambiguities, as are their converse — small communities and nature herself. Although New York City most flagrantly flaunts its dangers and attractions, one must ask why Americans so often looked at cities with anxiety — an anxiety deeply embedded in the national psyche. Thomas Jefferson, for instance, feared for the character of city dwellers. They would, he said, depend for their survival on bankers, merchants, and manufacturers, and dependence on the uncertainties of urban capitalism breeds a vulnerability to demagogues. He would prefer a nation of self-sufficient farmers, closer to nature, to assure an enlightened democratic citizenry. Nature (domesticated), he believed, acted as an inherent good. Responses to cities today are not unlike Jefferson's. Civic unrest, amorality, and the artificiality of man-made environments are frequently cited as city problems — as if much the same could not be said of smaller communities. Still when the social ills of small communities are conceded, Americans tend to blame cities for their baleful influence. Do cities, in some peculiar fashion, infect the otherwise pure of heart? The constant consciousness of cities, even among those who utterly disdain their presence is, as we shall see, an admission of their determinative historic role.

Concomitant with negative perceptions of the city is a consensual view that America's institutional development — at least until the twentieth century — was determined by the accessibility, conquest, and settlement of relatively unclaimed (by whites) western lands. Might that not be putting the cart before the horse? That is to say, might not the conquest and settlement of the West represent a flight from the city, or more properly what the city seemed to symbolize, since in actuality most western expansion was undertaken by immigrants, farmers, or other persons living outside cities? And what the city symbolized, beyond its presumed negative associations, was authority. For were not cities, both European and American, centers of concentrated governmental, financial, and religious power? *Escape West* implied escape from the overarching authority of city institutions — an authority that restrained, taxed, and defined individuals according to social class.

The first West for Europeans was the East Coast of the North American continent. But, in general, as the nation expanded westward to the Pacific, American cities to the east appeared to appropriate the mantle of authority that European capitals once knew. By contrast, the aura of "West" would from time to time assume trans-geographical meanings, that is to say, areas apart and away from cities — perhaps, strangely, even east of cities, upstate, downstate, frontier, forests, small towns, villages. By distancing themselves from cities, Americans liked to imagine themselves distanced from authority, awakening to a new sense of independence. Surprisingly, some among the authority figures they fled applauded. At the nation's start, for example, Presidents Washington, Adams, Jefferson, and Madison knew well the history of worker-peasant uprisings in European cities, and with the specter of the violence and egalitarianism of the more recent French Revolution fresh in their minds, they welcomed an open, unclaimed West as a means of defusing class tensions in overcrowded cities. (This is not to say they could have been altogether easy about western farmers who twice in the late eighteenth century rebelled openly against paying government excise taxes and debts owed to eastern banker creditors.) Still, however varied their reasons, the rulers and the ruled, the governing class and the governed, more often than not at cross purposes, were usually at one about the desirability of the western expansion as opposed to the perils of the city. But as wilderness and frontier receded toward the end of the nineteenth century, cities and the West began to assume an additional, ambiguous, mythic baggage. Professor Frederick Jackson Turner, in a widely publicized 1893 address, declared western frontier settlements the historic guarantor of democratic institutions, his implication being that the closing of the frontier boded ill for the republic. Meanwhile nostalgic cultural references in the popular press portrayed the West as exemplifying the moral vigor and masculine energy of a younger American republic, now sadly dissipated by the presence of cities whose inhabitants lived lives of sybaritic decadence or proletarian barbarism. Pejorative allusions to cities were not, however, without their ironies when settlements in the West began producing the very phenomena for which the West was presumably intended as anodyne. Indeed, the very successes of western settlement caused western cities to spring up whose governing institutions were in large part modeled on those of eastern cities — which in turn catalyzed further waves of western emigration until at last it appeared there would be no more West to settle.

Despite such ironies, the rise of new cities was not always seen as a necessary evil. However much Americans claimed they detested cities, they also served paradoxically as a source of pride. Financial, cultural, and religious institutions were, after all, signs that high levels of civilization had been achieved. Fragmented visions of cities prevail to this day, but what makes the ambiguity especially odd is that, in addition to their usual mixed images, cities have paradoxically lately begun to assume the positive mythology of the West. Beginning in the 1890s (at about the time the census bureau announced officially that there no longer existed an extended unbroken western frontier) southern and eastern European immigrants began seeking in cities dreams long associated with the West: independence, personal freedoms, economic opportunity. They were joined, too, by vast numbers of rural Americans, white and black, displaced from their homes by technological advances, agricultural depression, and racial persecution. Although none would claim these groups got along famously with each other or with longer-established city dwellers, they are now frequently envisioned (often sentimentalized) as heroic, very much as were earlier generations of western emigrants. Just as early westerners had to subdue amoral untrammeled nature and "lawless" Indians, so must city newcomers deal with indifferent or hostile slums, lumpen gangs, and cruel or exploitative landlords and bosses. In the popular literature, lone rangers with John Wayne–like integrity, no longer able to find respite or to repurify themselves in open country, revert to cities as Philip Marlowe-like private eyes fighting crime and corruption. Moreover, the ordinarily exalted West may now on occasion be depicted as mean, bleak, narrow and provincial. One need only think as far back as Mark Twain or to more contemporary writers like Raymond Carver or Larry McMurtry, or to present-day films and documentaries deploring the West's ecological damage and the "genocidal" treatment of Indians. Finally, this peculiar reversal of East-West perceptions extends to individual freedoms. Whereas once the West inevitably tested an individual's resources for survival, a corrupted West may now compel him to conform to hypocritical standards.

The city serves as a countercultural vision — not despite but because of its seeming indifference to personal behavior, not despite but because of its seeming anarchy — allowing individuals psychological space to attain their possibilities without fear of societal disapproval. The very "formlessness" of cities may be viewed as a challenge to create structure, neighborhoods, or political, ethnic, social communities not unlike pioneers who dominate nature to create property and communities. If an open West once seemed to beckon persons who might otherwise crowd into cities, the cities may now relieve the distressed countryside of their dispossessed. But unlike previous settler generations, the new city dweller cannot hope for self-sufficiency in a corporate environment. Perhaps Jefferson's dream of an agrarian nation (impervious to the wiles of demagogues) never really had much of a chance in a nation determined from the start to become rich.

Few would dispute that New York's early history diverges considerably from that of other Atlantic coast cities. And yet in a curious way, New York history anticipates much of what concerns Americans today. Like other East Coast cities, New York was, as we have seen, the West for seventeenth-century Europeans departing their countries. But unlike other cities, New Amsterdam (as it was first called) could not very securely establish itself as a community ruled over and populated by a single ethnic or national or religious group. Try as they might, the city's Dutch governors were unable to persuade their Netherlands stockholder-employers to limit settlement to persons of Dutch origin and preferably to members of the Dutch Reform Church. As a consequence, when in 1664 the British took possession of New Amsterdam, the population consisted of sizable numbers of native Indians, Walloons, Finns, Swedes, Dutch, Irish, Jews, Huguenots, and Africans, not to mention varieties of religious worship. It is said, furthermore, that one could hear spoken on the streets of the newly named New York eighteen different languages. British rule contained no less diversity, and by the time New York was absorbed into the new American nation, immigrants from all parts continued to pour in. Meanwhile persons of black African ancestry — consisting of perhaps twenty percent of the population in the eighteenth century —

increased in number (though in lower percentages) over the next two centuries, especially after World War I with large infusions from the American South and the Caribbean. The city's ethnic proportions change constantly but never its heterogeneity. This is not to suggest that New York is or ever was a melting pot. Not quite. Still, in its fashion the city always was and remains a concentrated image of the country's population diversity. The writer who writes of a particular ethnic group senses constantly the hovering presence of others.

Obviously, a city with its plethora of subcultures is not always a happy microcosm of the nation at large. From the start, New York has had its share of lawlessness, poverty, civic corruption, racial and social tensions. What makes the city work — when it does — are the truces, the small compromises different groups make among themselves and one another. In their fashion interfusions of these sorts produce a kind of peculiar New York culture — and within the fluctuating culture, the writer discovers the ever–American struggle of the individual to realize himself in an ever-shifting community that makes demands on his freedom. The problem for the New York writer, often enough, is how to uncover the myths that explain his experience.

Complicating the problem is that the city looks to be without tradition. Rather, in fact, the city appears to be forever rebuilding itself, reinventing itself, reconstituting its image. Perhaps *this* is the tradition. To be sure, New York was not founded on ideological or religious or political grounds, and thus in later years has never had to bury or live up to romantic cachets associated with its birth. New York, pure and simple, was established to make money for its Dutch stockholders, and its moneymaking proclivities remain a constant lure. Newcomers have arrived for mainly economic opportunities (though often these are illusory), and shifts in population are generally determined by the flow of money in and out of the city. Freed of illusion and sentimentalities, while at the same time recognizing economic needs as essential for survival, New Yorkers have built a complex culture intended to slake the spiritual and aesthetic needs of its diverse, often restive communities. No other city has produced so rich a culture because, paradoxically, the main business of the city is not culture. And yet in no other city does there linger so strong a cultural consciousness of the mother countries of immigrants, not to mention the Southern cultures of migrating blacks. As a result, about the time of the decline of America's Old West, epiphanies of New York as a kind of hybrid cosmopolitan frontier town begin to emerge. By 1917, with America's entry into World War I, very nearly all New York narratives embrace thematic myths often associated with an idyllic American West alongside traditional mixed images of urban life.

Which elements of post-frontier myths an author appropriates (or reconstructs) depend on his predisposition. The city, so large and seemingly random, offers an abundance of choices. The city as a savage amoral Wild West (meshing sometimes imperceptibly with ancient visions of cities as evil and corrupt)—or the city as an imagined New West offering American dreams of self-renewal, self-reinvention, individualism, and promises of prosperity. Often, not surprisingly, some authors appear to embrace both views. In this fashion, by enlisting New York lore to accord with personal experience, the author may alter or redefine the city's mythology—the way the world looks at the city, the way the city looks at itself. Processes of the imagination produce reverberations.

As this book proposes, New York authors who trace their ancestry to antebellum generations interpret with variations city post-frontier mythology one way, immigrants another, African Americans yet another, and first-generation American Jews yet another. And not unrelated are authors who produce images of the city as failed romance, as fantasy, or magical promises unfulfilled. Not surprisingly, other authors convey self-contradictory love-hate western themes in projections of the city as a panorama or ship of fools where social and cultural conflicts resemble those of the larger nation. In extremis these myths may turn violently on themselves, describing death or defeat as a final resolution. But even here the city's singular vitality cancels out a gloomy prognosis—and New York lives on, however compromised, in readers' minds. Clearly, none of the books discussed fits easy definition, nor is that my intention. Art eludes strict classification and by its very nature embraces more than any single point of view. Yet segments of these works illustrate certain constants and paradoxes of New York City mythology, especially during the last hundred years.

Before proceeding, a few general remarks follow about what is not in this book. First, my regrets for writers omitted. Their numbers are countless. To name only a few: Mary Gordon, Ring Lardner, Jay McInerny, John O'Hara, J.D. Salinger, Edward Lewis Wallant, and John A. Williams. In the main they are skilled artists who may be as worthy as or superior to some of the writers selected, but for reasons both of focus and diversity I have here reluctantly relegated them to honorable mention. They do not add much to my main argument, that is, the constancy of New York myths and the variety of their interpretation as well as what they tell us about the larger

America. Doubtless readers will note, too, that for the most part the authors chosen are not native-born New Yorkers but come from elsewhere — foreign lands or other parts of the American continent — and so it is not unreasonable to suppose that they arrived with already formed expectations.

Second, this book does not embrace all literary genres. With the exception of the plays discussed in Part III, very nearly all the works examined are novels or short fiction. Depending on their length, novels may, of course, take as their purview an entire society. But even Jane Austen, who dwells on the insular gentry of provincial life, reveals by indirection much of a larger world. And twentieth-century writers like James Joyce and Virginia Woolf, who probe as no authors did before them the inner souls of their protagonists, uncover in the process busy and complicated societies.

Finally, though sorely tempted, I do not include mystery or detective fiction. Oddly, New York City has not produced as much in the way of these kinds of books as one might expect. Perhaps this is because of the constant mobility of its population, its changing ethnicities, and its ever-shifting, expanding or contracting neighborhoods. To catch a crook somebody has to stand still. In Chester Himes' *Blind Man with a Pistol* his cop heroes simply give up. To be sure, there are first-rate Ed McBain police procedurals and traditional cerebral "locked room" detective fictional sleuths like S.S. Van Dine's Philo Vance, and Rex Stout's Nero Wolfe, but the latter seldom, and then only reluctantly, leave their premises. Rarely do these authors invoke as much of the diffuse energies of New York as, say, Raymond Chandler and Walter Moseley manage for Los Angeles, Elmore Leonard for Detroit, Robert Parker for Boston, or Dashiell Hammett for his 1920s dark, brooding western cities. (When Hammett turns to New York in *The Thin Man* in 1934, much of the élan is missing.) The one notable exception may be the above-mentioned Chester Himes, whose tough guy hard-boiled thrillers portray a Harlem Babylon of tumultuous streets, teeming tenements, whorehouses, Caribbean cafes, drug dens and the like in vivid almost surreal detail. Still, for all their spirit, Himes and other masters do not satisfactorily encompass the variegated urban myths of twentieth-century American cities. Disgust and anger are usually the only emotions their iconic heroes are likely to display. Indeed, the tough guy subgenre must of necessity sacrifice character for action — but for our purpose, exchanges of character and environment tell the essence of city dreams.

In light of the foregoing, I have selected several "post-frontier" authors and works, some celebrated, some less well-known. Among the latter I relate something of their contents and when relevant I conjecture how the lives of these authors may relate to their New York writings. What they have in common are assumptions about the character of the city. What distinguish them are the elaborations and constructions they have built on these assumptions. In effect, they have both enhanced and modified city mythology. Although the present study does not pretend to any in-depth criticism, clearly the way authors present their material confers meaning. It follows that some critical judgments are in order. The myths of New York are America's dreams and dilemmas writ firsthand both large and small, and what we make of them tells us much about ourselves.

PART ONE: MYTHMAKERS

1

The Old Guard

Henry James, Edith Wharton, Louis Auchincloss

When a carefully attired Henry James disembarked at Hoboken's New York harbor in August 1904, he could not be sure whether or not this would be his last American visit. He had sailed as a passenger on the massive SS *Kaiser Wilhelm II* on the pretext that he would be writing an American travel book of sorts, but he was perhaps also searching for his American roots. It had been twenty years since his last sojourn in New York, and by now most of his life had been lived abroad. His brother William, a celebrated Harvard University philosophy professor, regarded Henry's disposition as being a bit too delicate for the American environment and tried subtly to dissuade him. But Henry was adamant. He wanted to see the country of his birth and particularly parts he had never before visited — like the American South and California. Along the way he agreed to meet the promising author Edith Wharton at her recently built mansion in the Massachusetts Berkshires. Finally, before departing for Europe, he would take a closer look at New York City, the city of his youth.

Although James in his fiction had glossed over the way people made their money, he was himself rather good at managing his finances. He was in fact perhaps the first serious American author to support himself entirely by his writing — and so for this journey he had arranged beforehand to deliver paid literary lectures countrywide and to further negotiate with his publisher a revised edition of his novels.

The American Civil War had weakened the grip of New York's antebellum Protestant upper class — a class to which James once belonged — displaced, often enough, by descendants of Irish immigrants and upstart western capitalists. The latter, as it happened, were more intent on buying than imbuing their culture — that is, buying, in the main, European art treasures — just as their daughters bought or acquired husbands of Europe's aristocracy. Indeed, such women would become the great subject of James's novels. Perhaps another unstated reason for James's return was that he would like to scrutinize them on their native ground, or more particularly, in the new capitalist capital, New York City.

James's most popular New York fiction up to this time was the novel *Washington Square* (1881) whose events take place in the years prior to the Civil War. It was a short work dealing with the relationships between an upper middle class doctor, his daughter, and her feckless suitor. Despite certain bittersweet qualities, there is also present a kind of nostalgia for a bygone age. Now he would be most interested in persons of his own class in his own time. What were they like? What would *he* have been like had he stayed behind? Particularly intriguing is his 1886 novel *The Bostonians*, relating in large part the adventures of a dispossessed Mississippi writer-lawyer who comes to New York to restart his life. Calling on socially prominent New York relatives, he finds them mindlessly self-indulgent. But in the course of events Basil Ransom falls in love with a young woman in New England who he believes is being manipulated by ferocious Boston feminists. Was Ransom, with his antiquated notions of the importance of "ideas" and the "place" of women, a removed surrogate for James? Perhaps to a small degree he was — James writes about him with a kind of detached bemused sympathy. Ransom had at the least some very fixed views at a time when so many traditional beliefs were being undermined.

Yet Ransom's prospects are dubious, as are his immediate New York environs, portrayed here by James as "perhaps expressive of a rank civilization." His living quarters suggest something of the looming larger city, decadent yet at the same time primordially menacing. Literally and symbolically, Ransom inhabits a "somewhat decayed mansion" whose shabby rooms command a view of the "fantastic skeleton of the Elevated Railway overhanging [the] street which it darkened and smothered with the immeasurable spinal columns and clutching paws of an antediluvian monster." At the novel's conclusion, Ransom perhaps only tentatively manages to wrest away from her radical women mentors the woman he wants to marry, but he has not otherwise made much of a success of himself in the great world beyond.

Despite its title and its several New England settings, the novel does in a fashion capture the essence of what the New York novel would become. Ransom, the postbellum Southerner, looks to the city as a kind of West in his endeavors to put away the past and begin a new life — but like the frontier West of old, there are hints here and there that his new environment is fraught with dangers. Still, for the most part, *The Bostonians* is a novel of manners, a novel of society, as poor Ransom learns to circumvent not only peculiar groups of women but an ossified New York upper class of rather silly Europeanized pretensions.

New York was not, however, a city of Europeanized culture and when James returned in early 1905 (having now seen other parts of the country), he had little faith it ever would be. A collection of magazine essays about his American journeys — published afterwards as *The American Scene* (1907) — tells of his impressions, the most interesting of which deal with New York. Above all, it appears, he was astonished, overwhelmed by the city's immense "ingurgitation" of immigrants — especially east European Jews whom he tried his best to understand. But in the final analysis, they left him uneasy. For one thing, how would their Yiddish garble affect, influence his beloved English language? On a visit to New York's Lower East Side with its "bristling fire escapes," he admires the energy of the Jews, their intelligence, their will to prevail, but he fears now for his own foreignness. It was not only Jews, of course, but all those others crowding in from Ellis Island:

> It is a drama that goes on, without a pause, day by day and year by year, this constituting visible act of ingurgitation on the part of our body politic and social, and really an appeal to amazement beyond that of any sword-swallowing or fire-swallowing of the circus.... [The American-born citizen] had thought he knew before, thought he had the sense of the degree in which it is his American fate to share the sanctity of his American consciousness, the intimacy of his American patriotism, with the inconceivable alien; but the truth had never come home to him with such force.... I positively *have* to think of him, as going about ever afterwards with a new look, for those who can see it, in his face, the outward sign of the new chill in his heart. So is stamped, for detection, the questionably privileged person who has had an apparition, seen a ghost in his supposedly safe old house.

Beyond feeling himself an outsider, he hotly resents being dispossessed of what was once his:

> ... that loud primary stage of alienism which New York most offers to sight — operates, for the native, as their note of settled possession, something they have nobody to thank for; so that *un*settled possession is what we, on our side, seem reduced to — the implication of which, in its turn, is that, to recover confidence and regain lost ground, we, not they, must make the surrender and accept the orientation. We must go, in other words, *more* than half-way to meet them.... This sense of dispossession haunted me....

But if he feared what he saw as the loss of possession of his city, he was equally appalled at members of his own patrician class whom he felt had surrendered to their worst get-rich instincts. He called them "monsters of the mere market" who had transformed the face of the city from what he remembered as pleasingly livable to something dehumanizing — all in the service of profits. Skyscrapers were likened to "giant pins" scattered across the landscape overshadowing churches, banishing neighborhoods and indeed New York's past:

> Crowned not only with no history, but with no credible possibility of time for history, and consecrated by no uses save the commercial at any cost, they are simply the most piercing notes in that concert of the expensively provisional into which your supreme sense of New York resolves itself. They never begin to speak to you, in the manner of the builded majesties of the world ... with the authority of things of permanence.... One story is good only till another is told, and sky-scrapers are the last word of economic ingenuity only till another word be written. This shall possibly be a word of still uglier meaning....

Sans history the city had reverted to a barbarous state of nature, a symbolic savage Wild West, untouched by saving graces or the mitigating domesticities of civilization. These would be James's harshest words.

And yet, for all that, he was conflicted. He journeyed around other parts of the city and found architecture that pleased him, pockets of neighborhoods he could warm to. His next grand undertaking would be a final revision of what he regarded as his major works. The whole enterprise, he speculated, would take him several years. Prior to his departure for Europe, he requested his publisher, Scribner's, to call these books the New York Edition, which title, he hoped, conveyed "sufficient dignity and distinctness" to the greatness of his "native city."

Three years after his departure, James's "The Jolly Corner" appeared in the December issue of the *English Review*. The tale tells of Brydon, a returned expatriate (clearly James's alter ego), who confronts in his old New York home a horrifying apparition, a projection of sorts of what he might have become had he remained in America. What he sees gives off the look of the crass new class of millionaires. Brydon shrinks in terror, indeed very nearly faints. The imagery in this story unconsciously refers back to his New York essay in *The American Scene* where James speaks of "the questionably privileged person who has had an apparition, seen a ghost in his supposedly safe old house." The difference in the two pieces is the identity of the ghost. In *The American Scene* the ghost is the outsider in the city, the alien, the immigrant. In "The Jolly Corner" the ghost is James himself.

As things turned out, James did once more return to America — in August 1910 — accompanying his sister-in-law and dying beloved brother, William, who had lately visited him. Not long after their arrival William died, and James, deeply depressed, sought psychiatric help. He had been staying in New Hampshire and Cambridge, William's family homes, but would on occasion visit New York. The city at least temporarily restored him. New York, he wrote a friend, appeared "a very extraordinary and terrific yet amiable place, as to which my sentiment is of an hourly impression of its violent possibility and of a sneaking kindness for its pride and power (it's so clearly destined to be the agglomeration of the world!) born of early associations and familiarities." Was it the chameleon nature of the city that acted on the Master's temperament — or was his large imagination projected on New York? We cannot know. Two partial autobiographies published several years later seldom alluded to his hometown.

James departed New York in August 1911. His passage to Liverpool marked the last of his American journeys. A month earlier he had called on Edith Wharton at the Mount, her Italian villa in Lenox, Massachusetts. Their friendship, begun in 1904 during James's previous American sojourn, saw James presuming a kind of literary mentorship. He was nearly twenty years her senior and by now a highly regarded author. The forty-year-old Wharton, on the other hand, had published only a handful of poems and a couple of collections of short fiction. Her first full-length novel, a historical work, was printed in 1903. Their compatibility had of course something to do with their common background — they could both trace back a century or more their New York ancestors. Wharton, at the time, hoped that any linkage with James might enhance her literary career. She had long sought James's approval, although privately entertaining reservations about some of his writings. James, for that matter, was not excessively fond of her work. "DO NEW YORK," he wrote her early in their correspondence, as if to warn her away from her propensity to write fiction with European settings. He leavened his advice with the implicit admission that his own writing suffered from a lack of "FIXED" place. Yet, despite his counsel, he felt years later that she had not taken his advice sufficiently to heart. In 1910, when for all practical purposes Wharton had expatriated herself to France, James wrote her sister-in-law that "Edith should be tethered in her native pasture even if it reduces her to a back yard in New York." And again, two years later, he addresses her directly: "Your only drawback is not having the homeliness and inevitability and the happy limitation of the affluent poverty of a country of your Own (comme moi, par exemple!)." Still, whatever their differences, they enjoyed one another, both sharing in a curious way a view of Europe as *their* reverse West — a place apart and away from raw and grasping New York, a place where they could discover themselves anew in a cultural milieu not given over entirely to business success.

One other thing that James and Wharton did have in common is that they both wrote about the "old families" and the very rich as experienced insiders — that is, as persons born and reared as patricians — rather than as outsiders writing about the rich as, say, Fitzgerald or Dreiser or Marquand. The reader senses nuances, observations, assumptions that those outside the pale might not otherwise make. But granting as much, their works differed in significant ways. James's best fiction had to do with Americans abroad; indeed, he could not, as he himself conceded, deal as an artist with the ferocious fluidity and mobility of American life, let alone New York. He needed the tottering stability of a European class system against which he could measure his characters' psychology. Conversely, Wharton knew *her* fragments of New York life well. She had lived in the city on and off until middle age and observed acidly the several gradations of what was then known as Society. The geographical boundaries of her experience tell us something of her limitations. She saw little of New York beyond Fifth Avenue and its narrow strips of traversing streets. Her north-south boundaries were equally confined, extending from Central Park to Washington Square. And yet her perceptions, like those of James, however circumscribed, fit like pieces into a mosaic in the city's larger mythos.

To understand Wharton's New York, it is helpful to look at the ways her life and work converge. She was born Edith Jones in New York in 1862, the youngest of three children of enormously rich parents, George and Lucretia Jones. Like James she spent much of her childhood and youth in Europe and Newport, during which time she read prodigiously, and her proclivities, especially for French literature, would last a lifetime. Her young womanhood was, however, marred by disappointments. Although she enjoyed the company of two suitable young men, neither of them asked for her hand in marriage. (One of them, Walter Berry, who later became a lifelong friend, may have introduced her to "Darwinian" sociology, which she would later apply to portraits of her native city.) Edith's subsequent marriage to the amiable but listless and nonintellectual Teddy Wharton turned out to be an anguished non-carnal fiasco — and they were eventually divorced after eight years. Edith's only passionate affair transpired in Europe in 1911 with the expatriate bisexual journalist Morton Fullerton.

One brings these matters up because Wharton to some degree seems to have associated her personal disappointments with the character of the city. At their best, none of her seemingly desirable fictional male characters have the strength, courage, energy, or moral vigor to resist the corruption of their patrician class or to defend themselves against crude but determined outsiders who seek opportunities in the city. New York was indeed their new West and Wharton links this observation to an implicit social Darwinism. Her failed "heroes," unable to cope, bequeath the city to the barbarians. The myths of the decadent city revert to the myths of a barbaric West. Wharton herself gave up permanent residence in New York in 1907 and moved to France.

Edith's mother hoped she would not become a writer. It was not appropriate, she believed, for someone of Edith's social standing. Not just marital stress but Lucretia Jones's disapproval doubtless contributed to the two nervous breakdowns Wharton suffered in the 1890s. The self-conflicted characters of her fiction, male and female, are reflections of Wharton's own ambivalence. As an author, she had, after all, violated the cultural code she knew best. One reads Wharton at the start of her career as both a dissenter and a conformist, even as she writes nonfiction. Her very first book, *The Decoration of Houses* (1897), which she produced with the architect Ogden Codman, suggests ways of ridding houses room by room of their Victorian clutter. She would replace the clutter with the understated ostentation of the stately edifices of France and Italy. An underlying idea here is that the basic character of a house is its architecture and that massive overstuffed furnishings conceal character. In essence Wharton would substitute a simpler kind of decoration for more conventional kinds, though she by no means advocates that the rich give up their displays of wealth. Put another way, she would only *reduce* rather than eliminate the "conspicuous consumption," a term Thorstein Veblen would employ two years later in his celebrated *Theory of the Leisure Class*. Still, the only persons who could benefit from her counsel were the very rich who owned the clutter and the houses in the first place.

Wharton's literary works follow along analogous lines. Her female protagonists endeavor to free themselves from stifling New York class-based strictures, conventions and formalities, but often to no avail. To survive they must adapt to the demands of their social class. One of her first stories, "Souls Belated," set paradoxically in Italy, tells of a once-married New York woman who desires to live unmarried with her lover. He refuses, and finally they prepare to reenter New York society as man and wife. Wharton's finest

"Darwinist" novel, *The House of Mirth* (1905), portrays a spirited heroine unable to shake off the weight of her upper-class New York upbringing. In the end she perishes and, as we shall see, Wharton here uses much botanical imagery as if to say that impersonal societal mechanisms are at one with the amoral powers of Nature. Free will is illusory.

Wharton's social Darwinism extended at least once to persons outside her social class. In 1892 she wrote the novella "The Bunner Sisters," which, however, she could not get published until 1916. In this piece her sympathy reaches out to the lower-middle-class sisters of the title as they sink gradually into poverty. The dreariness of their surroundings determines their destiny:

> The house of which the Bunner sisters had annexed the basement was a private dwelling with a brick front, green shutters on weak hinges and a dressmaker's sign in the window.... On each side of its modest three stories stood higher buildings, with fronts of brown stone, cracked and blistered, cast-iron balconies and cat-haunted grass-patches behind twisted railing.... The middle of the street was full of irregular depressions, well-adapted to retain the long swirls of dust and straw and twisted paper that the wind drove up and down its sad untended length; and toward the end of the day, when traffic had been active, the fissured pavement formed a mosaic of coloured handbills, lids of tomato cans, old shoes, cigar stumps and banana skins cemented together by a layer of mud, or veiled in a powdering of dust....

Theirs is a melancholy existence drained of any gaiety or beauty which perhaps only persons of an aristocratic sensibility can experience. One thinks in this regard of Lily Bart, the central figure of *The House of Mirth* written perhaps a dozen years later, who chooses (unconsciously) to die rather than live a life of genteel poverty.

Wharton's first collection of stories was given the Darwinist title *The Descent of Man,* but Edith, an avid reader of French novels, might also have drawn her determinism from the novels of Zola. One of the books Wharton admired was Robert Grant's naturalistic *Unleavened Bread* (1900), which tells of an amoral Midwestern woman, Selma White, who marries three times in a relentless drive for social success. Despite Selma's unfortunate character, one suspects Wharton may have had a sneaking admiration for women of Selma's sort, who in their single-minded pursuit of success become a kind of force of nature. Afterwards Wharton would herself write of other such ambitious women. "The Other Two," which was probably written in 1903 or 1904, tells of a social-climbing woman from the point of view of her third husband. Not only is Waythorne gradually disabused of sentimental preconceptions about his wife's past, but he also learns he must accustom himself to the occasional presence of her first two husbands. Alice Waythorne is quietly triumphant, and the reader suspects she has used each of her husbands as stepping-stones.

The House of Mirth (1905) was Wharton's first New York novel and Lily Bart, a product of New York society — unlike Alice Waythorne, the outsider of "The Other Two" — must succumb to its inexorable rules. Long conditioned to wealth, she suddenly discovers she has very little money left and as a consequence finds herself conflicted between her material needs and her finely tuned sensibilities. She knows she could marry any of several wealthy bachelors but at the last moment turns them away, knowing they are vacuous, self-seeking, or predatory. Throughout the novel Wharton portrays in partially Darwinist terms a young woman whose nature and upbringing make it impossible for her to live any kind of life other than the kind she has always known. She was an "ornament," a "victim of her environment," an aptly named "Lily":

> Inherited tendencies had combined with her early training to make her the highly specialized product she was: an organism as helpless out of its narrow range as the sea-anemone for the rock. She had been fashioned to adorn and delight.

Lily is well aware of herself; she responds almost passionately to objects of beauty and regrets her meager capacity for compassion for the poor. It is the dinginess of their existence she cannot abide. Hers is as much an aesthetic reaction as anything else.

Her indecisiveness and impulsive behavior assure her decline. Especially intriguing are Wharton's observations about the various gradations and cliques of New York's very rich as Lily sadly stumbles down the social ladder. The one man who could possibly save her, the lawyer Lawrence Selden, shares her sensibilities but is himself too hesitant. Ironically the two recognize that the social class to which they are both emotionally bound is devoid of moral values. Lily's decline is inevitable, but Wharton does not take a wholly detached view of her world. High society, for all its pretensions and self-deceptions, its presumed morality and standards, is informed ultimately by money. Lily dies because she has no money — pure and simple. Although Wharton would have regarded the notion as absurd, her vision of capitalist acquisitiveness agreed largely with the city's most radical socialist critics.

Wharton's most monstrous creation was the ravishing Undine Spragg, the central figure of Wharton's *The Custom of the Country* (1913), who has come with her parents to New York from Euphoria, Illinois. (Several of Wharton's other "western" vulgarians come from places named Debs, Aeschylus, Hallelujah, and Lohengrin.) In the course of the narrative Undine marries and casts off husbands in America and Europe (as well as her simple good-hearted parents) until she acquires the immense wealth she evidently desires. Among her victims is an honorable New York aristocrat who ultimately commits suicide and a French nobleman whose ancient chateau she plunders. Finally, Undine remarries her first husband, another Midwesterner, who has become even richer than he was when she had first married him. Despite her beauty, her ruthlessness, philistinism and greed are so extreme that it is hard to imagine that any of her husbands could have long tolerated her. But for Wharton, only persons of that sort were fittest to survive the New York jungle.

It is often claimed that Wharton softened her view of New York after living abroad many years. Most frequently cited is *The Age of Innocence* (1920), set in the 1880s, which tells of a love affair never consummated because the young man in question is engaged to be married and the woman he desires, an American-born countess, was once married in Europe to a scoundrel. New York society tacitly informs them their affair is unacceptable, whereupon the countess returns to Europe. It was a period, Wharton suggests, when principles and standards were at least sternly enforced, however quaint or cruel. Several other works Wharton wrote abroad contain much the same message: *The Mother's Recompense*, for example, or "The Old Maid." Indeed, much of what Wharton wrote while living abroad used New York as background. But on the whole they read little better than slick magazine fiction. James was right. Wharton would have been better advised to remain "tethered" in a New York backyard.

As regards her nostalgia, one notes that the New York she speaks of in more gentle tones was a New York that existed before she was born ("The Old Maid") or a New York she could remember only as a girl. And yet even in her autobiography, written a few years before her death, she speaks of the "intolerable ugliness" of that old New York, "its untended streets — the narrow houses so lacking in external dignity, so crammed with smug and suffocating upholstery." As for the now changed twentieth-century city, she was no less repelled. She even tells us Henry James (who, as we have seen, had a far more ambivalent reaction) "hated the place: its aimlessness, ugliness, its noisy irrelevance...." Perhaps a letter quoted by her biographer, R.W.B. Lewis, conveys passions she was never able to quite overcome. On a visit to the city in 1911 she gazes out her hotel window, viewing New York as a kind of hell: "The brick and iron landscape of this appalling city ... looks like a Mercator's pro-jection of hell — with the river of pitch and the iron bridges, and the 'ele-vated' marking of the bogie and Blackwell's Island opposite for the city of Dis."

Missing in both Wharton and James is what men (and occasionally women) actually do to make or maintain their fortunes. James in his fiction makes of these omissions a virtue — that is, to know how money is made is to distract the reader from the moral, ethical, and psychological issues his characters face. Suffice it to say, often these figures take their New York (or New England) wealth abroad to test subconsciously their American souls. New York is thus no longer an issue. In Wharton's case, the men and women she portrays are unproductive. (Idleness is a virtue among the very rich, says Veblen.) To be sure, her men quite often journey to Wall Street as investors or lawyers or financiers, but because they have so much money to begin with actually being there does not seem to matter a great deal. They do what they do because it is the thing one does. The reader never actually sees them managing their affairs.

This circumstance makes for one of the chief differences between the men and the women of James's and Wharton's New York and that of Louis Auchincloss. In the latter's works one views his characters going about their business, making decisions of all sorts in their clubs, in their law offices, in their banks and brokerage firms. Even certain high offices of government, the military, and the Episcopal Church are scrutinized. Auchincloss is, of course, of a later generation (born in 1917) and post–World War I mobility into the realms of the upper classes was made considerably easier. And yet among the arrivistes there are still many who endeavor to adopt or adapt themselves to the culture of the "old families." Needless to say the old families, too, mod-ify their behavior to survive the demands of changing times. The intermix-ture of old and new, the East and West, is what Auchincloss likes to write about. In this respect he evidently believes that the ways people make their money, and the ways they dispense the money they have made, throw a great deal of light on the social, moral, and psychological issues that also concern the works of James and Wharton. Finally, Auchincloss does not always confine himself to his own times but reaches back on occasion to the years of James and Wharton. Indeed, he makes himself their contemporary.

Like his patrician predecessors Auchincloss was reared in wealth and privilege. He is a descendant of one of New York's "old families" extending as far back as the early nineteenth century. One of his ancestors, Philip Hone, was a one-term antebellum mayor who later made his fortune as an auction-eer. Auchincloss is clearly proud of this connection and uses the name Hone in several of his stories to depict thematic associations with an earlier New York. More to the point, he is not embarrassed to suggest the political and commercial roots of the New York aristocracy. Perhaps another reason Auchincloss is unafraid about writing about "money" is that for many years he has worked as an attorney at New York law firms whose upper-class clients derive their income from a variety of business investments. He is thus knowledgeable about the nitty-gritty of high finance and even the role it plays among the presumed non-moneymaking elite like Episcopal churchmen.

In addition to his professional activities Auchincloss served long years as the head of the Museum of the City of New York, a task which no doubt enhances his knowledge of lives lived parallel to those of James and Whar-ton. And yet, as we shall see, his perceptions differ although he respects and defers to their work. (He has in fact written excellent essays about both writ-ers.) Importantly, too, he has experienced life beyond the confines of his class — most notably as a naval officer during World War II. Nor did the end of war remove him from the wider literary life. He would for some time after-wards meet in Greenwich Village with other postwar American authors — Vance Bourjaily, Gore Vidal, William Styron, and James Jones, among others. Although he writes about the social class he knows best, no one could accuse him of being blind to the world beyond.

It should not surprise then that wars and political and cultural issues serve as background events in Auchincloss's fiction, but he is mainly inter-ested in competitive relationships within families and institutions and how lives not immediately involved are affected. Ultimately all things in Auchin-closs boil down to a question of power, because his families and institutions are themselves rich or once-rich or prestigious. To be sure he portrays wan-ing Protestant influence, but for him white Protestant New York still figures as a symbol of mythic authority where high culture, ancestry, and principle remain important issues.

Some titles of the fifty or so books he has written (several are works of literary criticism) suggest the centrality of the city: *Skinny Island, Portrait in Brownstone, Tales of Manhattan.* Very nearly all his books convey some New York settings wherein large problems are posed, probed, or resolved. The famous Massachusetts boys' school in *The Rector of Justin*, for example, is financed in large part by New York alumni. Other issues take on different colorings as the culture of the city shifts over long periods of time. Auchincloss is particularly good at this as he gives voice to traditionalists, the young, the rebellious, and the newly arrived in their conflicts about values or the meaning of events. Quite literally he divides several of his works into segments, allowing his characters (often women) to speak for themselves or at the very least convey their points of view through the voice of the narrator. Typical is *Portrait in Brownstone* where several members of an "old" family discuss and dispute certain crises in their lives from the turn of the century until the 1960s. Their views are by no means monolithic, but they do come together from time to time to preserve what they regard as their honor and their responsibilities.

In *Portrait*, a publicly observed kiss at the Metropolitan Museum in 1903 impels the upper-class family of the "compromised" young woman involved to pressure her to marry the young man who behaved so audaciously. The resulting marriage has widespread social, psychological, and financial implications not simply for the couple but for their relatives and associates. In the course of time the overall culture shifts gradually, impinging subtly on the culture of the rich. Over the years Ida, the "kissed" woman, submits to her husband's domination and adultery, but by the 1960s she acquires new confidence in herself. Not only does she gain control of family matters, but she even chooses an appropriate woman for her son to marry.

Auchincloss's New York, then, is made up of generations of "old" extended families, often renewing themselves with "outsiders," symbolic or flesh-and-blood Westerners, who may or may not be rich. Like Ida, however, the families demand appropriate choices. Seldom are Catholics or Jews admitted to their inner folds — which is not to say they are necessarily anti–Catholic or anti–Semitic (though they may be). They may simply prefer their own kind. In a sense, too, Auchincloss's New York writing is much like American Southern literature with its emphasis on family and on family relationships and mythic remembrances of a grander past. His is a city where many still venerate the past, as opposed to James's assertion that New Yorkers deny or reject their history. In "The Landmarker," Auchincloss tells of an elderly gentleman who wanders the streets seeking remnants of an earlier, nobler time in a city now so given to change:

> Happily for him, however, the past did not prove a sterile pursuit.... In a curious way his need to retreat to it seemed to have a democratizing effect on his attitudes. Anything that shared now in the dignity and grandeur of that greater age — a church, a station, a hotel or a store — shared similarly in his

widening affections.... Lefferts, who had once walked by the Lady Chapel of St. Patrick's Cathedral and Commodore Farragut's statue in Madison Square without turning his head, was now happy to pass a morning traveling underground to the center of Brooklyn for a glimpse of the Gothic gates of Greenwood Cemetery.

It was as if he and the old by-passed city had found each other in a golden twilight. As he stood looking up at Louis Sullivan's terra-cotta angels with their outstretched arms, high on a cornice over Bleecker Street, or wandered amid the chaste Greek porticos of Snug Harbor, or took in the faded grandeur of Colonnade Row in Lafayette Street, he felt a tremendous upsurge of spirit.... The very mass of the surrounding city, the engulfing, amorphous, indifferent city, like a huge sow smothering of her own offspring, gave to his searches some of the excitement of a consecrating act, as though, a monk in a desperate age, he was solacing his soul by lighting little candles in darkest corners.

Clearly not all Auchincloss's upper-class characters, past and present, are admirable. Some are cruel, dishonest, self-absorbed, envious, vulnerable, and generally morally wanting. But at their best (even financiers and lawyers!) they are honorable and patriotic, with a sense of duty — persons whom James and Wharton might at first sight distrust. Several are endowed with an obstinate Protestant faith — something rare in contemporary American letters — that makes them appear at times unbending. The Rector of Justin, for example, relentlessly intrudes on an affair between his daughter and her lover in an effort to reprieve the Christian soul of the young man. On the other hand the male protagonist of *The Venus of Sparta*, an upwardly mobile, "successful" banker who has semi-passively played by the rules all of his life, undertakes a final Dionysian fling before destroying himself.

Yet, even when religion is not made explicit a kind of stubborn morality governs the behavior of his protagonists. They do make moral choices, independent, often enough, of community opinion. Examples abound in Auchincloss's fiction and several assume political dimensions. One comparatively late work, *Honorable Men* (1995), is illustrative. After having endured some difficult confrontations with his culturally conservative parents, a sexually tormented, guilt-wracked youth radically transforms himself into a decisive, near dogmatic adult. The irony here is that the morality he now assumes is often as rigidly hidebound as the kind he had ostensibly rejected. World War II and the Vietnam War serve partially as background and moral balance sheets for the protagonist, as well as for his wife, his wayward offspring, and his mistress. None of the persons in the work is portrayed as altogether sympathetic or unsympathetic. Each has chosen a moral stance not always ideally suited to all situations. The power struggles within the families reflect, in their way, the larger cultural and political conflicts within their City — indeed their nation.

In an earlier novella, *Arnold & Degener, One Chase Manhattan Plaza*, a young attorney opts to work for the New Deal, much to the horror of his conservative Republican associates. When he returns to his law firm after many years of government service, he attracts new business because of his Washington connections. The ideals and values of the prodigal lawyer and those of his colleagues are not unmixed with pride, egotism, and compromise. In sum, what Auchincloss has done in this and many of his other New York writings is deal with one of several popular perceptions of the city as an insulated class-bound community whose upper classes cling stubbornly to bygone Europeanized aristocratic illusions. But rather than satirize them or deplore their "decadence," Auchincloss reveals them in full panoply, with qualities attractive and undesirable — and often a mix of the two. In a word, he humanizes them, suggesting implicitly that they are, after all, mirrors of ourselves.

No one would today claim — least of all Auchincloss — that he writes with the wicked satiric precision of Edith Wharton — nor, for that matter, does he communicate the brilliant imagery of Henry James. There are no bristling fire escapes in Auchincloss's New York. And yet he does have a sharp eye for detail — the look of a room, the contours of a table, the texture of a painting, or a sensuous vista of a New York summer colony in Maine or Long Island. To be sure, he is a successor of James and Wharton but he is more tolerant, more democratic, and, dare one say, more open to experience than his great predecessors.

2

❧❧❧

Immigrants

ABRAHAM CAHAN, PIETRO DI DONATO, MARIO PUZO, OSCAR HIJUELOS

All the while the new century saw James and Wharton worrying the moral and aesthetic issues of New York's old order, a burgeoning Jewish eastern European immigrant community began extending itself beyond the borders of New York's Lower East Side. James, as we have seen, looked in their direction somewhat aghast. Wharton, if she thought about them at all, would have been appalled. Her own social class was bad enough, thank you. As for the immigrants themselves, it is safe to say they knew little of the worlds of James and Wharton and could not have cared less. Theirs, for the moment, was a struggle to gain a foothold in America, and New York — or what they knew of it —*was* America.

But what they knew of it was itself being transformed by their presence. Prior to the 1880s, eighty thousand Jews (mainly of Germanic and Sephardic origin) constituted 4 percent of the City's population. By 1910 their numbers had increased to a million and a quarter, now making up 25 percent of the population.

Still it was not simply the Jamesian ancien régime that imagined itself socially and culturally miles apart from the newcomers. German Jews, some of whose forebears had come to New York in the 1840s and 1850s, were themselves dismayed. Some among them viewed the immigrants as little more than superstitious primitives whose demeanor and proximity threatened their status. Anti-Semitism was not unknown in New York nor indeed in the larger America, especially in the Midwest and the South where populist tracts portrayed Jews as symbols of exploitative urban capitalism. The city's assimilated Jews were thus of two minds. On the one hand they tried hard to assure themselves and their gentile neighbors that they were not all like their Russian, Polish, Romanian, and Hungarian coreligionists, and yet they did what they could to help ease these newcomers into the American mainstream. They advised secular education and contributed generously to settlement houses, charities, immigrant societies, and other supportive organizations aimed at assimilation. Whether or not they were motivated by compassion or self-preservation is of course an open question. But what they could not foresee or possibly imagine was that the immigrants themselves might one day outstrip their benefactors in economic and social spheres.

The latent and sometimes overt competition between eastern European Jews and their Americanized counterparts lies partially concealed as subtext in Abraham Cahan's first-person novel *The Rise of David Levinsky* (1917). In the course of his narration the "successful" garment manufacturer, Levinsky, lately risen from poverty, boasts of the superior skill and acumen of immigrants in the apparel industry. Indeed, Levinsky himself comes to employ an Americanized Jew who had mocked him on his way up. Yet, despite their achievements, the immigrants' aspirations were not so far-reaching as had been generally supposed. Like other Europeans, Jews had come to America to escape poverty and persecution, but they had little desire to blend in with the larger gentile world. The notion of a "melting pot" of various ethnic communities would have been to them an anathema. Ironically, a popular Broadway play celebrating intermarriage, *The Melting Pot* (1909), by an Anglo-American Jew, Israel Zangwill, flagrantly misrepresents their outlook. At one point near the end of Cahan's novel, the now rich Levinsky considers asking a gentile woman to marry him but at the last moment desists. Despite certain common interests, he believes the social and cultural gulf between them is too great. Cahan was himself both a leader and reflector of the Jewish working-class immigrant community. Born in Russian-controlled Lithuania in 1860, he came to New York at the age of twenty, barely escaping the czarist police who rightly suspected him of revolutionary activities. As a socialist and trade union supporter, he wrote for both English and Yiddish language publications and is today best remembered for his fifty-year editorship (begun in 1899) of the Yiddish daily *Forverts*, a newspaper in its early years devoted to helping immigrants adjust.*

---

*An early front-page feature, for example, tells how the game of baseball is played, with an accompanying diagram of the Polo Grounds. The paper also served as a forum for readers' correspondence about personal family problems. Cahan may well have drawn from these columns for David Levinsky.

From the start, purists railed that the Yiddish of Cahan's *Forverts* was too watered down, too simple, with Yiddishized American words, but this may also account for its popular appeal. Paradoxically Cahan would also print the more formal prose of classical Yiddish authors and was himself drawn to writing fiction. But he determined he would write in English, and aim as much for gentile readers as for immigrants. New York City would be his great subject — the "golden" West of rebirth but also a West of frontier individualism where Jews might well lose their cultural identity. Theoretically Cahan would have liked to displace the city's capitalist ferocity — indeed the country's — with a moderating socialism, and his newspaper urged something of this sort for its first few decades. (After a trip to the Soviet Union in 1923, however, he would become an impassioned anticommunist.) But one of the curious aspects of Cahan's early fiction is that he wrote very little about politics or labor unions. Nor did he have very much to say about religion or the high rate of delinquency among the children of immigrants. Still, if he ignored *these* problems he concerned himself with others equally important — alienation, the strains of poverty, ghetto love affairs, and, above all, the cultural dilemmas of immigrants endeavoring to become Americans. The picture is decidedly mixed.

No one would today claim that Cahan wrote an elegant English. His first pieces feel stiff and self-consciously literary — this from an author whose Yiddish newspaper prose would become so self-consciously nonliterary. The phonetic pronunciation renderings, too, are sometimes unfortunate, and yet from the start he wrote with a hard economy, not unlike the far better known (and far different) immigrant author Isaac Bashevis Singer, who would later publish nearly all his fiction in Cahan's newspaper. William Dean Howells, the grand literary authority of the mid–1890s, viewed Cahan as a forceful writer, as did the promising young author Stephen Crane. For his part, Cahan liked to think of himself as a "realist" in the tradition of Dickens, Maupassant, Zola, and Chekhov. But at the same time he was obviously aware that his American readers would regard his ghetto world as peculiar — and so there are occasional intrusive explications where he would, for example, asterisk a word like "kosher" and give its meaning in a footnote at the bottom of the page, or sardonically describe a provincial young woman as "a true daughter of Israel," implying her knowledge of the world was limited to the reading of a Yiddish version of the Five Books of Moses. Asides of this sort are not of course always confined to foreign ethnic minorities. Like Cahan, the African-American author Richard Wright would momentarily reach out to white audiences of the 1930s and 1940s to attempt to explain his characters' insular environment.

In 1896 Cahan published the novella *Yekl: A Tale of the New York Ghetto*, portraying a young sweatshop operator's uncertain American identity. Yekl had come to America in hopes of making enough money to send for his wife and son later on. The phenomenon of the male breadwinner arriving ahead of his family was of course not uncommon among other ethnic groups, but several years have passed since Yekl's arrival. During this time Yekl, who now calls himself Jake, has, little by little, cast off many of his old country's ways. The absence of external social restraints has unfortunately undermined his intentions. He has sexual longings, but more than anything else he wants to look and sound American. Thus when his wife, Gitl, finally does appear, looking and sounding like a "greenhorn," he feels ashamed and angry. Eventually he abandons her and their young child for a seemingly "Americanized" young woman whom he had met some time before at "dancing school." Still, Yekl-Jake is not quite emancipated. A religious divorce is arranged and Gitl, the reader is given to understand, will eventually marry a worthier, "educated" young man while Jake is now bound to marry (unhappily) the hussy he no longer desires.

Thus in *Yekl* Cahan reveals the insidious breakdown of subjective restraints, given the new freedoms the city offers to even the most tradition-bound newcomer. The ghetto of the Lower East Side, despite its seeming homogeneity, is necessarily impinged upon by varieties of life beyond its borders. Some, like Yekl-Jake not very sure of themselves to begin with, stumble in their new environment. Others maintain an underlying integrity like the far more conservative Gitl, who will at one point nonetheless cast off her traditional headgear, loosen her hair, and buy a fashionable hat. The city frees her to marry for love while for Yekl-Jake the city will always be a kind of limbo. Cahan here has produced a two-edged vision of the city's New West freedoms on the immigrant soul.

Yekl's New York is a city constantly on the move — a city where ancient religious moorings are loosened. The reader picks up images, sounds, and smatterings of ghetto voices — families and couples doubling up in tiny rooms in tenements, overflowing barrels of garbage, fire escapes "festooned with mattresses, pillows and featherbeds," thronged steps, stoops and sidewalks. Here are not simply harsh and precarious conditions but inhabitants socializing, entertaining themselves, seeking solace or escape. Much is pathetic, admirable, even funny, but in odd ways curiously touching. Yekl-Jake tries out American slang, and likes to talk about baseball and boxing, although the reader intuits he is bewildered. And then there is the dancing school he and others attend in order to dance like an American. To be sure, they are exploited, but it is a place where young people can mix outside the purview of their religious elders. At the same time Cahan is not averse to satirizing traditional customs. During the divorce proceedings the venerable old rabbi attempts to discharge "his duties of dissuading the young couple from their contemplated step as scrupulously as he dared in view of his wife's signals to desist and not to risk a fee."

Two years after the publication of *Yekl*, Cahan published a collection of five stories which, though most stand up in their own right, play on themes already touched upon. "The Imported Bridegroom," the title story of the book, tells of Asriel, an elderly prosperous widower who returns to his Russian village where he manages to find a brilliant young Talmudic student whom he brings back to New York to marry his daughter. Flora, his New York daughter (who reads Dickens), is appalled at the idea of an arranged marriage and covertly sets out to subvert the young man by introducing him to the enticements of the city — that is, to libraries where he may read the works of secular authors. Not only does her future husband soon lose his faith, but he now joins with small groups of scholarly non–Jews to study the writings of positivist philosophers. Ironically Shaya has become as intensely intellectually and emotionally engaged as he had once been as a Talmudist.

The vision of New York as a land of rebirth fails Asriel. He is heartbroken. To all intents and purposes the city has not only robbed him of a daughter and a prospective son-in-law but has also robbed them both of their religion. "America is treife [tainted] to me, I can't show my head. The world is dark and empty to me. All is gone, gone, gone. I am a little baby.... I want to be born again." He proposes marriage to his religious housekeeper, promising they would set out on a journey to Palestine. Paradoxically it is Shaya who is reborn. Only the less impassioned Flora appears ready to live in the city of ambiguities.

Cahan's other stories portray the effects of New York's poverty on romance and marriage. Young families break up, relationships are unconsummated. Yet, in Cahan's fiction, education for women, as much as for men, may be a way out. In this regard the city does not discriminate — and some old-country attitudes may be beneficial. The value most honored in European shtetls was religious learning; surely only a slight shift to worldly matters may aid in survival. By the same token, secular education simultaneously liberates and defeats. "A Providential Match" tells of a crass uneducated factory worker who has saved enough money to pay passage for a desirable mate. Hannale would be well above Rouven's status in Russia. But when Hannale arrives in New York, he discovers she has fallen in love with a "college" fellow whom she met in steerage. Rouven has lost his money but Hannale will marry for love.

Cahan published his New York novel, *The Rise of David Levinsky,* in 1917, eleven years after his short story collection. By now, well established as editor of the largest Yiddish newspaper in the world, he could view Jewish New York with more perspective. That is to say, he might write now not only about the struggling immigrant but also about the "successful" businessman who emerges from the struggle. As social history, the novel is without parallel. Assuming the voice of Levinsky, Cahan tells us something about his constricted youth in Russia and carries through to his penniless arrival in the steaming New York ghetto of the 1880s, his menial beginnings as a peddler, his sweatshop days, his shaky start as a factory owner and salesman of his own goods, and finally his success as a prosperous apparel manufacturer. Along the way there are failures of a sort: his relationships with his fellow immigrants are mainly superficial, and with American gentiles uneasy; his love affairs end unhappily.

More suggestively, Levinsky's story deviates thematically from the usual pattern of American rags-to-riches literature. For one thing, Levinsky is not altogether likable. On his course upward, he may deceive, betray, and manipulate. No one would mistake him for a Horatio Alger hero, nor does he himself feel his triumphs fulfill him. One thinks in this regard of James Weldon Johnson's 1912 *The Autobiography of an Ex-Colored Man* (much of which takes place in New York), whose protagonist's "rise" depends on the concealment of his African-American identity. Both books question the dream of upward mobility, the ethos of self-congratulatory American success stories, and foretell the curious role of the city as creator and destroyer of identity.

One achievement of Cahan's novel is that, despite all, the reader wishes Levinsky well. Like everyone else, he experiences his share of embarrassments, insults, and frustrations. Yet he is unstoppable, and one admires his energy and, surprisingly, his keen social and cultural perceptions. Above all he is honest about himself, and closes his account on a melancholy note. What has his wealth gained him? He is lonely, without family, and retains in his consciousness residues of ancient ghetto fears of the gentile world. The individualism nurtured in the roiling city has by the same token severed his links to a supportive Jewish community. Levinsky's New York, like his life, is a bittersweet conundrum.

The Italian peasant immigrants of Pietro di Donato's *Christ in Concrete* and Mario Puzo's *The Fortunate Pilgrim* are a far cry from Cahan's Jews. However much the latter suffered persecution, they were in some ways better equipped to face the rigors of New York. Often enjoined by law from attending universities, owning land, or holding government office in their mother countries, Jews were compelled by necessity to practice skilled trades in crowded communities or partake of small mercantile and capitalist activities. Nor did their religion exalt poverty but instead encouraged individualistic (albeit Talmudic) disputatious reasoning. New York's seeming business competitiveness was thus less of a culture shock for Jews than for di Donato's or Puzo's rural Italians.

They came in numbers almost comparable to those of the Jews. From 1880 to 1920 the flow grew with increasing intensity. By 1920 they and their offspring constituted 14 percent of the city's population. At first, most were men — unlettered, unskilled peasants, many of whom would return to their native soil after a few years with earnings from factory or construction jobs. Despite this exodus, the city's Italian population was almost immediately replenished by the arrival of hundreds of thousands of others. At the start of the century, return immigration to Europe began to thin out and by 1910 Italian neighborhoods had sprung up in Brooklyn, Manhattan, and the Bronx.

Their prospects did not appear promising. Oppressed, despised, and exploited for centuries (and frequently ignored by their church), they arrived understandably suspicious of all governmental institutions and by extension even institutions designed to benefit them such as trade unions, schools, and settlement houses. Only the church was grudgingly accepted, but even here the priesthood appeared to belong to the Irish who had come to America decades earlier. What did stand them in good stead were strong traditions of family and group loyalties, their respect for the dignity of labor, and, above all, their historical capacities to face up to very hard times.

The myths clash in Pietro di Donato's autobiographical *Christ in Concrete* (1937): New York as the city of broken hopes and dreams and New York as a succoring extended Italian family of nature's peasant outcasts. After his immigrant father's accidental death on a shoddy construction job, Paul, the novel's twelve-year-old protagonist, leaves school circa 1923 to become a bricklayer in order to provide for his widowed mother and eight brothers and sisters. Physical hardships, squalid living conditions, accidents, death, and extreme poverty plague the family from the start, yet they endure just as their forebears long endured hardships in their native Abruzzi. For Geremio, the father, New York is no better than Italy. Trapped one day on a girder, he will die when a loosened hopper pours concrete over him. He thinks bitterly of his life of "worn oppression." Always "there had been hunger and her bastard the fear of hunger." Yet, at death, his last thoughts are of his wife and children. His sacrifice, harrowingly described, is likened to Christ's:

> He paused exhausted. His genitals convulsed. The cold steel rod upon which they were impaled froze his spine.... The icy wet concrete reached his chin.... Savagely he bit into the wooden form pressed upon his mouth. An eighth of an inch of its surface splintered off. Oh, if he could only hold out long enough to bite the smallest hole through to air! ... He is responsible for his family! He cannot leave them like this! ... This could not be the answer to life! He had bitten halfway through when his teeth snapped off to the gums....

For Paul, his new role as father-provider will also require that he minister to his grieving mother, Annunziata, as well as to an uncle crippled by the fallen building. Neither the city's welfare bureaucracy nor the church relieves Paul of his burdens. Fortunately the crew of immigrant workers with whom he works becomes a rough-and-tumble family of sorts. (One of the workers is in fact his godfather.) Annunziata, too, has the sympathy of immigrant wives and widows to help sustain her. That the immigrants have one another is their only salvation as the city resonates with attributes of stone — cold, indifferent, and impervious. The unseen rich and powerful rule the city while the health and the lives of the immigrant workers are constantly being sacrificed in the relentless drive to create monstrous skyscrapers. The Italian workers view a city devoid of grace.

> Morning-born senses brought vividly the solarized city into ken. Sharp against sky's light-light blue concave stood the architectural stance buildings — now tall and pointed — now squat and square — now sandstoney buff in ornate rolls — now with jail-bar severity — ugly — and never beautiful.

Even language betrays differences between immigrants and the soulless city. When Paul and his fellow workers speak to one another in Italian, they express themselves in poetic rhythms and metaphors. When non–Italian New Yorkers speak English, the words issue as argot, crass or debased.

In some regards *Christ in Concrete* is very much a novel in accord with the fashionable proletarian fiction of the Depression thirties. Workers for the most part are salt of the earth; and somewhere in the murky background are the ruthless capitalists who exploit them. And yet, despite tired conventions, one senses not only the author's genuine compassion, but also his admiration for his immigrants. Not long removed from the land, they retain in their beings nature's great love of life. Italians are not just victims; they dance, they drink wine, they make love, they wed, they even feast when money is available. They bring warmth to an otherwise cruel environment.

Di Donato moved away from the city in 1930; some seven or eight years later, he would write his book. But images of the city years stayed in his memory. New York for him stood as the concentrated image of the larger world. The rich and the powerful were the enemy, bent on using or rejecting ordinary humanity. During World War II di Donato became a conscientious objector, and remained an antagonist of the "system" until his death in 1992. He wrote six other books — one about Mother Cabrini — but none of his others expressed the passion of his first.

As a rule of thumb, nearly all novels about the immigrant experience are written by the children or grandchildren of immigrants. This, however, is less true of first generation male Italian-Americans, who are expected to find gainful employment rather than to indulge in the unreliable arts. Thus the autobiographical writings of di Donato and his successor, Mario Puzo, are phenomena not just because their authors are men but also because their subject choices are often viewed as the province of women — family and the care and rearing of children. (According to the author Gay Talese, Italian men are especially guarded about family matters.) In di Donato's case, as we have seen, Paul, the central figure, becomes father to his siblings while simultaneously reaching out to a metaphorically extended family of Italian immigrants. A quarter of a century later, Mario Puzo would publish his autobiographical *The Fortunate Pilgrim* (1966), focusing on Lucia Santa, an immigrant mother, and her efforts to bring up her six children. Here again New York plays its role both as a hard taskmaster and as a supportive Italian community. If poverty and the lures of cosmopolitanism tear families apart, immigrant neighborhoods help provide cohesion.

Although Puzo's novel centers on Lucia Santa, it also tells at some length about the lives, fortunes, and thoughts of her children. Some of course fare better than others, some are sad, some prosper. One son, Gino, seems modeled on Puzo; one son, Lorenzo (Larry), moves insidiously, almost inadvertently, into a life of crime; and a daughter, Ottavia, marries unhappily. But their stories always revolve around Lucia Santa. She is the bravest, perhaps the shrewdest, despite poverty and peasant ignorance. Puzo tells us that she was so humiliated by poverty in her native Abruzzi that she came alone to America, married by proxy to a New York City Italian immigrant whom she had once known as a child. She bears him three children before he dies on his job. She gives birth to three more children by a second husband who goes mad and years afterwards dies in an institution. Lucia Santa carries on.

Lucia Santa's America is New York. It is the only America she knows, and yet, in its peculiar way, the city is also part Italy: "Each tenement was a village square, each had its group of women, all in black sitting on stools and boxes" exchanging gossip, memories and opinions. To be sure they complain often enough about America, remembering the strict moral codes of their ancient Italian villages, but their complaints are really directed at the bewildering varieties of behavior the city tolerates. In truth they love the city. Like the West of old, it promises hope and opportunity for them and their descendants. Near the start of the book, Puzo makes the analogy explicit. They are pioneers:

> *Mannagia America!—* Damn America. But in the hot summer night their voices were filled with hope, with a vigor never sounded in their homeland....
>
> The truth: These country women from the mountain farms of Italy, whose fathers and grandfathers had died in the same rooms in which they were born, these women loved the clashing steel and stone of the great city, the thunder of trains in the railroad yards across the street, the light above the Palisades far across the Hudson.
>
> Audacity had liberated them. They were pioneers though they never walked an American plain and never felt real soil beneath their feet. They moved in a sadder wilderness.... It was a price that must be paid.

But if they are pioneers, they are also cowboys. At the novel's start, the time is 1928 and Lorenzo, a "dummy boy" carrying a lantern for the New York Central Railroad, rides his horse through the streets of the city to warn traffic of oncoming north-south trains. A few years later an overhead pass would be built and scouts like Larry would become obsolete. But for now he evokes romantic images of the West. Indeed, for Larry, the city is the heroic West of American movies.

> Larry Angeluzzi spurred his jet black horse proudly through a canyon formed by two great walls of tenements, and at the foot of each wall, marooned on their separate blue-slate sidewalks; little children stopped their games to watch him with silent admiration.

As straight and as arrogantly as any western cowboy, he sits on his mount and will later sleep in a stable "cowboy-like on a prairie of stone." Larry's dreams are, however, also dreams of women and American riches. "He would be powerful. He would make his family rich. He dreamed of wealthy young American girls with automobiles and large houses...." In contrast, his half brother, Vincenzo, sees the city as hell:

> A watcher on the western wall of the city, everything weighed down his soul and spirit, the wasteland of railroad yard, steel tracks, deserted box cars, engines giving off dirty red sparks and low hoots of warning. The Hudson was a black ribbon beneath the cragged Jersey Shore.

Over the years Lucia Santa, now mother and father to her brood, embraces within herself her children's diverse visions, addressing her sympathies, her angst, her fury, her love to one and then to another. She is of course not always sure of herself, dimly aware on occasion that her old-country outlook may hinder her children's development. She scorns her daughter's desire "to be happy." Happiness, for Lucia Santa, is not the business of life. Nor do poetry or literature, "fairy tales," enhance one's capabilities of facing hardships. Nonetheless, the traditional disciplines she does wield preserve the family. Ceremonies as unremarkable as family dinners (lovingly described), as well as more ritualized wakes, weddings and funerals, save the family from their worst instincts. However much her children have strayed, however much they suffer disappointments, none is as alienated as Cahan's David Levinsky. Ironically, the Italian city that has kept them together for so long has succeeded only too well. The family, having acquired some wealth at about the time of World War II, moves out to the suburbs.

Puzo's sensitivity to Lucia Santa and her generation were, he concedes, closely drawn from memories of his mother and the neighborhood he grew up in. He was born in 1920, roughly ten years after her arrival in America. Her first husband, a brakeman for the New York Central Railroad, died, leaving her three children; she had three more by a second husband who abandoned her. Mario educated himself (despite his mother's skepticism) in city schools, in city libraries, settlement houses, and finally as a GI in World War II. His first novel, *The Dark Arena* (1955), deals with American air force personnel in postwar Germany, and he wrote his "true" family novel, *Pilgrim*, while working as an editor for a business management magazine. Financial success came ironically with his subsequent crime family "godfather" novels of the 1960s, 1970s and 1980s, designed mainly for mass consumption. But of all his works, his favorite was *Pilgrim*. Surely it was his most deeply felt and imagined, opening up vistas of city life rarely portrayed. Puzo died in 1999.

The influx of immigrants from eastern and southern Europe came to a near halt with passages of legislation in the 1920s establishing prohibitive quotas from these regions. Only after World War II would new laws ease such restrictions. In the interim, New York continued to lure large numbers of persons from outside the North American mainland, chiefly from the Caribbean islands and Latin America. Although many arrived from rural areas, unskilled and uneducated, others — especially Cubans and Dominicans — came in large part from middle-class or propertied backgrounds. It does not of course follow that such advantages always assure success elsewhere. Sometimes a little alienation helps. Immigrants too immersed in their own culture may be unable to adapt to very different demands elsewhere. A case in point are the first two novels of the Cuban-American writer Oscar Hijuelos, whose immigrants misread New York as the golden West while their offspring experience New York as something akin to a Wild West.

Our House in the Last World (1985) spans the years 1929–1975 and with a large cast of supporting characters relates the adventures of the Cuban immigrant couple Alejo and Mercedes Santinio and their American-born sons, Hector and Horacio. The opening section of the novel, "Cuba 1929–1943," tells of the families of the protagonists, their courtship, and their decision in the midst of World War II to depart for New York. Mercedes descends from mercantile gentry now in greatly reduced circumstances. (Her father had once been a wealthy timber merchant who brought up his children on a large estate.) Both parents come from Spain and dream and sentimentalize and wax nostalgic about their younger Spanish years. Mercedes inherits her parents' romantic traits along with what one assumes are native Cuban folk beliefs in magic and ghosts and spirits. Her hobbies extend to reading movie romances, and when she first meets Alejo she is working in the box office of the Neptune cinema in a small town in Oriente province. She especially idealizes her deceased "Victorian" father who in reality periodically beat her as a child. Like him, she would write poems about nature, myths, and an imagined glorious Hispanic past. So embedded is she in her private worlds that when she reaches New York, a city of stone, glass, and concrete, she retreats in confusion from its possibilities.

Alejo, in his own way, is no less a romantic. Although he comes from a family that owns small farms, he has no aptitude for crop calculations and likes to think of himself as an aristocratic Lothario. He arrives in New York expecting to make a lot of money, but because he has no head for business he quickly dissipates whatever little money he had. At first he takes a series of unskilled jobs but eventually works his way up to cook and salad man at a luxury hotel. Yet, as the years pass, he loses all ambition, preferring the drinking camaraderie of kitchen help and neighbors to improved status as a hotel employee. Frustrated and without knowing why, Alejo will drink more and more, beat and bully and even rape his wife as he tries to live up to his Latin fantasies. He and Mercedes live out the rest of their dreary lower-middle-class lives on the edges of Harlem.

Hijuelos nowhere suggests that all Cubans are unable to adapt to the city. Quite the contrary. Friends and family of the Santinios orient themselves to the business climate of New York and later become successful in real estate. Mercedes and Alejo are, however, too locked into their own Latin romantic proclivities. They measure a harsh city almost entirely in terms of their Cubanness. In the course of time, Alejo deteriorates into a barely functioning alcoholic. Mercedes meanwhile sinks deeper and deeper into childhood dreams.

Their children, however, save them from their worst self-destructive instincts. Horacio, tough and cynical, and Hector, dreamy and poetic like his mother, reluctantly mediate between their parents and the jungle realities of New York. Periodically abused, neglected (and in the instance of the younger son, Hector, occasionally overprotected), they nonetheless adapt themselves to the dangerous city streets, where they learn to survive fighting neighborhood toughs and authority figures like the police and schoolteachers. Ironically, while his sons face daily perils, Alejo likes to plunk himself down in front of his television set to watch Wild West adventure programs. Ultimately both boys will escape their own city "Westerns." Horacio, like Puzo's Gino, flees into the safer, more civilized realm of the army and Hector becomes a writer. At the end of the novel Hijuelos allows Mercedes and the two brothers (Alejo is by now long dead) to speak for themselves. In their fashion, they forgive one another.

Hijuelos's next book, *The Mambo Kings Play Songs of Love* (1989), although better known (it won a Pulitzer Prize) is in some ways less successful. It narrows in almost exclusively on two immigrant brothers, mambo musicians, whose personalities somewhat resemble those of the brothers in his first novel. But their arena of experience is confined mainly to music and sex, which makes for a good deal of repetition. What the novel inadvertently does reveal is a city (and a nation) without memory, forgetful and indifferent to the past, too busy and too preoccupied with constant change.

Mambo Kings tells of the arrival in New York City of Nestor and Cesar Castillo who, in the course of a few years, become famous as the Mambo Kings for their songs and performances. In the short run, their Cuban-ness serves them well. But the popular culture is a fickle mistress, volatile and unpredictable and the brothers are not always prepared to meet her changing demands. Sadly they are soon forgotten. If the city remembers too little, the brothers remember too much their earlier lives in Cuba. In this sense their Cuban past becomes a liability in a city given over to constant rebirth.

The younger brother, Nestor, sensitive and poetic, is forever unhappy. Though married and father of an American-born son, he is still obsessed with memories of an unhappy love affair in Cuba. His celebrated ballad "Bella Maria de mi Alma" relates his love for the Maria he left behind. Cesar, conversely, is outwardly "macho," often flamboyantly garbed, a hedonist and womanizer, more attached than he realizes to his family in Cuba. Both brothers read several times an inspirational book called *Forward America*, whose message is that success in America requires a positive attitude. The brothers' lives stand in pathetic counterpoint to the book's title. When his younger brother dies in an automobile accident, Cesar declines into sickness and drink. Although *The Mambo Kings* relates their interactions with other ethnic groups throughout the city, the brothers' sensibilities remain stubbornly Cuban. This is what defeats them. An indifferent city simply swallows them.

Hijuelos, who was born in New York City in 1951 of working-class parents, would write another novel portraying immigrant families — this time, Cuban-Irish who settle in Pennsylvania. (There is an Irish strain in Hijuelos's family background.) *The Fourteen Sisters of Emilio Montez O'Brien* (1989), perhaps as a reaction to the male perspective of *The Mambo Kings,* unfolds from the point of view of several generations of women. But *Sisters* does not project the manic intensity of Hijuelos's first two novels, and he would return in a subsequent work to the New York of his parents and his own growing up years. *The Empress of the Splendid Season* (1999) covers much the same ground as *Our House in the Last World.* Lydia and her husband, Raul, who met and married in New York, are somewhat less bewildered in their new environment than the protagonists of *Our House*, but nonetheless they are not quite able to elevate themselves much above the working class. Raul is a waiter and Lydia, for most of her New York years, is a cleaning woman who comes face to face with a variety of better-off New Yorkers. Their children, Rico and Alicia, cope with the same social turmoil and tensions, especially in the late sixties and seventies, in the same marginally deteriorating neighborhood as did the brothers in *Our House.* The main focus, however, is on Lydia, her workaday world, her uneven relationships to her children and husband, her notions of elegance and sense of propriety, her fantasies about movie stars and even her employers. Like Mercedes in *Our House,* her perceptions have been determined by her small town upper-middle-class upbringing — which of course prevents her from truly assimilating. But what sustains her is her community of Hispanic neighbors. They socialize; they support one another and do what little they can to communicate their values to their children. Here we find a gentler, more sympathetic picture of Spanish immigrant Harlem than in Hijuelos's earlier works. And yet what his immigrants have come for in the city of great expectations they never find. For Hijuelos's immigrants, as for those of di Donato and Puzo, the city looms as an ever tantalizing enigma. If they seldom realize their dreams, their children do, by writing about their parents' bitter lives. The myths of the city work in curious ways.

3

Black Manhattan

James Weldon Johnson, Nella Larsen, Richard Wright, Ralph Ellison

One of history's grander ironies is that the African-American presence in New York reaches farther back than that of some of the city's "oldest" families. New York's first two centuries saw a much larger percentage of black residents (as high as 20 percent) than in subsequent years. The relative decline in the first half of the nineteenth century (to less than 2 percent in 1860) came as a result of many causes, not least of which were severe economic and social barriers and fierce racial antagonisms, especially among working-class Irish immigrants. If during the Civil War Southern slaves could anticipate manumission, New York blacks would suffer mob attacks and lynchings. Nor would they fare much better in the War's aftermath. Immigrants pouring in from all parts of Europe began displacing African Americans in their neighborhoods and work sites — and it was not until the World War I years that the black population would begin to return proportionally to numbers comparable to those of colonial times. Little wonder that African-American perceptions of post-frontier myths of New York differed qualitatively from those of other inhabitants.

And yet, for all that, the African-American presence in the city figured strongly if not dominantly in the early twentieth century. While whites viewed blacks as social and economic problems, black New Yorkers looked at the white majority as indifferent and unjust. Still, in some peculiar fashion, there developed a disfigured conflux of cultures in black and white worlds in music, dance, and theater, and by 1912 (with the publication of James Weldon Johnson's novel, *The Autobiography of an Ex-Colored Man*) in literature.

It is fitting that Johnson should be the first serious black author to depict the city, because earlier in his career he was involved in writing song lyrics and producing black musicals ("coon shows") for the New York theater. These were bits and pieces of vaudeville sketches, song and dance acts, and minstrel-like caricatured comedians who performed for both black and white audiences. Blacks and whites would, however, view the performances differently. Both audiences would laugh and enjoy the simple-hearted, happy-go-lucky "darkies" who pranced and strutted and shuffled across the stage, but blacks also recognized implicitly that the stylized creatures they were watching poked fun at white perceptions of black life — and might indeed poke fun at white pretensions by caricaturing them in blackface. The ever popular cakewalk, for example, a staple in some turn-of-the-century black musicals, was understood historically by blacks as a parody of white Southern plantation dances. As performance pieces New Yorkers initially regarded these as peculiarly Negro entertainment, but in time adaptations of the cakewalk became immensely popular among other segments of the population countrywide, all of which suggests the two communities, black and white, sharing and diverging in their perceptions. But just as importantly, even in the popular arts, blacks felt the need to assume stereotypical roles to please and deceive and mock their white audiences. The principles of shame, deception, self-deprecation, and mockery lie at the heart of Johnson's *Autobiography*. *Autobiography* is not, of course, the only Negro novel about "passing" at the start of the century. There were several others, but none so sophisticated. Indeed, Johnson himself achieved his "success" several times over before publication.

Born in 1871 of upper-middle-class parents in Jacksonville, Florida, he attended Atlanta University, practiced law, and taught school before arriving in New York in 1899, where, as noted, he wrote song lyrics with his brother and several other composers for black musical theater. By 1906 he had begun serving in consulships in Venezuela for Theodore Roosevelt's administration and would later on perform similar duties under President Taft. He returned to New York in 1913 to edit *The New York Age*, a conservative black weekly, and remained in the city more or less permanently thereafter. *Autobiography*, which draws in part on his songwriting years, was begun in 1905 and thus reflects a fin de siècle city. On publication the novel was widely assumed to be true, and, to reinforce the impression, its authorship was left anonymous until 1927. It would be Johnson's only novel although he wrote several other books afterwards, the best of which are accounts of black cultural life in New York (*Black Manhattan*, 1927) and an autobiography (*Along This Way*, 1933).

In addition he served as executive director of the NAACP in the 1920s and later taught at Fisk University. He died in 1938.

As we shall see, *Autobiography* deals with New York as a site of interchangeable racial identities. But Johnson is ambivalent regarding what black identity means. In some ways *Autobiography* is a protest novel, but it protests as much against injustices inflicted on middle-class blacks as it does about racial prejudice generally. Odd as it may sound, he writes, "refined coloured people get no more pleasure out of riding [Jim Crow railroad cars] with offensive Negroes than anybody else would get."

At the very start of the novel, the protagonist-narrator establishes himself as a cultured, sensitive figure unfairly linked to the coarser elements of his race. Indeed, his father is a white Southern aristocrat who has shipped his black mistress and their son north to Connecticut, presumably to avoid embarrassment. As a schoolboy the narrator, who loves Beethoven, is suddenly shocked to learn he is black and therefore barred from partaking of the social and cultural activities to which other children are invited. From here on the novel becomes episodic. As a young man, he goes South to attend a black college but loses all his money and ends up working in a cigar factory in Florida. Later he comes to New York, earning a living as a pianist in a black night club. (The club was apparently set in Jimmy Marshall's hotel in New York's Tenderloin district, where black artists, musicians, and writers would sometimes gather. In fact, Johnson lived in the hotel when he first came to New York.) A wealthy white patron of the club who enjoys both his music and his company takes him to Europe where he sees for the first time his white Southern father and his father's wife. The narrator does not inform his father of their relationship and on his return home he travels South again, this time to gather black folk and ethnological material in rural areas. In Alabama he witnesses a terrible lynching whose black victim is horribly burned to death. Frightened and revolted, the narrator returns to New York, passes himself off as a white man and eventually becomes a wealthy real estate investor. Somewhere along the line he falls in love with a beautiful (blond) young woman to whom he reluctantly reveals his racial secret. Though hesitant, she eventually marries him, but after a few years she dies, leaving him a daughter and a son to whom he is deeply devoted. The novel ends with his confession that, despite his business success, he has deep and uneasy feelings of loss. He believes, he tells us, he has sold out his musicianship, talent, and scholarly ambitions for a mess of pottage.

The novel has its shortcomings. Some events are too telescoped, some implausible (the wealthy white patron, for example), and because *Autobiography* is obviously directed at white audiences there are many asides and digressions where the autobiographer tries to explain aspects of black life or rails against the injustices he and others of his social class must endure. Still, *Autobiography* is a groundbreaker. Like Abraham Cahan's Levinsky, the speaker is not an altogether attractive character. Besides being a bit of a snob regarding lower-class blacks, he is irresponsible, abruptly leaving behind a fiancée when he loses his factory job in Florida. But above all he lives in fear: fear of telling his mother about the loss of college money, fear of telling the New York police about a murder he witnesses in his nightclub, fear of the South after the lynching, and fear of revealing his racial ancestry to the woman he loves. Indeed, it is not at all clear whether he tells his offspring of their African-American blood. All of the above, of course, is understandable — but hardly heroic.

Although all the narrator's fears are carried into his New York life, it is clear the city nonetheless offers him options for another beginning. And if there lies new life ahead for the narrator, New York also allows other kinds of possibilities for African-Americans — possibilities perhaps unimaginable at that time elsewhere in America. The city does grant breathing space to black artists, sportsmen, businessmen, and musicians, however limited their circumstances. Some of the best portions of the book tell of the narrator's adventures in what Johnson called New York's "black Bohemia" (in some ways a cultural frontier as dangerous and attractive as any in western mythology). Pictured are gambling rooms, cafes, and cabarets frequented by black entrepreneurs, gangsters, sportsmen, intellectuals, and musicians. Here, at least momentarily, blacks and whites exist on equal if precarious footing. White people of all social classes attend these places and black men are seen escorting white women. If miscegenation follows from such fraternizing, it would not be as it had been in the caste-ridden South, between dominant white males and subordinated black women (the autobiographer's parents, as a case in point). Of course none of this is spelled out in Johnson's novel — it may well not have been his conscious intention — although his black narrator does eventually have such a union with a white woman. Thus, despite his understandable melancholy, his newly adopted city suggests varieties of choice which may one day render "color" irrelevant.

The blurring of color lines was not, however, regarded as a burning issue for most fin de siècle white New Yorkers. If they thought about it at all, they would probably have subscribed to the generally accepted view that persons were "colored" if they inherited even the smallest quantity of African blood. The consequences of being "colored" were, however, another matter. At the start of the Wilson administration (a year after the publication of Johnson's novel), racial segregation deepened in housing, the professions, the civil service, and the arts. Blacks in Manhattan neighborhoods quickened their movement north (begun as early as 1902) from the midtown and Tenderloin districts to large areas of Harlem. Meanwhile, black theater productions were no longer being produced on Broadway. The black response simmered for several years, but then, perhaps fueled by America's participation in World War I (in which black soldiers served honorably) and reaction to postwar racial violence nationwide, Harlem's African-American community exploded in outrage, averring racial pride and black nationalism. A growing number of artists, intellectuals, composers, musicians, poets, and authors converged on Harlem, producing works mirroring the community's aroused self-awareness. The Harlem Renaissance, as the period of the 1920s came to be called, exhibited superior talents, yet, ironically, much of the Renaissance output served only to accommodate revised white perceptions of "color."

In lieu of earlier images of easygoing darkies or barely restrained violent savages (see, for example, Thomas Dixon's novel *The Clansman*, 1905, followed by the popular 1915 film, *The Birth of a Nation*, based on that book), blacks were now noble primitives, pure of heart, hedonistic, and uncontaminated by the new acquisitiveness, neurosis, and materialism of the white postwar generation. In curious ways, blacks concurred. The cultural critic Alain Locke, in a celebrated book of essays, hailed the "New Negro." Poets and novelists like Langston Hughes, Claude McKay, and Jean Toomer sang of the majesties and mysteries of the peasant and proletarian African-American soul; artists and sculptors like Aaron Douglas and Sargent Johnson extolled the dignity and the African-ness of their subjects; and black leaders like W.E.B. Du Bois and Marcus Garvey (though ideological antagonists) described a new militancy. The city which liked to think of itself as providing the ambiance for all this creativity was perhaps too self-congratulatory. True, themes of renewal and independence rang across the entire black community, but the roles blacks assumed were often the roles ambivalent white audiences desired to satisfy their own suppressed longings. Harlem's celebrated Cotton Club suggests an apt metaphor. Downtown white audiences would throng the club to listen to the genuinely wonderful Duke Ellington and his "jungle rhythms." Black chorus girls sang and danced exotically. Blacks had suddenly become Nature, authentic and "real," no longer threatening. Most black customers were, however, barred.

A much overlooked African-American writer whose works did not appear to conform to the celebratory Renaissance spirit was Nella Larsen. For her, the seemingly various identities New York offered were illusory, if not porous. At first glance her novels appeared as the conservative rear guard of African-American writers. Like Johnson's ex-colored man, her heroines are middle class, torn between affirming their African roots and "passing," attracted to the ease and cultural treasures of the white world, and yet drawn inexorably to an earthy African-American life. Of her two published novels (she is said to have written unpublished works), *Quicksand* (1928) is the better known. The plot's settings are mainly the American South, New York City, and Copenhagen, Denmark. It is not so much a New York story as a story about a sensitive, intelligent young woman's struggle to discover and fulfill her psychological needs. That she is a mulatto of course complicates matters, especially in communities that want to define her in terms of her color. But New York City seemingly differs, offering her the freedom of several identities, and yet even these, as we shall see, draw her into the quicksand of fixed roles. The novel is a protest novel only in the widest sense; it is not only the white world that seeks to define her, but black people as well — not to mention her own vaguely conflicted consciousness derived in part from both communities.

As the novel opens, Helga Crane is about to resign her faculty position at a Southern college because she is fed up with its mediocrity, its genteel pretensions, and stuffy atmosphere. She will also leave behind her somewhat priggish suitor, James Vayle, and the college president, Dr. Anderson, about whom she has ambivalent feelings. Early hints of Helga's buried passionate nature are the vivid clothes she wears, which her colleagues think most inappropriate. They "felt that the colors were queer; dark purple, royal blues, rich greens, deep reds, in soft luxurious woolens, or heavy clinging silks." Helga, whose deceased mother was Danish, goes first to Chicago to visit her mother's brother, but her American aunt receives her coldly. Later, however, she finds work as an assistant to Mrs. Hayes-Rore, a leading YWCA lecturer. Their business takes them to New York, where Helga becomes the companion and housemate of Anne Grey, a young Harlem widow. Anne, who professes to champion black causes and to despise white people, hypocritically (but unconsciously) adopts white cultural standards:

> She hated white people with a deep and burning hatred ... [but] aped their clothes, their manners, and their gracious ways of living. While proclaiming loudly the undiluted good of all things Negro, she yet disliked the songs, the dances, and the softly blurred speech of the race.

Although Helga sees through her, she cannot but admire, indeed identify with, Anne's elegant taste in clothes and furnishings, or, as Helga puts it, her "aesthetic sense." But Helga would also like to imagine herself an anonymous New York African-American. On first arriving in Harlem she would bask in her own blackness. If she could only lose her singularity in the grand diverse mass, "the gorgeous panorama of Harlem. Like thousands of other Harlem dwellers she patronized its shops, its theaters, its art galleries, and its restaurants, and read its papers.... And she was satisfied, unenvious. For her this Harlem was enough." Still, below the quotidian Harlem there lies a pounding heart. At one point Helga attends a black cabaret, a dark and sultry "subterranean room" where musicians play driving sensuous music and patrons dance "violently twisting their bodies or shaking themselves ecstatically." Here Helga sees Dr. Anderson (her erstwhile president) dancing with a girl who responds to the "jungle rhythms" with "grace and abandon," arousing in Helga "primitive feelings." Restless and uncertain of herself, Helga now comes to think of Harlem as provincial. Quite unexpectedly, however, she comes into money left her by her Chicago uncle and she leaves for Copenhagen, where she is welcomed warmly by her Danish relatives. But soon she discovers that she is regarded as an exotic African trophy rather than what she is. What is she? Who is she? Spurning an aristocrat's offer of marriage she returns once more to New York, where she at last gives way to her desire and attempts to establish a liaison with Dr. Anderson, who by now has married Anne. He is tempted but ultimately rejects her, causing the anguished Helga to stagger alone down rain-swept Harlem streets seeking respite. She enters a storefront church and swoons under the spell of its ecstatic congregation and its hypnotic minister. At the novel's close, she is once more living in the South, now the minister's wife, physically and emotionally exhausted by the offspring she must produce for him year after year.

It is clear from the start that Helga has long attempted ways to suppress her sexuality. Her New York City experience suggests several possibilities. She could adopt the life of the haute bourgeoisie like Anne. She could give up her sophisticated sensibilities and become one of the crowd on Harlem streets. She could allow her body to express itself as dancers do in the jazz cabaret. Or she could surrender her entire consciousness to the fervor of evangelical religion. None of these options truly fulfills her and she is sucked into the quicksand of her own contradictions in New York just as she would be anywhere else. The freedoms of Harlem are illusory.

Quicksand is an astonishing book. It is written with an economy of prose and a precision of language. But most striking of all is Larsen's creation of Helga, a rather complicated woman with quick and witty insights into most situations, though unable to understand herself. The ending, however, as some critics have noted, is a bit far-fetched. Anguished as Helga may be, one cannot imagine her giving herself over to the kind of life she chooses.

Yet Larsen's last years have been as enigmatic and puzzling as those of her heroine. Born in Chicago in 1893 of West Indian and Danish parentage she grew up in a white household until adolescence. (Her mother remarried after the death of her black husband.) As a young woman she studied nursing and worked for two years as a librarian in New York City. In 1913 she married a research physicist at Fisk University, but by the 1920s she had come to live more or less alone in New York. Among her friends was the writer Carl van Vechten, who advised Knopf to publish her work. *Quicksand* attained some notoriety at the time — it won a 1928 Harmon literary award — and Larsen followed that six months later with *Passing*. Shortly after, she won a Guggenheim fellowship and traveled about a good deal with a woman friend in Europe. She remained married for a few more years though long estranged from her philandering husband, and in 1931 she was accused of plagiarizing another author's short fiction. Since then no other work of hers has been found or published although she is rumored to have written other novels. From 1931 until her death in 1963 she worked as a nurse in New York City hospitals. No obituary noted her departure.

Passing, Larsen's other novel about upper-class Harlem African-Americans, tells a bit more about how the city is perceived. For one character, the near-white Clare, it provides an enthralling social life. For Irene, her similarly fair-complexioned friend, Harlem is a safe and secure place to bring up her family, no different (except for color) from other American communities. Irene's physician husband, Brian, however, views Harlem as simply another component of the racist segregated America he hates. For the most part the novel describes the complicated relationship between the two women, one of whom, Clare, has successfully passed herself off as white to deceive her bigoted husband. When Brian meets the dangerously adventurous, beautiful Clare (whose husband is often away from the city), Irene begins to fear for the stability of her marriage and will eventually cause Clare's "accidental" death. Although written in the third person, the narration unravels from Irene's increasingly dismayed consciousness, and there are subtle perceptions of both her attraction to and terror of her presumed rival. As for New York City, only Clare envisions her life in Harlem as promising new possibilities, new freedoms — and she sadly must die.

The sense of New York City as a place where one could forge new identities and thus free one's self for a new life serves as a subtext of Richard Wright's *The Outsider* (1954) and Ralph Ellison's *Invisible Man* (1953). Not only is it possible to reinvent oneself, survival for African-Americans demands an ever-changing persona. The horror is not so much that one is frozen eternally in an unfair identity (as portrayed in much black protest fiction) but that in New York one must shift constantly from role to role.

Wright and Ellison were sometime friends from the 1930s until Wright's death in 1960, but they differed publicly about what they thought should be the novel's mission. Wright argued that the novel should convey unsparingly society's generally negative influence on the human spirit, especially that of African-Americans. Ellison suspected such an approach. ("People who write sociology should not write a novel.") He would focus more on an individual's growing sense of self even when that person was interacting with a hostile white world. Yet both authors met, more or less, on the same grounds in their New York novels. Indeed, a curious reversal took place. In *The Outsider*, Wright, the social novelist, would become almost metaphysical in portraying his hero's plight — not in racial or sociological terms but as a universal human condition. Ellison, on the other hand, would lay emphasis on black culture and on the black community as being somehow redemptive. Probably neither author would have liked to admit that, despite their stated differences, their vision of the city coincided. Of the two, however, Wright's turnaround was the more radical.

Much of Wright's fiction prior to *The Outsider* drew on his responses to the brutalities of racism he experienced or witnessed or learned about during his lifetime. Born in Mississippi in 1909, he, his mother and brother (his father had abandoned them when Richard was very young) moved about from one Deep South community to another at a time when Jim Crow laws and violence were at their worst. At age seventeen, Wright managed to escape to Chicago, where he worked at odd jobs (among them the post office, one of the opening settings of *The Outsider*) and where later he would join the Communist Party. Whatever else its influences, the Party imbued in him a Marxist worldview enabling him to compose two of his most powerful works of fiction, *Uncle Tom's Children* (1938), a book of novellas that takes place in the South, and *Native Son* (1940), about an adolescent black killer in Chicago. Ten years after Chicago, Wright moved to New York where he became Harlem editor of the communist *Daily Worker*. But early in the 1940s he broke with the Party, believing it to be manipulative and deceptive. The break was more than political. There were psychological consequences. Not only did he lose longtime friends, but more importantly the Marxist substructure by which he had come to understand himself and his times was now largely loosened. In 1947 he and his wife and daughter moved to Paris (a second daughter was born in France), hoping to escape American racism. It was in Paris some years later that he finished writing *The Outsider*, which some critics felt at the time smacked too much of fashionable French existentialism. Be that as it may, Wright's choice of a New York setting for much of the novel allows his hero possibilities of dreaded freedoms unimaginable elsewhere in America. Wright would go on to publish one other novel in his lifetime and several works of nonfiction, but none so revealing of his pessimistic humanism.

To suggest Wright and Ellison shared similar views of New York is not to suggest their books are equally successful. Wright's is by far the more flawed, probably because having lost his faith in communism he could not find as strong a philosophical base on which to anchor his imagination. Indeed, he tried to marry his newly acquired existentialism to a kind of fictional naturalism more suited to a social novel. The attempt was surely admirable but ultimately unsuccessful. Ideas tend to overwhelm characterization, if not the very plausibility of the narration.

At the beginning of the novel Cross Damon, a Chicago postal worker, laden with guilt and responsibilities and anxieties about his wife, children, pregnant mistress, and pious mother, manages to extricate himself from a freak subway accident. Newspapers and police identify him as one of the dead and Cross determines to begin life anew elsewhere. He hides out in a hotel-brothel where quite by accident he encounters a postal worker who recognizes him. Fearing exposure, Cross quickly kills him and flees. On a train to New York, he meets Bob Hunter, a Communist dining car waiter who hails him as a race brother and Ely Houston, a white New York district attorney, who evinces great interest in Cross's lengthy disquisitions on the purposelessness of the universe, the meaninglessness of life and man's consequent sense of dread. Both Bob and Houston figure strongly in Cross's ultimate fate.

In New York City, Cross appropriates a name from a gravestone and pretends to a buffoonish stupidity in order to inveigle a birth certificate from credulous white city clerks. Reborn as Lionel Lane, he again meets Bob and with his help begins sharing a Greenwich Village apartment with Gil Blount, a white Communist, and his wife, Eva. Cross is aware that Gil and his Party cohorts do not value him as an individual but rather want to use him as a goad in their struggle against Gil's fascist landlord. Cross later observes his friend Bob (a Party member) being humiliated by Communist officials. Cross's belief is thus reinforced that, despite professed ideals, the Party exists chiefly as a body of power arrangements where serried ranks of the hierarchy wield absolute control over their subordinates. In truth the Party's hidden appeal is the lust for power that sits at the bottom of human nature.

Cross yearns for freedom but despairs that freedom depends on the subjugation of others. When Cross comes upon Gil and Herndon (his black-hating landlord) fighting, he kills them both. By now, Eva, who has fallen in love with him, believes Cross a persecuted victim. But when Cross tells her of his crimes, she commits suicide. As the novel nears its end Cross manages to kill yet another Communist, but not before an additional exchange of views (fourteen pages long) expatiating on existence, the value of human life (not very much), and the nature of man (at root, a bundle of "impulses and desires"). At long last, the city's district attorney and the Party (though not of course in cahoots) cotton on to Cross as a killer. Houston brings Cross's wife and children to New York to confront him, but Cross refuses to acknowledge them. Houston wonders at his heartlessness, but Cross is only following the logic of his ethos. Finally Party members, more convinced than ever of Cross's culpability, gun him down on the street and the dying Cross confesses to Houston that there are more and more people in the world like him who are tearing away at civilization's disguises and see life as simply a savage struggle for existence:

> Don't think I'm so odd and strange.... I'm not.... I'm legion.... I've lived alone, but I'm everywhere.... Man is returning to the earth.... For a long time he has been sleeping, wrapped in a dream.... He is awakening now, awakening from his dream and finding himself in a waking nightmare.... The myth men are going.... The real men, the last men are coming.... Somebody must prepare the way for them.... Tell the world what they are like.... We are here already, if others but had the courage to see us....

The true horror of his life, he adds, is that "in my heart ... I'm ... I felt ... I'm innocent...."

Although Wright paces his novel well, the plot is farfetched and much of the dialogue sounds unlikely. As regards his characters, several serve mainly as mouthpieces for Wright's ideas. That is to say, that despite their differing political and cultural stances, Communists, Fascists, Cross himself, and even Ely Houston, all basically look at life in much the same way. The world is without moral or spiritual design, a deplorable truth that individuals and societies attempt constantly to conceal from themselves. All history simply records the struggle for dominance, nothing more. To illuminate these insights a bit more, there are allusions throughout to Husserl, Heidegger, Jaspers, Nietzsche, Kierkegaard, Hegel, and Dostoyevsky. For our purposes it is worth noting that, although Wright completed this novel some four or five years after leaving America, he chose to play out his ideas not on foreign soil but on the amorphous terrain of New York City. And yet, where other writers would endeavor to reproduce for the reader the look or feel of streets, neighborhoods, and buildings, Wright projects a cityscape very nearly barren of detail. What we have is simply a third person narration from Cross's perspective. It is almost as if the environmental void requires the novel's characters to create and re-create their personae at will.

Consider, for example, not only the chameleon behavior of the police, Communists, and fascists, but also the various roles Cross casts for himself. For Houston, he is the alienated intellectual; for Bob, he is a race brother; for the city clerks, he is the black simpleton; for Gil Blount, he is a weapon in the struggle for Party dominance; for Eva Blount, he is the victim-lover; for Herndon, their landlord, he is the symbol of an inferior race; and for Cross's wife and children, he is the bourgeois breadwinner on whom they depend. Could Cross's scenarios be played out in any city other than New York? It could of course be argued that he resorts in extremities to an ancient African-American trickster tradition as a means of survival. Certainly the New York setting allows trickster behavior greater plausibility. Still, as we have seen, by granting him symbolic rebirth, the city also allows him the freedom to assume his multiple identities. In the end his freedoms are made possible because ironically others refuse to see him as simply a man. He is, in other words, what Wright's onetime protégé, Ralph Ellison, had earlier called an Invisible Man.

Ellison's *Invisible Man* came out a year before Wright's novel and reflects perhaps a more benign view of New York life despite the fact that the hero undergoes some fearful trials. In part the reason may lie in the revelation that the Invisible Man (his name is not given in the novel), like Ellison himself, comes to the city better equipped to employ African-American culture as a resource in confronting social tensions. Wright, as a youth in his constant peregrinations across Mississippi, seldom stopped long enough to sink roots and assimilate what was positive in black life. What he did see, he writes in his autobiography, was bleak and vapid — and white America was the enemy. Ellison, on the other hand, derived from a fairly stable family and grew up in a thriving black Oklahoma City community where black culture, he writes, melded easily with the wider mainstream American culture.

Five years younger than Wright, he was educated in public schools and later attended Tuskegee Institute, where he focused most on music and literature. From his earliest years, he writes, he was drawn to black music and he cites the Kansas City jazz musicians whom he knew in Oklahoma. When he came to New York in the mid–1930s he was determined to become a jazz trumpeter, but he also sought out Wright, whose published poems intrigued him. Wright encouraged him to write fiction and even helped pave the way for him in left-wing publications. Yet, despite their friendship, Ellison's first stories reflect little of radical doctrine, though they did on occasion deal with black-white conflict. By the early 1950s, however, the literary reputations of the two writers had taken a decided turn. Wright, now the expatriate, was largely dismissed as a protest author, while Ellison's star was on the rise. The differences in temperament and outlook between the two could not have been greater, and yet in the novels they published within a year of each other their treatment of New York City is in some ways remarkably similar. Both recognized, for example, that the city's peculiar racism paradoxically produced peculiar freedoms. But first the differences.

As regards their protagonists, Ellison's Invisible Man is very different from Cross Damon. The latter is a serious reader of iconoclastic western philosophers as opposed to Ellison's hero who, for the better part of the novel, resembles a Candide-like innocent. Unlike Cross, who from the start of *The Outsider* knows how the world works, the Invisible Man becomes aware of his invisibility in New York only after a series of initiatory adventures in the South. In a sense, the city in its blindness and indifference to his humanity educates him as to his invisibility, whereas Cross educates the city that invisibility may produce a murderous rampage.

Another major difference between the two novels lies in their structure. Where Wright fashions his book as straightforward narrative fiction, Ellison's work reads like a picaresque jazz blues score, the refrain of which comes at the end of each of his hero's adventures — a riot, an explosion, an upheaval, a disturbance or trauma of one sort or another. Ellison signals this approach at the start of the novel where he depicts his first-person narrator hiding out in a Harlem basement as he plays a phonograph record of Louis Armstrong, "What Did I Do to Be So Black and Blue?" Although the narrator does not tell us much more about the recording, the reader imagines Armstrong reciting his several woes and closing each account with the song's title. This, in a manner of speaking, is what the narrator must ask of himself as he mulls over the disastrous results of so many of his past endeavors to assume the roles the white world would impose on him. In New York, as we shall see, the black man's role-playing possibilities proliferate, but they come at the peril of obliterating his soul. Crouched in a basement, the Invisible Man is literally invisible to the people who walk overhead and metaphorically invisible to those who fail to see him as he is. But who is he? Here in his retreat he will reconsider his situation. His tale up to the present constitutes the bulk of the novel. The first portions of *Invisible Man* tell of his life in the South where, as a schoolboy, a high school valedictorian, and as a college student he attempts unconsciously to play out the various racial fantasies of the surrounding dominant white world. Each of these ends in a near catastrophe not only for the protagonist but often enough for the whites whose expectations cannot be realized. When the narrator comes to New York seeking employment, his consciousness begins to change. After a series of rebuffs by business executives who believe him a troublemaker, he manages to get a job in a paint factory.

Here the Invisible Man (and the reader) begins to learn that African Americans have always been essential to the nation's growth as well as to its historical underpinnings — and that these truths are mainly hidden from public view. (The paint, often used to cover national monuments, is called optic white because below its illusory white surface lie several drops of black.) The narrator next learns of African Americans' equivocal relationship to organized labor when he becomes inadvertently involved in a conflict between his ancient black supervisor, Lucius Brockway, and white unionists who traditionally keep blacks from joining their ranks. Brockway thinks him disloyal, they struggle, and meanwhile the machinery they are supposed to be tending explodes. When the Invisible Man awakens in a hospital operating room, doctors are busying themselves with his brain; but, try as they might, they cannot quite deprive him of fragments of his cultural heritage. The hero escapes and flees to Harlem. In metaphoric fashion the protagonist had thus recapitulated black history in the city in which he has sought opportunity.

In Harlem, the narrator observes dreadful economic deprivation. At one point he witnesses a poor elderly couple and their pathetic belongings being evicted onto a sidewalk — and so aroused is he that he delivers a fiery spontaneous public denunciation, causing enraged onlookers to return the unhappy pair and their furnishings to the vacated quarters. Subsequent episodes deal with the narrator's uneasy relationship to a romanticized black nationalism (as exemplified by Ras the Exhorter, an exotic African-garbed street corner orator who exhorts blacks to violent rebellion) and the Communist Party (cited in the novel as the Brotherhood), which recruits him to employ his suddenly discovered eloquence to persuade other blacks to join the Party. But he later discovers that Brotherhood leaders view him and indeed other African-Americans as instruments to be manipulated for the enhancement of Party power. (Here the novel anticipates Wright's *Outsider*.) More significantly, the narrator comes to reject the Brotherhood's (Marxist) philosophy of history which fails to account for the African-American's past or for that matter his continued presence. Traumatized by the sudden violent death of his friend Clifton, a black street vendor, he retreats to a subway where he awakens to new "ahistorical" insights while observing a group of black youth:

> I stared as they seemed to move like dancers in some kind of funeral ceremony, swaying, going forward, their black faces secret, moving slowly down the subway platform, the heavy heel-plated shoes making a rhythmical tapping as they moved. Everyone must have seen them, or heard their muted laughter, or smelled the heavy pomade on their hair — or perhaps failed to see them at all. For they were men outside of historical time, they were untouched, they didn't believe in Brotherhood, no doubt had never heard of it; or perhaps like Clifton would mysteriously have rejected its mysteries; men of transition whose faces were immobile.

Eventually a Harlem-wide riot erupts, houses and apartment buildings are burned to the ground, stores are looted, and the narrator finds himself perceived as the enemy, by both the Brotherhood and the followers of Ras. He dons a disguise (about which more later) and ducks into a manhole, pursued, as it happens, by white hoodlums. If his New York experiences up to now are a symbolic run-through of African-American history, the Harlem uprisings of 1943 are Armageddon.

Although the above is an extremely condensed synopsis of a richly detailed, lyrically related, sometimes comic novel, the events described highlight a convergence of city myths — the city of violent frontier chaos and social inequalities, as well as the city of intellectual perceptions and new West possibilities of renewal, rebirth, and changed identities. And yet the city's ultimate absurdity is that by denying blacks their place in the sun blacks are made free to create and re-create themselves. Ellison does not stop there.

Invisibility so permeates the American culture that blacks may become invisible to one another. In the heat of the Harlem riot the fleeing protagonist, who has donned a wide-brimmed hat and dark glasses, finds himself constantly being stopped on the street and addressed as someone named Rinehart. But the Rinehart people profess to know always differs in his calling. For some, he is a numbers runner, for others, a gambler, or a lover, or a "spiritual technologist," a Seer of the Unseen. In effect the Invisible Man is disguised as Rinehart, who is himself apparently a man of many guises. But who was Rinehart? What was the rind and which the true heart? Whatever his identity, his "world was possibility ... [a] vast seething hot world of fluidity," and Rinehart designs himself in as many images as he wishes. The Invisible Man is thus not without hope. Perhaps soon he will emerge from his underground place and discover his true self. At the very least his New York life has intensified his existence, aroused him to a consciousness of his invisibility. What next?

In 1994 Ellison died before completing his second novel. Judging from what has since been published (a friend and editor has put together manuscript fragments of the novel Ellison had been writing, published as *Juneteenth*, in 1999), Ellison had not yet resolved the issues his Harlemite refugee pondered many years earlier.

4

First Generation or Jews Without Money

SAMUEL ORNITZ, MICHAEL GOLD,
HENRY ROTH, ANZIA YEZIERSKA,
DANIEL FUCHS, DELMORE SCHWARTZ

Not unlike Southern blacks, impoverished eastern European Jews at the start of the century looked to be a pariah nation. As we know, African Americans with their long history of racial woes grappled with New York myths in their own fashion. Jews, as we shall see, would resort to other strategies. Still, it is a curious twist of history that both African Americans and eastern European Jews would in the course of the next hundred years influence so much of the city's culture.

Anti-Semitism in America was obviously not so volatile as black-white racial antagonism, but from the start the image of the Jew even in the nineteenth-century imagination seldom configured favorably. In American letters he was frequently depicted as ruthless, acquisitive, underhanded and untrustworthy (in short, a Shylock)—unless of course he converted to Christianity.* Indeed, in 1654 New Amsterdam's Dutch Reform governor, Peter Stuyvesant, tried to bar Jewish immigrants from Brazil on grounds they would threaten the homogeneity of the colonists' Christian worship. (To be fair, it should be noted also that Stuyvesant loathed Quakers, Baptists, and Congregationalists, and barred entry to Lutherans and Catholics.) He may not have known that several of the stockholders of his employer, the Dutch West India Company, were Jews. In any event, company stockholders overruled Stuyvesant since in fact they rather

*See Louis Harap, *The Image of the Jew in American Literature*, 1974.

liked the idea of infusions of the capitalist spirit which Jews were presumed to possess. Stereotypes persist, not always favorably, however, and one can imagine the alarm many native-born white Americans — Brahmins and populists, workers, farmers, and industrialists — felt at the huge incursions of eastern European Jews who, beginning in the 1880s, all seemed to be settling in New York. These Jews, with their peculiar foods, dress, diction, and religious practices, were not like the earlier generations of German and Hispanic Jews whose appearances seemed at least more in accord with mainstream American life. And as noted in an earlier chapter, even German Jews were dubious about their newcomer coreligionists. To be sure, Jews, like other immigrants, confronted myths of reborn identity even before they reached American shores. But, unlike other immigrants, they were a despised ethnic minority within their mother countries and hence often confined to separate communities where they would produce for themselves an insular, integrated culture.

How would they fare in a more tolerant New York? In *David Levinsky* we saw how the protagonist, an immigrant, becomes a successful businessman by shedding little by little his ghetto observances. As a general rule it was not that easy for adult immigrants to release themselves from a culture that had nurtured them all their lives. It would remain for their offspring to strive for American dreams. Would this require that they wean themselves from all that their parents had taught them? Possibly a clash of values lay in the offing. For now, however, the first business of the children was to rise above their parents' straitened circumstances. Still, who could foretell that an economic depression would strike at American dreams thirty years into the upcoming century? For Jews, meanwhile, struggles to seek places in the new American sun would produce variations on New York myths. The present chapter intends to devote itself to some of the writings of that first generation of eastern European Jews, the children of immigrants, or themselves immigrants whose childhood and youth were lived in New York.

One of the first novels to deal with escape from the ghetto is Samuel Ornitz's *Haunch, Paunch and Jowl* (1923). Set in the late 1890s and in the first decades of the new century, it is a lively first-person account of a scoundrel's ascent from Lower East Side poverty to fashionable Jewish Riverside Drive prosperity.* Although the novel obviously owes something to Cahan's *Rise of*

---

*To most New Yorkers today the term East Side signals the middle class and upper middle class areas east of Fifth Avenue. For purposes of clarity I try to make the present-day distinction: the Lower East Side generally means those areas south of Fourteenth Street and east of Third Avenue.

David Levinsky, it fits more easily into a kind of American rogue's progress genre wherein rotten heroes tell their stories without an iota of remorse. In this respect *Haunch* may be a precursor of some of the short stories and novellas of Ring Lardner or the later novels of Jerome Weidman and John O'Hara. Put another way, it sends up Horatio Alger rags-to-riches tales or, better still, Benjamin Franklin's not altogether truthful autobiography. The great joke of course is that it turns upside down bourgeois shibboleths and laughs at the simple pieties of the masses. To succeed, all the hero really need do is dissemble. In sum, Ornitz embraces and very nearly unites antithetical New York myths. Yes, success in New York is achievable, upward mobility attainable, and one's identity renewable, not in spite of but *because* the city is itself so immoral. Yet, if Ornitz expresses a point of view not startlingly original, he does amaze with profusions of the New York experience that relate to his hero's dubious career. We read not only about the miniature interweavings of ghetto life but also of New York's larger public life — its civil service, its police, its religious institutions, and even its ethnic politics.

As a child, Meyer Hirsch lives in a crowded tenement flat with his working class uncle, his mother and his tubercular father, a sewing machine operator who finds sporadic work in sweatshops. Meyer tells of his childhood years shuttling between home, his cheder (a decrepit religious schoolroom), and the lures of a gang, the Ludlow Streeters, whose feats over the years graduate from pranks, to petty crimes, to ethnic battles with "Irishers," to outright criminal activities. Meyer sticks with the gang through the early years of his adolescence and remains in touch with many of its members and former members throughout the novel. Some become killers and professional thugs, some doctors, others social workers, popular entertainers, union organizers, and businessmen. At the onset of his teen years, Meyer attends public school (he did not have to work very hard) and afterwards the City College (much more demanding), and in due course becomes a rather shady lawyer who, when convenient, aligns himself with Tammany Hall. His ultimate prize at the novel's end is a New York State judgeship. As the novel unfolds Meyer makes alliances and sheds alliances within rival Jewish organizations and charities, the Democratic and Republican parties, emerging labor unions, and unscrupulous garment manufacturers. In short he is ambitious for himself alone and as he grows older, fatter, smugger, and richer his enemies allude to him as Haunch, Paunch and Jowl. Yet, despite his overall repellent behavior, Ornitz grants him a few saving graces. He may pretend to himself that only the material things in life are desirable, but he is not unmoved by, or disdainful of, the idealism of a few of his friends, nor even of the poems some of them write. Oddly, too, although Meyer regards himself as a tough-minded realist, he is not immune to romantic or sentimental yearnings. On these occasions his inner life seems to be in conflict with his other needs for position and power. It must be said, however, that Meyer does not always get everything he wants. One of the women he desires throughout the book constantly eludes him, and Meyer's ambition to run for mayor is thwarted because of fears that it would become publicly known that he has lived unmarried with a woman for many years — to whom, incidentally, he had not always been faithful.

Apart from its bildungsromanish character, *Haunch* is rather good at portraying some of the new century's popular culture. At one point Meyer joins other Ludlow Street teenagers to form a singing-dancing troupe who eventually get to perform professionally. He tells how songs are composed (almost by committee), what audiences they are aimed at (working-class Jews and Irish, and middle-class slummers), and where they are performed (in clubs, cafes, and rathskellars from the Tenderloin to Chinatown). Descriptions of such places, as we shall see in chapter five, are also vividly created in Stephen Crane's *Maggie, Girl of the Streets*. Finally Meyer tells us how much of the vitality of American popular music derives from African-American sources. Indeed, Ornitz (via Meyer) appears to be one of the few white authors who in the early 1920s willingly acknowledge positive black contributions to "mainstream" American music:

> Ragtime has the whole country jogging. From the World's Fair in Chicago it sent syncopated waves bounding across the length and breadth of the land. The negroes had given America its music. Soon the white man started stealing the negro's music and making it his own. There was money in the negro's music. Cultured people snickered at it. Boston, which at this time still claimed to be the center of culture, stuffed its ears. Musicians, who ruled and confined their art with religious dogma, raised their hands and voices in horror and denunciation. The elite, the elect, the polite, the ultra-fashionable, and their aping followers, despised ragtime and complacently decreed its early doom. But ragtime had the vitality of a people's music and the whole country hummed, sang, whistled, two-stepped and cried for more doggerels and maddening tunes.

No one could mistake Ornitz's book as straightforward realism. Embodied in much of the prose are ideological messages which, fortunately for the reader, seldom intrude in what is otherwise a swift-moving narration. In effect he tells us that capitalism erodes, distorts, and compromises human lives not simply in terms of material necessities but in terms of character and morality as well. Meyer speaks of what happened to average fellows who looked for economic salvation in business or the professions:

> A few rubs of the rough-grained world wore away the idealistic tenderness.... It did not take them long to see that the straight and narrow path was long and tortuous and ended in a blind alley. There was nothing in the conspicuous example of American life to inspire anything else. Politics stank of corruption and chicanery. Big business set an even worse example.... The order of the day was — PLAY THE GAME AS YOU SEE IT PLAYED.... It was a sordid generation, a generation creeping out of the mud into the murk. There was not as yet an American identity. There was yet to rise up an American standard.

Meyer himself feels trapped. "I had taken root in the morass." When Meyer speaks thus, he steps out of character because of course he is himself the most flagrant example of everything he deplores. At other times Ornitz may put in the mouth of a secondary character viewpoints that reinforce his anticapitalist animus. In some instances he does not care much if what he says offends Jewish readers — as when he holds responsible some Jews for fostering anti–Semitism. Here is Avrum, one of Meyer's erstwhile socialist friends, who after conceding the horrors of Jewish persecution in Russia casts blame not only on the czarist government but on Jewish moneylenders and traders: "We must tell our people ... that these traders and moneylenders, the leaders and controllers of our community, this minority of profit-takers are the root causes of the pogroms.... Is it not easy to be incited against the persons who have been systematically wronging you? Stop the wrong, the first wrong, and you will end the ultimate wrong." It follows then that Ornitz would level similar kinds of criticism at rich Jewish businessmen ("allrightniks") who, having fled poverty, now often enough exploit their unfortunate brethren still mired in ghettos. Nor will he spare their wives, "plump and fat women who blandished the extremes of the latest styles in clothes, trying to out vie one another; and were never seen without a blinding array of diamonds on ears, breasts, fingers and arms...." As for the allrightnik men, their "faces were puffed and sleekly pale; their bellies stuck out as the show windows of their prosperity." They interpret life in terms of moneymaking. Their entire identity revolves around conspicuous consumption. Ornitz will not even grant them gestures of generosity: "Show. Show ... Even in their charity. Charity was another outlet for display. Pompous, righteous beneficing ... Show."

How finally shall we assess this book? Oddly, despite its raw urban subject matter, there are flourishes of modernism. Meyer, in telling his story, will occasionally resort to streams of consciousness which seem remarkably to antedate the writings of James Joyce and Virginia Woolf. He is also perhaps self-consciously aware of his literary forebears. Meyer's life is divided into seven "Periods," with introductory epigraphs as far-ranging as Jean-Jacques Rousseau and Saint Luke. Sometimes, too, the symbolism wears itself on its sleeve. Meyer's Yiddish "love name," Ziegelle, which means little goat, also suggests a goat's antisocial character. Meyer's friend Beryl explains that "nothing bothers a goat and that makes people angry. A goat manages to get along where other creatures perish.... He is for himself; unfeeling and befriends no one." Perhaps here Ornitz overreaches for symbolic significance, but nonetheless *Haunch* does not deserve the neglect it has suffered. In his massive study of eastern European Jews in America, *World of Our Fathers* (1976), the critic Irving Howe has written that with the atrophying of Yiddish culture and the passing of the immigrant generation there would be no more Jewish-American literature. Howe may be right, but Meyer's cynical manipulation of some of New York's self-congratulatory myths informs us that Jewish-American literature at its first flowering was surely capable of uncovering some rather nasty truths.

Of Ornitz himself not much is known. He was born in 1890, the son of a prosperous dry goods merchant. But unlike his brothers, who followed their father into the family business, he became a committed socialist who at the age of twelve delivered fiery speeches on New York's Lower East Side streets. The novel *Haunch* was evidently drawn on some of what he had learned as a social worker for the New York Prison Association as well as for the Brooklyn Society for the Prevention of Cruelty to Children. But six years after the publication of *Haunch* he looks to have given up hopes of remaining a novelist; he took up employment as a screenwriter in Hollywood. None of the films he wrote are particularly noteworthy — although one of these was *Imitation of Life*, adapted from a novel by Fanny Hurst about a black girl who tries to pass as white. One wonders whether the divided loyalties of the heroine struck the screenwriter as corresponding to his own situation. Still, Ornitz never really tried to conceal his political sympathies. He was one of the founders of the left-wing Screenwriters Guild, and in 1947 he was sentenced to twelve months' imprisonment for refusing to answer questions the House Un-American Activities Committee (HUAC) put to him. He thus joined other screenwriters sharing the same fate who later became known as the Hollywood Ten. Upon his release Hollywood studios refused to reemploy him and he spent the rest of his years writing fiction. He died in the Los Angeles Motion Picture Country Home in 1957.

In some respects Michael Gold's *Jews Without Money* (1930) covers much the same span of years as *Haunch* as well as much the same material. One major difference is that Gold's autobiographical novel — it reads more like a memoir — focuses almost exclusively on lives on the Lower East Side. Another difference is that the hero of Gold's book, who incidentally shares the first pen name as the author, fails to rise much above poverty. Though Gold (né Irwin Granich) was himself a dedicated Communist — this was his only novel — he rarely editorializes until the book's last hortatory paragraphs prophesying a workers' revolution that would displace the Messiah of his childhood religious upbringing. Where Ornitz and Gold diverge most, however, are in their prose tones. Ornitz's Meyer is after all a cynic-realist who plays the ruthless and amoral game of life as he sees it. Gold's Michael, on the other hand, cares deeply and passionately for almost all the people he writes about. It is perhaps odd to say of Gold, who liked to think of himself as being a scientific Marxist, that he has written a novel of love, not of the romantic love of men and women, nor of the love of the impoverished humanity that engulfs him (although there is some of that), but of a deep love for his immediate family and especially his mother:

> My humble funny little East Side mother! How can I ever forget this dark little woman with bright eyes, who bobbled about all day in bare feet, cursing in Elizabethan Yiddish, using the forbidden words "ladies" do not use, smacking us, beating us, fighting with her neighbors, helping her neighbors, busy from morn to midnight in the tenement struggle for life. She would have stolen or killed for us. She would have let a railroad train run over her body.... Mother! Momma! I am still bound to you by the cords of birth.

As an addendum to the above, it must be said that Gold also emits intermittent howls of rage at persons or forces he believes exploit the poor.

On the whole, Gold manages to avoid sentimentality, relating whatever he wants to say in straightforward declarative sentences juxtaposed to narrative images that give themselves over to emotional resonance. Hemingwayesque? Gold and the redoubtable Ernest would probably have hated each other, but there is an unlikely kinship of style. Here, for example, Gold tells of a disastrous fight with a neighborhood gang on a desolate empty lot. What follows is not exactly the retreat from Caporetto, but on its small scale it serves its purpose. He begins by describing the site of the warfare as being on "shabby old ground, ripped like a battlefield by workers' picks and shovels,

[a] little garbage dump lying forgotten in the midst of tall tenements...."
Michael and three of his friends are playing tipcat under a blue April sky.
"The air was warm. Yellow mutts moved dreamily on the garbage. The sun
covered the tenements with gold. Pools of melted snow shone in the mud.
An old man smoked his pipe and watched us." Suddenly they are attacked
by a gang of about fifteen boys who swoop down on them "like a band of
Indians." It was a massacre. "Abie and Jake were buried under a football pyra-
mid of arms and legs. Stinker, who had earned his nickname because he would
whine, beg, weep and stool-pigeon his way out of any bad mess, howled for
mercy." Butch, the formidable gang leader, pummels Michael. "It was a duel
between cockroach and a subway train." When they are finally allowed to get
to their feet, Butch sneers at them, "Listen, you guys ... this dump belongs
to us Forsythe streeters, see? Get the hell out." Michael and his friends scoot
off. "Our shirts were torn, our stockings chewed up, we were muddy and
wounded and in disgrace."

Strictly speaking, *Jews Without Money* is not a novel about growing up.
Some segments of the book omit Michael almost entirely and instead devote
themselves to portraying young Michael's East Side world. These passages
seem aimed at gentile readers, telling them who Jews are and how they lived
in the century's first years. Some passages tell of the city as if addressed to
foreigners: "New York is a devil's dream, the most urbanized city in the world.
It is all geometry angles and stones. It is mythical, a city buried by a vol-
cano." But it is also a city populated by other impoverished ethnic groups —
Irish, Italians, Chinese, and Negroes whom Jews constantly confront not only
on streets but also in tenement buildings and factories. Some of Michael's
statements are too generalized to be taken seriously. Jews, he says, are not
drunkards, after which he describes a wine cellar he visits with his father
where some of his fellow Jews appear to be rather tipsy. Or again: Jews in the
old country were never gangsters. (Evidently Michael never read Isaac Babel's
Odessa stories about Kric, the gangster chief.) Still, not all Gold's East Side
Jews are heroic or noble or hardy proletarian survivors of barely tolerable circumstances. He tells as well of small entrepreneurs, real-estate speculators,
violent criminals, pimps, and whores who, as often as not, exploit Jews and
Christians alike. Nor are his Jews always so tolerant of their Christian neighbors. He tells of a crowd of Jews jeering and booing in front of a church porch
where a Lutheran clergyman appears to be cleaning an icon.

But Gold's tales of the squalor and horrors of the Lower East Side can
also be tempered by nostalgia. The dreary, broken, garbage-strewn lot on

which he plays "blazes" romantically in memory. "No place will ever seem as wonderful again," he writes. He remembers picnicking with his parents in Bronx Park and on occasion watching his younger sister and other street children dance to the music of an Italian organ grinder: "Her pigtails fly, as she jogs in and out of the mazes of a Morris dance. There are other dark skinny girls. Their little bodies are aflame with rhythm." The entire street enjoys the spectacle:

> Some of the prostitutes have left their "business" for the moment and watch with gentle smiles. The cop leans against a lamppost and smiles. A grim old graybeard with a live chicken under his arm is smiling at the children. A truck driver slows down and watches them dreamily as he rattles by. Mothers watch from tenement windows. A fat important little business Jew, bursting like a plum with heat, mops his face and admires the children.

Nor is Gold himself immune to American myths, American dreams. The boy Michael buries himself in Buffalo Bill stories and imagines himself a western hero as he wanders boldly and foolishly into dangerous Italian streets. And even New York at its most hellishly hot evokes a kind of surreal poetry. Tenants scramble to sleep on tenement roofs on scorching summer nights.

> Sometimes the wind stirred from the Atlantic. Sometimes the hot fantastic moon looked down, and remembered us in the Arabian desert. Some nights it rained. The heavens suddenly split, the thunder rolled down the Brooklyn Bridge. We saw the lightning, like a stroke of insanity, as it created huge nightmare vistas of an unbelievable city of towers, New York.

Jews Without Money was the only novel Gold would produce, although in the 1920s he worked as a reporter and as an editor of radical publications such as *The Liberator, The Masses,* and *The New Masses.* He began his writing career in 1917 as a poet and a few years later assumed the pen name of a Jewish Civil War soldier who fought "to free the slaves." In the late 1920s he cofounded with the playwright John Howard Lawson the New Playwrights' Theater, modeled, they believed, on theaters in the Soviet Union. However, apart from his novel, Gold was best known for his cultural criticism, especially during the pre–World War II years. In the main, most of the articles, reviews, and essays he wrote — frequently in *The Daily Worker*— excoriated Trotskyites and authors whom he regarded as hopelessly mired in ossified bourgeois attitudes. He was especially vitriolic toward Marxist or leftist authors who diverged from current party-line communism. Although for the most part he skirted the issue of literature as propaganda, he felt that fiction should, in one way or other, express or advance the cause of proletarian revolution. There is no evidence at this writing that he ever changed his mind. He died in New York in 1967 at the age of seventy-four.

How on earth does one ultimately classify Henry Roth's *Call It Sleep* (1934)? It is at one and the same time an immigrant novel and a growing up in New York novel; it is a modernist symbolist work with drumbeat echoes of Freud, Joyce, and T.S. Eliot; it is a naturalistic account of Jewish life during the country's first decades in Brooklyn and on the Lower East Side; it is a book whose religious strains contain strong undercurrents of mysticism; and finally, I would argue, it is a book about language — not only about language at levels of dictionary meanings, but in a larger sense language as gesture, facial expressions, sounds, and tone, much of which David Schearl, the child protagonist of this novel, tries to ingest. Indeed language seems at times independent of what the central drama of the novel relates, as Roth sometimes goes outside David's immediate experience to record mosaics of voices.

But *Sleep* chiefly concerns itself with David's widening sensibility. In 1907 he has emigrated with his mother from eastern Austria and lives for the next seven or eight years in the Bushwick area of Brooklyn and in Manhattan's Lower East Side. David's father, who had left for New York before David's birth, meets his two-year-old son and wife upon their arrival at Ellis Island. At first David's only language is Yiddish and he must not only attempt to understand the strained relationship of his parents but also learn the highly inflected Yiddishized English of neighborhood children. A major problem Roth faces is rendering in English the spoken Yiddish of immigrants with all its nuances, imagery and hyperbole as well as recording the debased English they and their offspring speak. Compounding these complications are the voices, diction, and dialects of a gentile New York world which may on occasion act as a kind of choral attendance on David's life. Clearly, David's understanding expands as he grows older, but he is still a child with a child's limited knowledge and experience. In this respect one thinks of Joyce's *Portrait of the Artist as a Young Man.** Although Roth never specifically cited this work as an "influence," Joyce's youthful hero's developing consciousness corresponds in its way to what Roth would attempt. As for David, it is not until he allows, or resigns himself to granting, the mélange of sounds that engulf him, however incoherent and discordant, to

*Roth in his later years would denounce Joyce's work as casting an antihistoricist influence on contemporary writing. Another of Roth's influences was T.S. Eliot, whose anti–Semitism he also came to deplore.

coexist in his consciousness that the novel tentatively resolves itself. But before dealing in closer detail with Roth's negotiations of language, it would be well to recite further some of the contents of the book.

It is apparent from the start that David's father does not like him, nor is he particularly fond of David's "greenhorn" mother. Albert Schearl in the book is constantly angry or abusive and at times violent. He is unable to hold a job for very long, nor can he get along with his fellow workers. Genya, David's mother, is as protective of David as she can be, but she has the added burden of trying to mediate between her volatile husband and her raucous, indelicate sister, Bertha, who, before marrying, comes to live with the Schearls. David himself is in a constant state of anxiety, not just because of his parents' precarious marriage but because of the demanding rabbi at the cheder he attends and because of the strange and hostile gentile children he confronts. One of the central dramas of the book revolves around David's relationship with a gentile boy, Leo, who David envies as being unencumbered and whose Christian amulets, a scapular and a rosary, David believes possess a kind of magic that would free him of his fears. In order to ingratiate himself with his new friend, David leads Leo to his cousin Esther, who "plays dirty" with him in a cellar. When David's role is found out, he flees his violent father in terror and attempts to produce an effect similar to the explosive burst of flame that allowed Isaiah to invoke God. In David's Talmudic imagination an angel had pried open Isaiah's mouth with a hot coal. David, anticipating a similar miracle, plunges a metal milk jug dipper under an electrified streetcar rail, but rather than a miracle occurring, the resulting explosion knocks David unconscious as well as arresting all streetcar traffic up and down the line. Alien Christian voices surround him as he gradually regains consciousness. If David does not attain direct contact with God, he has at the very least submitted peacefully (if only temporarily) to the mysteries and dangers of a world he cannot quite fathom.

The above summary can only suggest David's New York childhood and the suppleness and vibrancy of Roth's prose. Beyond narration certain words serve as a force underlying thematic passages of time. Each of the novel's four sections, The Cellar, The Picture, The Coal, and The Rail, thus advance well beyond literal meanings. On a looser level, a mastery of language (English) becomes essential for immigrants to navigate New York. David's mother, for example, is rendered almost immobile because she can barely pronounce the name of her street. She speaks in Yiddish of her frustration:

"Boddeh Stritt ... It's such a strange name — bath street in German. But here I am. I know there is a church on a certain street to my left, the vegetable market is to my right, behind me are the railroad tracks and the broken rocks, and before me, a few blocks away is a certain store window that has a kind of white-wash on it — and faces in the white-wash, the kind children draw. Within this pale is my America...."

Likewise, when David cannot find his way home he is unable to communicate his address to adults who try to help him. On occasion a Yiddishized English may convey a lurking sexuality fraught with menace and fright. A crippled girl, not much older than David, takes him into a darkened closet. Babies come from the "knish," she tells him. "Between de legs. Who puts id in is de poppa. De Poppa's god de petzel. Yaw de poppa." David flees, but regardless of language he cannot escape the omnipresence of sex.

As one instance, Leo displays disturbing images of the Virgin Mary and of Jesus wearing what David takes to be a loincloth. But it is within David's family that sexual tensions are highest. David senses that a friend his father brings home for several dinners will attempt to seduce Genya — and when at a later time the Schearls move to Manhattan, David's enraged father rips apart the "erotic" drawers his Aunt Bertha has purchased. To be sure, there is the usual family romance. David's father becomes more and more envious of Genya's affection for her son and begins to convince himself that David was sired by a "goy." Meanwhile, within the house there are reminders of suppressed sexual and Oedipal moments. David's mother brings home a picture of a pastoral setting that recalls long-ago country trysts with her Austrian lover, and some time afterwards David's father brings home a pair of bull horns that evoke in him long-ago memories of the farm animal that killed his own father.

Toward the end of the book Roth takes us more and more outside David's immediate outlook. In a set piece we see David's squat and rather ungainly cheder instructor, Reb Yidel Pakower, waddling along the street immersed in his own random thoughts, which range from how America has disengaged Jewish children from their heritage to his own fears about David's Jewish legitimacy. Was David's father a goy?:

What was going to become of Yiddish youth? What would become of this new breed? These Americans? This sidewalk-and-gutter generation? He knew them all and they were all alike — brazen, selfish, unbridled. Where was piety and observance? Where was learning, veneration of parents, deference to the old? In the earth! Deep in the earth! On ball playing their minds dwelt, on skates, on kites, on marbles, on gambling for the cardboard pictures, and the older ones, on dancing, and the ferocious jangle of horns and strings and jigging with their feet. And God? Forgotten, forgotten wholly.... Not one could speak the tongue without a snuffle or a snort — except this child, David, this bastard, God have pity on him, a goy's spawn, a church organist's. Hi! Hi! And it is strange that true Yiddish children of pious parents should prove such God-forsaken dolts and this one — only half-a-jew — perhaps not (I could have found out then and there, but —) circumcised — an iron wit. God's ways. Hidden.

And finally Roth captures for us fragments of conversations (mainly about sex and sexual betrayals) in beer saloons, warehouses, tenement apartments, sidewalks and the like just before David plunges the milk ladle into the rail. (Even the hot coal thrust between Isaiah's lips appears to be suggestively erotic.) Here one thinks of Flaubert, who in his novels introduces seemingly unrelated images and voices alongside major dramatic actions — or, perhaps even more immediately, the protagonist's search for God amidst the spiritually disfigured denizens of the "unreal city" of T.S. Eliot's *Wasteland*. How reconcile seeming opposites? How reconcile the God-seekers with the rest of a soiled humanity? In Roth's novel, David will in the end leave them all be and call it sleep.

Despite spottily good reviews, Roth would not publish his next novel for another sixty years. He was eighty-eight in 1994 when there appeared the first of what would become a quartet of autobiographical novels Roth called, under a collective name, *Mercy of a Rude Stream*. (At this writing two more are said to be in the offing.) These purport to follow the first twenty-one or twenty-two years of a new protagonist, Ira Stigman, highlighting accounts of his religious and secular education, his jobs, his tormented sexual encounters, his developing intellectual interests, and a love affair of sorts with a college instructor who encourages him to become a writer. Most of the action takes place in Jewish East Harlem and in Greenwich Village, and the books are written from the perspective of an old man looking back on his life. In reality these works follow much more closely Roth's growing up years than *Call It Sleep*. It would be unfair, however, to compare *Mercy* with *Sleep*, whose main focus is on a child's developing consciousness of himself and his surroundings. Still, in one respect, the *Mercy* books do resemble *Call It Sleep* in that their protagonists, David and Ira, both come under Roth's moral scrutiny. How innocent is David Schearl? How guilty is Ira Stigman?

A conceit in the *Mercy* books is that from time to time the Roth–Ira Stigman character probes his computer for the psychological and moral consequences of his behavior. Indeed there are several moments when Ira and the computer engage in heated colloquies. Again the City plays an overtly dele-terious role on first-generation American Jews, separating them from their own old-world traditions — just as the fictional Reb Pakower of *Call It Sleep* had feared. As Ira becomes more and more adjusted — "assimilated" would be too strong a word — to a relatively heterogeneous New York, he becomes more flagrantly dismissive of Judaism. Indeed, as a growing boy he sighs with relief that he no longer need attend religious classes. According to his biographer, Steven G. Kellman, Roth is supposed to have said at one point in his life that America's greatest gift to the Jews is that they no longer need think of them-selves as Jews. But then, not long after the end of World War II he appears to have changed his mind, rejoicing in his ethnicity and announcing strong Zionist sympathies. Roth departed New York in the late 1930s, abandoning Edith Walton, the college teacher who had long supported him. Oddly, he came to feel himself more a Jew in gentile American environments than in New York Jewish neighborhoods. Although he never really came back to live in the city, the city remained amazingly alive in his literary imagination.

It would be daunting to enumerate all the jobs Roth held in his life-time — among them, in no particular order, were toolmaker, plumber's assis-tant, boxer, psychiatric aide, Latin teacher, and waterfowl farmer. In none of these did he seem to have excelled, although he managed apparently to pro-vide some support to a wife and two sons. The grand question remains, of course, of how to account for the sixty-year hiatus between his novels, surely the greatest gap in literary productivity. Actually he did attempt another novel after *Call It Sleep* and seems to have written a good deal of it before he him-self destroyed it in a panic of despair. It had to do with the travails of a union organizer. Roth during those dreary years of the Depression joined the Com-munist Party and came to believe his writing failed to convey the proper rev-olutionary spirit. (Roth himself was at one time beaten up trying to organize dock workers.) Whether Roth's conversion to communism rendered him cre-atively sterile, as he sometimes claimed, for so long a period is questionable. He did after all write a few intervening short stories, articles, and other pieces. Roth himself, however, conceded that a novel is a sustained emotional under-taking. A more likely reason for what some critics call Roth's lengthy writer's block was a constant ever-present gnawing sense of guilt. Not only does the Roth–Ira Stigman figure tell his computer of an incestuous relationship with his sister, two years younger than he, but he also carried on another liaison with a cousin. The revelation of these affairs in the second of the *Mercy* books, he believes, liberated him to write more expansively, although his "tainted" sister, sixty years after their trysts (who, incidentally, typed *Call It Sleep*), pleaded with him not to write about their illicit encounters. In any case, whatever the competing virtues of producing a work of art as opposed to not exacerbating one's elderly sister's anxieties, Roth was first and last a writer, and the multiple contradictory strains of City themes sear through each of his books.

As a general rule, twentieth-century first-generation New York City Jewish writers — especially Ornitz, Gold, and Roth — came to regard the religion of their "old country" fathers as burdensome, or at best something to be set aside in order for them to realize their American-ness. To be sure, their attitudes reflected the usual generational conflicts (aggravated no doubt by the city's seeming attractive alternatives), but there were substantive reasons as well. Much of the religious education to which so many of them were subjected in dismally shabby quarters seemed to them rote and tedious. They believed, as a consequence, that the American ideals they sought were divorced from traditional religious demands. Specifically they felt that religious Judaism failed to address their life experiences as well as the exciting challenges of the new American environment. Nor did Christianity appeal to them as a replacement — indeed, conversion seems seldom to have occurred to them. Memories of past Christian persecutions were too deeply imbued in their culture, and American anti–Semitism too immediate to regard organized Christianity with anything but extreme skepticism. Agreed, a few Jews did convert, as does one character in Ornitz's *Haunch, Paunch and Jowl,* but they did so often enough in the belief that church attendance would be socially or economically advantageous. Thus the three authors we have so far dealt with looked to radical solutions to reach for their American dreams. Their new religion became Communism and it would take the post–World War II years before they might even allow to themselves that not only had their communist god failed but also that the fountainhead of their ideology, the Soviet Union, revealed itself as capable of oppressing Jews as any other regime. Readers need not of course demand that authors relinquish their ideologies, religions, or political beliefs, but the effectiveness of a work of art depends on its transcending fixed codes. If the business of literature is life, life is too messy, too amorphous to surrender altogether to predetermined systems of thought. In spite of themselves, and in spite of their politics, Ornitz, Gold, and Roth were artists.

Anzia Yezierska is another writer who would concur in an antireligious outlook in her novel *Bread Givers* (1925). She arrived in New York in the early

1890s, one of a family of ten, and grew up in the city's Lower East Side. The New York she brings to *Bread Givers* tolerates dreadful poverty but also allows for a way out by the city's public education, thereby offering mythic possibilities of a new identity. Her heroine, Sara Smolinsky, shares the Jewish reverence for learning but now the education she yearns for is secular. The suffering she undergoes is brought about not so much by a barely tolerable poverty, but by a Torah-driven father who regards all women as mere appendages of men: "It says in the Torah that only through a man a woman has existence. Only through a man can a woman enter Heaven." Reb Moisheh Smolinsky browbeats his saintly wife, who only occasionally rises to defy him, and devotes practically all his time to studying Jewish law, leaving it to the womenfolk to provide for the family. In the course of the novel he compels Sara's three older sisters to marry unsuitable men they do not love. But Sara, the remaining unmarried daughter, rather than submit to tyranny, leaves the parental home, finds sweatshop jobs, and manages to attend night school classes. Afterwards she enrolls in college somewhere outside the city (how she affords this is not explained), and returns to New York economically independent (also unexplained) to become a public school teacher. Shortly after her arrival, her mother dies but a happy ending of sorts may be in the works. There looks to be a romance in the offing with her school principal — she had apparently frightened away two other men who thought her too aggressive. In short order, along with her two married sisters, she comes to the financial rescue of her ungrateful father, now remarried to a greedy widow.

The Bread Givers is not a particularly elegantly written novel — the Yiddishized English Yezierska occasionally produces sometimes works and sometimes doesn't — but it is relatively rare in city literature because it tells of the Lower East Side experience from a woman's point of view. Yezierska doesn't spare us some of the raw events in her heroine's life: the numbing family disputes about money, the pathetic attempts to clean and decorate the Smolensky family's Hester Street flat, the travails and humiliations of a single woman finding work and food and living space in New York's slum neighborhoods. And finally, but not least, there are the heroine's inner conflicts between the traditional Jewish family-centered roles that women are expected to play and Sara's desire to strike out on her own. These conflicts are not as easily resolved as some feminist critics would have us believe. For all Sara's yearnings for independence, we see she also seeks a Jewish husband, albeit someone who respects her as a person. Perhaps just as significantly, even after she achieves her longed-for independence she remains inexorably drawn to her family and especially her father, who believes, as we have noted, that all women are lesser beings. In the end, nonetheless, Yezierska's novels differ from those of the other male authors we have so far looked at. They, we know, deplored the extremes of the city's capitalist individualism which they believed lay at the heart of urban pathologies. Yezierska, surely no apologist for capitalism — indeed she lived for a while at the socialist Rand Institute — celebrates some of that individualism as a means of liberation.

It is not immediately clear how much of *Bread Givers* is autobiographical. There are conflicting accounts of Yezierska's birth date and country of origin. According to one source, Alice Kessler Harris, she was born in Russian Poland and arrived in New York at the age of eight. As regards her other writings, they contain much the same material as *Bread Givers*: Lower East Side Jewish women yearning to escape poverty and dreaming of bursting through their own stifling cultural restrictions. Men in these stories are either contemptuous, unattainable, or unsuitable. In one of Yezierska's novels, *Salome of the Tenements* (1923), Sonia, the heroine, describes herself as an "ache of unvoiced dreams and the clamor of suppressed desires." It would therefore be nice to think that in her own lifetime Yezierska achieved her dreams, but, unhappily, only a few of these were realized. To be sure, she had begun publishing short stories as early as 1915 and a collection of these, *Hungry Hearts* (1920), was bought by Hollywood and converted to film. She subsequently sold the film rights to *Salome*, but despite these successes she returned to New York where she felt her true subject matter lay. There were by now two unsuccessful marriages and an aborted love affair with the philosopher John Dewey. But although her output in the 1920s was relatively productive (five novels among several other writings) she published little afterwards and her works during the Depression decade were all but forgotten. She did find some employment on a WPA project during the thirties but produced only one other book in her lifetime, a memoir, *Red Ribbon on a White Horse* (1950), whose title recalled her father's Yiddish wisdom: "Poverty becomes a wise man like a red ribbon on a white horse." Yezierska herself died in near poverty in 1970 in New York City.

Perhaps the most comprehensive novelist of first-generation New York Jewish life was a Brooklyn high school teacher, Daniel Fuchs, and judging from his writings he was nowhere near being seduced by Communism. The first of his three city novels, *Summer in Williamsburg* (1934) was published the same year as *Call It Sleep* but drew even less attention than Roth's book. At first glance it looks to be more ambitious than *Sleep*—though not so determinedly modernist. Roth, as we know, focuses chiefly on the consciousness of a growing child, while Fuchs's book dwells on a relatively large number of inhabitants, most of whom live in a tenement house in the Williamsburg section of Brooklyn, and tells how their lives intertwine and interweave with their environment. The conceit of a tenement house as somehow containing a cross section of the larger community was not necessarily original with Fuchs. Elmer Rice attempts quite the same thing in his play *Street Scene* (see chapter nine), but Fuchs's novel deals with a far larger cast of characters — children, adolescents, impoverished tradesmen, widows, janitors, gangsters, unemployed actors, intellectuals, would-be scholars, and a few affluent Jews who live in the dreamland of upper Manhattan — not to mention their opposites, pious old men who gather together in Williamsburg tenement cellars to discuss and argue about the Talmud. He may also tell of Williamsburgers' less dramatic moments, but even when crimes, suicides, and tenement building fires occur they seem part and parcel of the day-to-day life of the community. The novel genre allows Fuchs to pursue the lives of the marginal poor at some length, and among these he concentrates more on Philip Hayman, a young man of twenty-one who seeks some kind of hidden order in what looks to him to be Williamsburg's formless existence. Why, for example, does a seemingly stable, well-liked neighbor decide to kill himself? Philip consults Miller, one of the old men in the building. Miller's answer could serve as a recipe for the novel:

> You must pick Williamsburg to pieces until you have them all spread out on your table, a dictionary of Williamsburg. And then select. Pick and discard. Take, with intelligence ... and with a patience that would consume a number of lifetimes, the different aspects that are pertinent. Collect and then analyze.

Miller is a thorough-going materialist. People, he continues, are like the atoms that constitute the physical world, but "they do not belong to one type but are variously commingled. The ultimate product, man, therefore moves mysteriously, but he is the scientific outcome of cause and effect." Philip is troubled. Does this mean that there exists in life no underlying morality, no independent truth, no realization of beauty? Miller does not give him much encouragement. Beauty, like the moon, he says, is an impersonal natural phenomenon, and on earth there is finally only one certainty and that is the reality of money. Philip cannot accept these views, but in a sense Fuchs's book is a young man's book, employing Miller's methodology for uncovering Williamsburg. Interestingly, Miller himself is a miser who derives his income from mourners by reciting prayers for their dead at Greenwood Cemetery.

Philip, Fuchs's fictional surrogate, goes far afield in investigating Williamsburg experiences, but no basic principle truly emerges that would make of these a unity. On several occasions Philip contrasts the morality of his elderly father, an honest, decent, and generous man, with that of his uncle, Papravel, a "successful" criminal businessman. Even Philip's brother, Harry, feels uncomfortable dealing with his uncle. When Harry tells his uncle that he cannot in good conscience work for him, Papravel responds:

> Everybody who makes money hurts people. Sometimes you can't see the people you are hurting, but you can be sure all the time there is always someone who gets squeezed if he is not ruined. That's the kind of world it is, and who am I to change it? ... But remember this, Harry, no matter where you go, no matter what business you'll be in, remember there will always be people who will live in rotten houses, who will have no money for a good time and who will die ten years earlier on account of you.

Papravel's version of the world in this novel does unfortunately appear to hold more than a grain of truth. There are everywhere described hurtful conflicts within families, ethnic street gang fights among adolescents — Jews and Italians, Jews and Irish — and duplicitous, bitter, squalid quarrels between men and women, husbands and wives. Nor do traditional political or religious institutions stand up very well in Williamsburg's relentless struggles for meaning. Philip admires the old Jews in his building who strictly adhere to ancient beliefs, but at the same time he feels that they are out of touch with the real world. Or perhaps they are part of a real world that deludes itself about its amoral nature. Nor are the supposed amelioratives that aim to lessen or cure over-all Depression miseries any more effective. Countryside "resort" getaways for Williamsburgers echo pretty much the same tensions and antagonisms Williamsburg residents experience in the City. Labor unions are run by gangsters, politicians and police are corrupt, and even members of the revolutionary Communist Party are hypocritically caught up in their own unworldly rhetoric. One of Philip's friends joins the Party in hopes of sleeping with one of its women recruiters. He fails. She betrays him for someone else.

One insightful observation Fuchs makes in this novel and, as we shall see, his two other New York works is the overall prevalence of the popular culture in people's lives. In the absence of religion or ideology or positive and supportive cultural institutions, Hollywood and radio offer Fuchs's Williamsburgers not only escape but templates of fulfillment. Take, for example, the vulnerable teenager Davy, whose ideas of wealth, heroism, manhood, and romance derive from a wonderfully absurd movie called *The Ace of Cads*. "It was a moving idyll and it was set among the fascinating rich of London, people who acutely impressed Davy because he wondered, do these people go to the bathroom?" As he leaves the movie house Davy says, "That's it, I wish to grow up fast." At the book's close, Philip (now even more obviously acting as Fuchs's alter ego) looks out on the Williamsburg streets and thinks it impossible to write a book that equals Williamsburg's reality. How does one truly depict people?

> These were people as God made them and as they were. They sat in the sunshine going through the stale operations of living, they were real, but a novelist did not write a book about them. No novel, no matter how seriously intentioned, was real.... What was all the excitement about? Philip asked himself. Literature was not reality. That was all there was to it. Writers who said otherwise were fakers, claiming more than they could do.

Fortunately for readers Fuchs does not altogether succumb to his fictional Philip's pessimism. He would write two more novels about the kind of people Philip believes novelists cannot truly write about. *Homage to Blenholt* (1936), Fuchs's second novel, is both very sad and very funny. Sad because so many Williamsburgers in the novel want to escape Williamsburg who, we suspect, never will; and funny because their attempts to do so are entirely ludicrous and misplaced. Again, one of Fuchs's main settings is a Williamsburg tenement building and once more Fuchs tells about what transpires within some of the apartments as well as about the misunderstandings, acrimony and friendships in the neighborhood as a whole. Interplays of relationships among tenants comprise a somewhat more focused world in this book than in Fuchs's first novel: there are fewer characters we must look out for and there is more of a centralized plot. Lovers are awkward and innocent. Parents, offspring, and siblings often at odds with one another are depicted as well as being very close. And children in their invented games, backbiting fights and betrayals resemble in miniature their more "serious" adult models.

The main character is Max Balkan, a young man in his twenties who puts off looking for a "real" job in hopes that big business will discover his innovative genius and employ him in a top rung position. He buttresses these hopes by writing advertising and promotional suggestions to industry executives who invariably reject them in polite form letter responses — although, truth to tell, some of his schemes sound rather imaginative. Still, in the last analysis Max is more a dreamer, a romantic, an idealist than he is anything else, despite the consensus of other tenants that he is really a schlemiel who refuses to give in to the plodding, dreary rhythms of Williamsburg life. His girlfriend, Ruth, another tenant in the building, also takes a rather dim view of Max's schemes — why can't he be practical, she asks — but Ruth's thinking is itself often filled with the sounds and images of a fantasy-ridden popular culture. At one point she dozes off at the beauty parlor as snatches of radio love songs, photos of crooners and movie stars, and titles of true confession and women's magazines flood her consciousness. Fuchs produces more than a page of these. The reader here may be forgiven if he thinks Max's rags-to-riches New York aspirations are no crazier than Ruth's sentimental daydreams.

Max is finally brought down to earth by two events — the first when he attends a turbulent, chaotic thug-dominated funeral for Blenholt, a corrupt, gangster-like City sewer commissioner who Max, for the longest time, had fantasized as a modern-day Tamburlaine. But Max is sadly disabused when the deceased Blenholt's henchmen attack outraged protestors. In the ensuing pandemonium, Max gets badly hurt. The second debacle occurs when Max discovers his imagined long-sought breakthrough with the directors of a nationally advertised onion company (he had suggested bottling onion juice) turns out to be another disillusioning experience. Max's father, a onetime actor in the Yiddish theater who is now reduced to wearing a clown costume with advertising sandwich boards on Williamsburg streets, unhappily observes his son's dreams die. Mr. Balkan, himself once a dreamer, recognizes "the clamorous demands of the world, its insistent calls for resignation and surrender, and he knew now that Max would never be the same again. Much had gone out of Max, aspiration, hope, life. His son would grow old and age-ing, die, but actually Max was dead already for now he would live for bread alone." The old man remarks to himself "that this death of youth" was among the greatest tragedies in America.

The third of Fuchs's New York books, *Low Company* (1937), came out only two years after *Blenholt*. Now the setting would no longer be Williamsburg but a place Fuchs calls Neptune Beach, a cross perhaps between Brooklyn's Coney Island and Brighton Beach. In a sense, however, he uses the same format that he employed in his two previous novels. Instead of a tenement house being the locale from which much of the narrative emanates, the center of action is now a combination ice cream parlor and cafe whose owner, Mr. Spitzbergen, figures strongly in the narrative. There are, however, no longer any young men or truth seekers or idealists or dreamers like Philip and Max of the earlier works, but chiefly immigrants and the children of immigrants clawing and embracing one another for sex and survival in the Beach's deteriorating neighborhoods. And, as in so many of the other novels we have looked at, there is a general sense that the physical environment functions as an agent of defeat. It is no longer simply a matter of money that erodes lives (although there is that, too) but surroundings that, to use Gogol's phrase, produce dead souls. Do surroundings create character or is character a product of a desolate environment? "On a rainy day you walked in black gritty mud. Nothing was solid, neither the pavements nor the foundations of the buildings. As the sands gave, the sidewalks broke and the houses on the pole foundations never stopped settling." There are bungalows "for the most part wooden in construction, once covered gaily with gray and green stucco or imitation brick surface now hideous with time and neglect."

What Fuchs does rather well here is set out a vast array of fictional figures — possibly more so than in his other novels — and provide them each with distinctive personalities. There are no modernist tricks here. Fuchs may tell you what they're thinking and how they're reacting, but even if the author were not so generous, the reader would have to admit, yes, that's consistent with what we know about them and what they would say. The title of the book is appropriate. Fuchs's universe does indeed appear to be peopled mainly by low company, "low" not only in the sense that they consist of shady businessmen, gamblers, outright hoodlums, and gangsters but "low" also in terms of social status: dishwashers, soda jerks, teenage vacationers, cashier clerks, marginal shopkeepers and the like. Although a few among the higher echelons act honorably with one another, they are for the most part socially irresponsible. That is to say, however they gain their wealth they hurt the larger community.

One of the principal plots in this multi-plotted book relates the struggle for dominance of the prostitution trade on Neptune Beach. A losing contender in the competition is Shubunka, depicted here as exceedingly fat and physically repulsive, his appearance being somehow the equivalent of the kind of business he engages in. And yet, even if he looks like a monster, Fuchs provides him with a few human traits. We may not like him very much but nonetheless empathize in his guilt and terrors. Another wretched creature is Karty, a former accountant so addicted to betting on horses that he will in desperation kill to get money to put down on the races. Still, with few exceptions, very nearly all the characters in this book, from gangster capitalists to dishwashers, sate their humiliations and frustrations with reinforcing support from America's popular culture. Hoodlums talk to each other and to their prey as if they have just stepped out of a pulp crime novel. Dorothy, a cashier in Spitzbergen's soda parlor, feeds her imagination on outlandish fantasies served up by lending-library romances, and Shorty, the balding soda jerk, envisions himself both as a film star romantic lead and as a movie tough guy. When thugs in the café slap him about, Shorty thinks about what he'll do the next time they come around:

> Biff! Crack on the jaw, butting with his head. Shorty would do it just the way James Cagney laid them low in the movies. While the guy was groggy, slam! Bang! A left and a right, two jabs over the heart and a finisher on the button. Those mugs were on the floor.

On the other hand, there's Shorty's boss, Spitzbergen, who entertains no delusions nor derives any comfort from the popular culture. When Moe Karty, working on his racing forms, demands more lights be turned on in the café, Spitzbergen retorts, with strong Yiddish inflections, "Tell me, Moe Karty ... how much you pay me I should give you light for the horses?.... Maybe you know how much my electric bill is? You think they give you electric for nothing? Thirty-one eighty! I can show you the bill!"

Low Company may well be the most successfully executed of Fuchs's novels. The several complications in all of his characters' lives are skillfully interrelated and in the end come together. Moreover, elements of suspense become especially dramatic as when, for example, gangsters chase Shubunka through the Brooklyn streets in attempts to gun him down, or when the desperate and penniless Karty corners and strangles Spitzbergen in an effort to get at his money. How then categorize this book? Surely it is no more a crime novel than *Crime and Punishment* is a crime novel. Like Fuchs's earlier books it is developed along the line of the silly movies he probably secretly loved, with their quick and alternating changes of scene. Yet, despite light touches here and there and compassionate portrayals of character, the novel seems to adhere to a dark mythic vision of the city. Or perhaps it would be best to simply regard it as a large slab of life with no particular message other than that the great stream of life goes on regardless of individual calamities and disastrous disruptions. Here is Fuchs on the day following Spitzbergen's murder:

> The storekeepers of Neptune Beach put the papers aside and grew prepared for the rush. It was too bad about Spitzbergen, but after all, business was business and a man had to make a living. It was a blazing sun, pouring thickly over the atmosphere which was heavy with dampness. It was like a steamy blanket. Their clothes were damp and chafing on their bodies. Going inside the stores, they scratched their chins thoughtfully and said it was a pity the soda man wasn't alive to enjoy the wonderful weather.

The Depression years in New York did not serve Fuchs as well as he would have liked. Although he published several stories in national magazines — among them *The New Yorker, Colliers,* and *The Saturday Evening Post*— he failed to receive the recognition he deserved. Even the few Marxist critics who read him viewed his writings as insufficiently ideological. Not until the early 1960s would his books be "rediscovered," and by then he had long departed the city. He was twenty-six when Hollywood beckoned, and so he headed West to turn out screenplays not so very different from the kind he had satirized in his novels. But unlike other major writers — West, Faulkner, Fitzgerald — whom Hollywood also had recruited in the 1930s, Fuchs seems to have adjusted better. He moved with his family to California, and by 1955 he even won an Academy Award for the screen play of *Love Me or Leave Me,* a biopic about the torch singer Ruth Etting. Other major successes followed. In the meantime, he continued writing short stories, only now about the film world, and a collection of these, ironically titled *The Golden West: Hollywood Tales,* would be published posthumously. Fuchs died in 1993 at the age of eighty-four.

If there is a common thread that runs through Fuchs's books as well as those of the other first-generation Jewish writers we have so far looked at, it is the desire to escape their dreary, broken neighborhoods. The New York American dreams of upward mobility and renewed identity remain, but, to attain them, unorthodox and unsavory means are sometimes required. Or, to put it another way, the myths of New York as the wicked city sit side by side with the myths of New York as a new world. In Ornitz's novel the protagonist succeeds by corrupt political processes. Gold's hero dreams of revolution. Yezierska's heroine is the exception. She achieves her dream by means of education, while Roth and Fuchs appear resigned, at least for the moment, to let conditions fester. In the stories of Delmore Schwartz, the next writer we shall be looking at, the heroes' dreams of escape are generally linked to an intellectual life — a life somewhat apart from the left-leaning politics so many other Jewish intellectuals embraced. Of course by the 1940s, with the advent of World War II, the waning of the Depression years, and accelerating assimilation, poverty would no longer become so central an issue in writers' lives. Meanwhile, the older immigrant generations had begun passing away and with them a distinctive Jewish American literature. Still, memories of the cruel struggles of years past remained deeply stamped in their children's consciousness.

It might be argued that Delmore Schwartz was himself partly responsible for the unmooring of Jewish-American letters, but it would perhaps be more accurate to describe him as a kind of transition figure who stands some-where between a community confined to a Depression mentality and a deter-mined desire to embrace Western aesthetics. To be sure, earlier writers like Roth and even Ornitz had employed modernist stream-of-consciousness tech-niques, but they did so mainly in the service of their ghetto subject matter. Schwartz's characters, on the other hand, overtly seek for themselves Euro-American high cultural attainments. In his heyday in the forties and fifties, Schwartz liked to think of himself as a poet and only secondarily as a writer of fiction or as a literary essayist, but today he is chiefly remembered for his extended stories. A major disappointment in the last years of his life was that he would sometimes be identified as a critic who applied severe modernist criteria to other writers' works rather than as the artist he believed he was. But it is primarily the melancholy stories he produced during the late Depres-sion years that we should look to for what they tell us about the perceived rifts and divided identities of a rising class of Jewish-American writers.

Schwartz garnered his fame in 1937 at the age of twenty-four with the publication of his story "In Dreams Begin Responsibilities." It appeared in the first issue of the anti–Stalinist *Partisan Review*, a journal edited mainly by Jews and devoted to lofty standards of literary and political writings. The nar-rator in Schwartz's story tells of a dream that he was in a movie house watch-ing on-screen critical moments of his father's 1909 courtship of his mother. From time to time the narrator cries out to them to sever the relationship right then and there; don't they know their marriage will be a disaster and their children monstrous? At length an usher rushes up to him, dragging him out to the lobby and telling him that it is impossible to arrest an unrelenting past. The dreamer wakes up on a winter morning with snow on the ground. On a literary level the film's surreal march of fearful portents resembles some-thing out of Kafka (one of Schwartz's favorite authors), while at the same time Schwartz uses the American movie house not only as Fuchs does, as a site of fantasy and wish fulfillment, but as a warehouse of personal histories. But most importantly, for our purposes, the story tells of the anguished dis-tance between the narrator and his parents' generation.

"Screeno," unpublished in Schwartz's lifetime, is another of Schwartz's stories that uses a movie house as a main setting. A listless and bored young man, Cornelius Schmidt, of high cultural sensibilities, decides to go to the movies. Wherever Schwartz's political sympathies lay, he clearly writes as if he believes that the movies rather than religion are the opiate of the people. As Cornelius approaches the theater entry, "a stream of people came out of the darkness of the theater looking like sleepwalkers." The movie house is itself a fantasy palace as he walks across "the eerie soundless plush carpet of the stupendous lobby from whose lofty top great chandeliers hung." And within the auditorium proper two thousand "entranced persons stare toward the white and black screen, ignorant of all else." The newsreel projects moving images along with the voice of an unseen commentator who sounds like the Oracle of Delphi. But in addition to its hypnotic atmosphere the theater also offers as an inducement for audience attendance a lottery (here called "Screeno") in which ticket holders are given cards with scrambled numbers. At one point a management employee will call out a random combination of these from the stage, whose winner is to be awarded more than four hundred dollars.

Here is where the central drama of the story plays out. The Screeno contest gets under way, and before long an embarrassed Cornelius discovers he holds the winning numbers. But as he prepares to collect the money, another figure in the audience, an elderly indigent musician, cries out that he also holds the winning combination. The management is determined not to give cash to two winners, and Cornelius, in a gesture of unprecedented generosity, offers to give his winnings to the desperate old man. Before leaving the theater, Cornelius informs a restless, semi-hostile, semi-indifferent, semi-philistine audience that he is a poet and recites a passage from Eliot's "Gerontion," the gist of which laments our vanities and illusions. And, once on the street, Cornelius remembers a fourteenth-century Scottish lay celebrating generosity of spirit as opposed to the desire for worldly goods: "Be rich in patience, if those in goods be poor.... Who lives merry he lives michtlily; without gladness avails no treasure." Whatever else the story may mean, the hero expresses an elitist sensibility considerably at odds with the bourgeois world in which he finds himself. And Schwartz, in this instance, happily mixes icons of the popular culture (the movie theater) with icons of the high culture (Eliot's poem and the Scottish lay). What saves Cornelius from an intolerable snobbishness is his youthful ardor. He is likable and his heart is in the right place, but he does indeed take himself very seriously, tokening perhaps a kind of insecurity about who he really is.

Something of the same may be said of Schwartz's prose style. Much of his writing betrays a stiffness, a literariness, as if he were very carefully watching himself. But then there are those rare occasions, as in his story "The Commencement Day Address," where he gives himself over to a poetic sense of the City at the start of a summer storm.

The rain began in earnest now. Drops spat and pelted; in the West lightning defined itself like a set of nerves; soft mutters of thunder arrived.... One had a returning sense of the metropolitan city, narrow and tall on all sides, full of traffic, accident, commerce and adultery, of a thousand drugstores, apartment houses and theatres, its belly veined with black subways, its towers and bridges grand, numb, and without meaning.... Meanwhile the mouse-gray evening entered imperceptibly above the street lamps going on and the sizzle of the taxis' tires on the wet avenue.

Two of Schwartz's other stories, "New Year's Eve" and "The World Is a Wedding," contain elements of a restrained self-conscious prose style as he tells of colleagues, friends, and other writers uneasy about themselves, frustrated that they have not realized their cultural ambitions, and unhappy that they are only partially able to connect with others. Still, as Schwartz's biographer, James Atlas, rightly observes, although stories such as these may be sardonic they are not really cruel. Somewhere, even at their most devastating, Schwartz's portrayals suggest elements of pathos.

Perhaps one of the things most poignant about Schwartz is that two of his culture heroes, Pound and Eliot, were openly anti–Semitic. Although Schwartz was not at all religious, he never tried to hide his Jewishness. Indeed he would occasionally celebrate it as identifying him as an outsider or as someone fashionably alienated. Nonetheless one wonders whether his adoration of their godships restrained him from expressing, say, the natural Jewish ebullience of Bellow (who incidentally not only greatly admired him but would years afterwards write a novel, *Humboldt's Gift*, where Schwartz serves as a major character named Von Humboldt Fleischer). These conflicts are nicely spelled out in one of Schwartz's stories, "America! America!" In the story Shenandoah Fish, a young poet recently returned from Paris, listens as his mother tells of the tribulations of their neighbors, the Baumans, whose male children are less "successful" in business than their immigrant father. But, surprisingly, their daughter, a polio victim for whom they had no hopes whatsoever, had married a doctor, one of the most revered occupations in the bourgeois Jewish-American social hierarchy. As Mrs. Fish tells her story, Shenandoah subconsciously (and almost contemptuously) remarks the code words, phrases, and platitudes of his mother's middle-class world. From time to time, Mrs. Fish will utter the words "America! America!" which means, to knowing Jewish ears, how ironic were our expectations of the new world:

> He had listened from such a distance that what he saw was an outline, a caricature, and an abstraction. How different it might seem, if he had been able to see these lives from the inside, looking out.... And now he felt for the first

time how closely bound he was to these people. His separation was actual enough, but there existed also an unbreakable unity.... He felt that the contemptuous mood which had governed him as he listened was really self-contempt and ignorance. He thought his own life invited the same irony.

In his own life Schwartz does not seem to have acknowledged Shenandoah's insight. His early successes as a writer may have both inflated and damaged his precarious self-esteem. Always emotionally volatile, he would weep, embrace, and quarrel with friends and colleagues. Above all, toward his last years, he was especially subject to periods of deep depression and unwarranted suspicions which in the end would cause him to lose university teaching posts and editorships of literary journals. His two marriages ended disastrously. He died alone, impoverished and friendless, in a New York hotel in 1966. He was fifty-three.

PART TWO: AN AMERICAN DREAM WITH VARIATIONS

5

Struggles for Space

Stephen Crane, James Baldwin, Ann Petry, Bernard Malamud

It is a commonplace that the rich and the poor, the landowner and the peasant, the slave and his master view their circumstances from different perspectives. The more fortunate classes justify their happier status by virtue of bloodlines, ethnicity, race, religion, or often enough self-referential assumptions of sturdier character. Their opposites, when not resigned to their plight, may of course express smoldering resentment or at times outright violence. But in cities like New York or Chicago where instances of upward economic mobility are sometimes perceived, the social order usually remains shakily stable. Moreover, as Stephen Crane observed — although obviously not the first to do so — the frustrated energies of the underclasses often turn them against one another rather than against their rulers. In other words, the poor may not always be as angrily class-conscious as some social scientists would have us believe. As we have seen, American cities serve as repositories of hope and despair and thereby provide opportunities to observe not simply the middle ground but the extremes of American society.

One obvious means of instruction is the novel, whose main business is to discover the actions, interactions, and thoughts of persons at particular moments in history. Yet the novel almost by virtue of its initial aims has its own limitations. Emerging and maturing in the eighteenth and nineteenth centuries, the novel was intended not simply to divert or entertain, but to inform the rising middle classes about themselves and to a lesser extent the larger world beyond their purview. But because for the most part both novelists and their audience were middle class, the perceptions and psychology of the lowest strata of society do not much figure in what they wrote. Rather, novelists (then and now) tend to deal with middle-class concerns, and even when they observe the poor, the landless, or the dispossessed, they do so from a distance, or from a patronizing ethos. Only with rare exceptions (for example, Dickens, Tolstoy, Hardy) do they get into the soul of the peasant or proletariat — which is why Stephen Crane's first two novels, *Maggie: A Girl of the Streets* (1893) and *George's Mother* (1896), look to be so extraordinary.

Although Crane did not entirely overcome a kind of voyeurism in his writings, he did manage to look at slum dwellers as integral to their environment with little or no reference to an external world. Only minimally does he tell us what they think or feel, but rather what they say and do, and it remains for the reader to understand their psychology as adaptations to their surroundings. The visions of a dark New York were of course clearly as real to Crane as they might be for most Americans, but he would regard any myths of a wicked city as cultural condescension rather than as evidence of immorality. In terse simple prose his fictional figures seem to regard as natural their compressed slum environments. Not only would he challenge the 1890s upbeat Protestantism of the American popular culture but he (and other writers in this chapter) would portray a city whose cluttered spaces reject the reforged visions of New York as a new open West of rebirths and transformed identities.

Yet, however subversive Crane's New York books may have appeared at the time of their publication, we may today view the novels as illustrative of an emerging Euro-American zeitgeist. Socialists and social Darwinists of all sorts were in the latter years of the nineteenth century dabbling in environmental and social determinism; and in literary fields, authors like Zola in France (*L'Assommoir* is said to have influenced Crane) and Hardy in England portrayed bewildered souls in unfeeling environments. And closer to home, there was Hamlin Garland, whose writings depicted the bleak conditions of Midwestern families (Crane would seek out Garland's friendship in New York), and, of course, Jacob Riis's *How the Other Half Lives* (1888), relating in photographs and graphic prose the plight and miseries of New York's poor.

How Crane arrived at his outlook is rather a matter of speculation. Surely he was rebelling against the strictures of his Methodist upbringing. Born in 1871, he was the youngest of fourteen children whose parents wrote pieces in Methodist publications denouncing drinking, dancing, smoking, gambling, and even the reading of novels. His mother was the niece of a Methodist bishop, and his father was himself a clergyman who died when Stephen was nine. As a youth Crane was educated in several Methodist schools in New

Jersey and in the Port Jervis area of western New York. Later he would attend Lafayette College in Easton, Pennsylvania, and Syracuse University in New York, but disastrous grades at both institutions persuaded him he was not suited for the academic life. As a result he turned to newspaper writing (some of which he had even done anonymously as an adolescent) and supported himself for the rest of his years as a journalist. He came to live in New York in 1891 with ambitions to complete his first novel, *Maggie*, which he had begun while a student at Syracuse. During the five and a half years Crane actually lived in New York he wrote feature newspaper articles, mainly about the city's poor, meanwhile tending as much as he could to his own literary pursuits. Among these would be his Civil War masterpiece, *The Red Badge of Courage*, which as we shall see bears stylistic and thematic resemblances to his New York fiction. In the course of his life Crane wrote short stories and poems — some of considerable merit — as well as firsthand battle accounts of the Greco-Turkish and Spanish-American wars, but none approached the intense psychological truths of warfare he imagined while living in New York. His last few years were spent mainly in England. He died of tuberculosis at the age of twenty-nine.

At first glance *Maggie* is familiar melodrama. A young woman, Maggie Johnson, living in a slum tenement with her dysfunctional family in what we may assume is the Bowery area of Manhattan, is seduced and afterward abandoned by her brother's friend. Her "disgraced" family refuses to take her back, nor are her working class neighbors any more sympathetic — leaving poor Maggie no alternative but to walk the streets. Scorned and rejected wherever she goes, she ultimately heads for the East River, where she drowns herself. The novel, however, differs from its moralistic predecessors in that Maggie is not seen as a sinner with only herself to blame, but rather the creature of a city that rejects as detritus the weak, the naïve, and the passive. In Maggie's New York, slum dwellers literally struggle for space on congested streets as well as in cramped tenement apartments. Indeed, the novel opens with a stone-throwing fight between the "howling urchins" of Rum Alley and Devil's Row. The struggle appears to be ethnic — one gang is Irish while the other is presumably white Protestant. But ethnicity is only an excuse. It is really a turf battle and suggests perhaps an ironic parallel to the recently announced closing of open spaces on the Western frontier. (Some years later Crane would write the short story "The Bride Came to Yellow Sky," reinforcing the notion that the mythic freewheeling romance of an open West is a thing of the past.) In any case it is clear in *Maggie* that Crane equates the slum's pinched spaces with what he would call the environment's enormous influence on human behavior. In a letter to Hamlin Garland he says of *Maggie* that it "tries to show that environment is a tremendous thing in the world and shapes lives regardless."

Crane sought his effects by a variety of means. He narrates his tales in the third person with seemingly simple words that give off an impression of objectivity. It is the kind of prose that Hemingway would admire in Crane for its avoidance of the florid literary style that so many nineteenth-century writers had affected. (Interestingly, both Hemingway's and Crane's newspaper-writing careers may have disciplined their prose by requiring them to tell their stories in as accessible a manner as possible.) The difference between them is that Hemingway's complexities often lie in what he deliberately fails to say, whereas Crane will diverge from the impersonal by coupling his deadpan prose with images that explode with a life of their own. Rain turns pavements into "tossing seas of umbrellas." Snow is depicted in theatrical settings as "pale green," and beer gardens are "hilarious halls." Buildings are anthropomorphized. At night saloons seduce or "smile" deceptive yellow light. In daylight tenements expel "loads of babies" through gruesome or "yawning open doorways." Some structures "careen" while others have eyelike windows that look out impassively at a troubled world. There are houses whose shutters are "closed like grim lips" and others with "sternness or solidity built upon their features." In effect these images become a kind of kinetic energy cajoling and pushing slum dwellers into smaller and smaller confinements. Human character, on the other hand, is often pictured in bright primary colors, somewhat akin to dominant humors or temperaments. There are red women, blue policemen, worms of yellow convicts, and blood-red mottled fists. Maggie herself is painted as a blossom in a mud puddle. Sometimes Crane will serve up expressionistic images alongside a picture of photographic realism:

> On a corner a glass-fronted building shed a yellow glare upon the pavements. The open mouth of a saloon called seductively to passengers to enter and annihilate sorrow or create rage.
>
> The interior of the place was papered in olive and bronze tints of imitation leather. A shining bar of counterfeit massiveness extended down the side of the room. Behind a great mahogany-appearing sideboard reached the ceiling. Upon its shelves rested pyramids of shimmering glasses that were never disturbed. Mirrors set in the face of the sideboard multiplied them. Lemons, oranges and paper napkins, arranged with mathematical precision, sat among the glasses....

Several chapters in both Crane's New York books begin with similar stage-like settings that tend to freeze space and prepare readers for the dramas contained within. In this way the flow of chronology is jolted forward as if one were flipping through the pages of a photo album.

Maggie herself does not emerge as a full-fledged character until chapter five, as the first four chapters are devoted to background circumstances that account for her fate. Other characters are portrayed as near fixed entities. That is to say, they do not evolve very much in Crane's framed scenes. They exist as individual types rather than as individuals — nor are they especially perceptive. None, by any means, is the salt of the earth. Each responds to his or her environment as if preordained. Maggie's mother, for example, is a raging alcoholic, furious at her children and working-class husband (who dies early in the novel) because presumably her suffocating tenement apartment grants her no other means of expression. Maggie's brother, Jimmy, believes he must fight Pete, Maggie's seducer, because in his limited world that is what older brothers are expected to do. He does not allow himself to worry much about the several women he has seduced. The naïve Maggie is herself impressed by Pete's brassy, vulgar, ostentatious garb, his virile braggadocio and the simple beer garden entertainments he takes her to. She is especially moved by implausible plays where the forces of goodness and virtue overcome evil. (One has a sneaking suspicion that Crane, against his better judgment, secretly enjoyed these quite as much as Maggie.) As for Christianity, it stands as a weak reed in the city's brutal environment. Few among the poor take salvation seriously. Early on, Maggie's brother chances to enter a mission church:

> He clad his soul in armor by means of happening hilariously at a mission church where a man composed his sermons of "yous." While they got warm at the stove, he told his hearers just where he calculated where they stood with the Lord. Many of the sinners were impatient over the pictured depths of their degradation. They were waiting for soup tickets.

And yet, if the Christian church fails the poor, the poor themselves display a most uncharitable Christianity toward Maggie, whom they condemn as a fallen woman. Their hypocrisy is compounded when, after Maggie's death, they "forgive" her. Readers may, however, wonder whether Maggie's other proletarian tenement neighbors would subscribe so uniformly to Victorian sexual codes — even in the 1890s. Theirs was, after all, a culture of survival, where Maggie's failed virtue would be regarded as something less than cataclysmic. In the final analysis, Crane, an outsider, may well have been projecting his own Methodist understanding of "respectability" onto an entire community. Nonetheless, no one could accuse him of romanticizing or sentimentalizing the poor. What he related he believed was the world as it was.

George's Mother was probably written shortly after *Maggie* although it would wait several years to be published. Like *Maggie* the novella outwardly fashions itself as familiar melodrama. A young man, George Kelcey, and his mother, recently arrived from the countryside, have taken residence in the same apartment house as Maggie and her family. (Indeed, on several occasions George lustfully fancies Maggie but cannot muster up the courage to speak to her.) In the course of time George, who has been nobly taking care of his pious widowed mother, degenerates under the influence of bad companions and the City's tumultuous streets. Clearly the countryside, from which the Kelceys have emerged, leaves them unprepared for the City's mixed messages. At one point George renounces the church to which his mother repairs for succor. But now even the church looks about to be crushed, its size and space lost in the City's immensity:

> In a dark street the little chapel sat humbly between two towering apartment houses. A red street lamp stood in front. It threw a marvelous reflection upon the wet pavements. It was like the death-stain of a spirit. Farther up the brilliant lights of an avenue made a span of gold across the black street. A roar of wheels and a clangor of bells came from this point, interwoven into a sound emblematic of the life of the city. It seemed somehow to affront this solemn and austere little edifice. It suggested an approaching barbaric invasion. The little church, pierced, would die with a fine, illimitable scorn for its slayers.

The sense of the anarchic world, in which George and his mother find themselves immersed, resonates as a theme in what would seem a very different kind of genre, Crane's war novel, *The Red Badge of Courage*. Here, another country youth, Henry Fleming, also undergoes disorienting experiences in unknown environments — although unlike George he finally acquires for himself a renewed identity. However else one would like to classify it, *Red Badge* is a psychological novel, and in this respect, too, *George's Mother* deals with shifting emotional responses to what amounts to the city's diverse battlefields. We observe Mrs. Kelcey sinking more and more into depression as neither her son nor her church nor her surroundings yield hope of New York's promises of a new life. Angry confrontations lie everywhere beyond the tiny flat she shares with George. Their neighbors, on the streets and in their houses, seem constantly to be fighting, cursing, shouting, and hurling missiles at one another — and even the larger city suggests warfare, where buildings loom "with a new and impressive massiveness like castles and fortresses." Nor is

George's mother herself entirely disengaged as she enters in symbolic struggle for space with the ever-encroaching dust in her apartment. Images of warfare abound in her ongoing losing battle to clean the flat:

> There was a flurry of a battle in this room. Through the clouded dust or steam one could see the thin figure dealing mighty blows. Always her way seemed beset. Her broom was continually poised, lance-wise, at dust demons. There came clashings and clangings as she strove with her tireless foes.... It was a picture of indomitable courage. And as she went on her way her voice was often raised in a long cry, a strange war-chant, a shout of battle and defiance.... Still it could be seen that she even then was planning skirmishes, charges, campaigns.

George, too, gives vent to frustrations, sexual and otherwise, as well as fury at what he comes to believe are his mother's unreasonable demands. He turns to liquor ("He was about to taste the delicious revenge of partial self-destruction. The universe would regret its position when it saw him drunk."); he quits his job; he joins on occasion with thugs who, when they are not fighting one another, beat up innocent passersby; and, worst of all, he verbally torments his mother, reducing her to shreds of despair. Crane succinctly penetrates George's sadism:

> He brooded upon his mother's agony and felt a singular joy in it. As opportunity offered he did little despicable things. He was going to make her abject. He was now uncontrolled, ungoverned; he wished to be an emperor. Her suffering was all a sort of compensation for his own dire pains.

Later, as his mother lies dying, George stares glassily at figures on the wallpaper, transforming them into mental images of terror and decay. The compressed dried up life of the slums has reached into his soul: "The pattern was clusters of brown roses. He felt them like hideous crabs crawling upon his brain."

In sum, Crane's New York is a kind of miniature metaphysics that he would come to adopt in much of his subsequent writings; that is, the city is a version of an amoral universe devoid of meaning and uncaring of the presences and sufferings of puny humanity. A poem he published in his 1899 collection, *War Is Kind*, says much the same thing.

> A man said to the universe:
> "Sir, I exist!"
> "However," replied the universe,
> "The fact has not created in me
> A sense of obligation."

Still, if Crane's New York would eventually produce for him a model of an indifferent universe, his graphic representation of the city's fragmented environments would become characteristic in much subsequent twentieth-century literature. Surely a frequent theme in New York life as well as New York letters deals with issues of living space. In a later chapter, we shall see that only a few years before *Maggie*, William Dean Howells' *A Hazard of New Fortunes* tells of the upper-middle-class March family's trek up and down Manhattan in quest of suitable living quarters. For later generations of authors, struggles for space become especially more pronounced in deteriorating neighborhoods like those in Harlem. Not only do the usual pathologies of poverty obtain, but problems are aggravated by New York's de facto racial segregation. The 1920s' popular romanticized (mainly white-authored) image of Harlem as a community of free and exotic earthy souls singing and dancing on every street corner gradually dissipates during the Depression years. Poets like Fenton Johnson and Langston Hughes and an emerging body of post–World War II authors tell of another Harlem whose residents live barely above survival levels. Whether or not present-day conditions have since improved remains a matter of contention, but the anguish of mid-twentieth-century writers cannot be doubted.

James Baldwin's black Harlem — which, surprisingly, he may on occasion link to Greenwich Village — lies somewhere in and beyond geographical space. In Crane, as we have observed, space is almost a physical entity, forever pushing and crowding slum dwellers into cramped places, as well as denying them means of escape. Although Baldwin expounds on some of these same issues, he also discovers pockets of relief, if not resistance. Put another way, Baldwin's Harlem/Greenwich Village pictures are not exclusively map-bound areas of social and cultural malaise, but regions that may at times transcend themselves. That is to say, one may also discover within their borders rare private moments or small communities of love, compassion, and comradeship. Finally, whatever Harlem's afflictions, black culture may nonetheless disinter the buried inner spaces of individual psyches where "perverse" libidinal yearnings exist alongside generally acceptable sexual expressions. White people, he comments, too often submit to taboos at the price of realizing their full humanity.

Let us begin then with Baldwin's first novel, *Go Tell It on the Mountain* (1953). The work describes one Sunday in the life of fourteen-year-old John Grimes (the name is suggestive) and his family. It is John's birthday although the greater part of the novel takes place during the family's attendance at a

Pentecostal church where the Grimeses' complicated and convoluted relationships reveal themselves to the reader. John's parents, Gabriel and Elizabeth, and his aunt Florence — each with Southern roots — had come to Harlem at different times. But New York, of course, did not produce for them a new life nor did it relieve them of ghetto stresses and interfamilial conflicts. The elder Grimes is a church deacon, but even in prayer he cannot overcome his anger, guilt, and suspicions, directed as much toward his family as toward an oppressive white world. He is especially resentful of John, his stepson, whose blood father died before John was born. Gabriel's sister, Florence, dwells in unhappy, bitter remembrances of a disappointing marriage while barely containing her antagonism toward her brother. Meanwhile, John's mother, Elizabeth, not only fears her husband but fears for all her children. John, whose physical presence affects them each in different ways, is himself troubled by an amorphous sense of unease. Near the end of the book, John is physically seized by paroxysms of the Holy Spirit in the presence of the entire congregation. Everyone believes John is saved, but John senses in the depths of his consciousness that more of himself is yet to be reborn.

Much of the novel is related in language closely attuned to the inner turmoil of Baldwin's characters. Several commentators have noted that bits of the prose appropriate the cadences and rhetoric of a Holy Roller Negro preacher — and indeed Baldwin did become a preacher at the age of fourteen. In any case, Baldwin's impassioned prose seldom works as well in his other writings and contrasts sharply with Crane's imagistic reportorial "objectivity." Where Crane and Baldwin most closely converge is in their depictions of the narrow spaces that constrict their characters' options. Maggie's passage, for example, leads inexorably to the river where she will commit suicide. John, we learn, had endeavored once before to explore the world beyond the ghetto, but when he tentatively ventured "downtown" he turned back, fearing hostile or condescending white people. A most striking metaphor describes John's attempts to clean the Grimeses' apartment. His efforts to stem the encroaching dust recall George's mother engaged in the same Sisyphean enterprise: "John hated sweeping this carpet, for dust rose, clogging his nose and sticking to his sweaty skin, and he felt that should he sweep it forever, the clouds of dust would not diminish, the rug would not be clean." And after he laboriously fills the dustpan, "he saw in the expanse behind him, the dust that he had raised settling again into the carpet...." Finally, both Crane and Baldwin portray their environments in much the same way. Houses do not rise in Baldwin's Harlem but crouch "huddled flat, ignoble, close to the filthy ground where the streets and hallways were dark, and where the unconquerable odor was of dust, and sweat and urine, and homemade gin." Windows in buildings stare out "like a thousand blinded eyes." On the Sunday streets Harlem men are "wrinkled and dusty ... muddy eyed and muddy faced" and harsh-voiced Harlem women "fight like the men." Some had passed the night drinking in bars, others in "cat houses or on the streets or on roof tops or under the stairs." Meanwhile, the detritus that runs along the gutters records the enclosed boundaries of Harlem's physical degradation:

> The water ran in the gutters with a small, discontented sound; on the water traveled paper, burnt matches, sodden cigarette-ends; gobs of spittle, green-yellow, brown and pearly; the leavings of a dog, the vomit of a drunken man, the dead sperm trapped in rubber, of one abandoned to his lust.*

And yet even within the contours of Baldwin's withered Harlem, there are some institutions that temporarily lessen tensions. Unlike Crane's contemptuous dismissal of mission churches, the Negro church to which John has surrendered himself has at the very least granted him expression of stifled passions, although he is not yet fully aware that in part these lie deeply embedded in his sexual nature. As we have already noted, he expresses these not so much in coherent language as in shouts and yells and in physical contortions. The congregation in turn responds, testifying by their presence to both his anguish and to his liberation, knowing full well their own internal sufferings. How long John will be saved is of course another matter. The price of salvation is a rejection of his sexuality. Early in the service, church elders admonish an adolescent boy and girl against walking about together unescorted. Ironically, John's ingestion of the Holy Spirit begins to awaken him to his own libidinal nature. His birthday has resonances beyond ordinary understanding.

When he was seventeen, in 1947, Baldwin departed Harlem for Greenwich Village in hopes of becoming a published writer. In the course of years he did succeed in finding magazines and journals that would print his pieces, mainly essays and short stories, the contents of which told of Harlem's deplorable living conditions and the terrible toll racism takes on blacks and whites alike. But Greenwich Village also gave him the opportunity to learn about the kind of African-American music he had been forbidden to listen

---

*Baldwin's detailed listing of street garbage anticipates Paula Fox's account in *Desperate Characters*. See p. 214. Like Crane's and Baldwin's working class figures, Fox's upper-middle-class characters are unable to escape a deteriorating city.

to as a child growing up in a religious household. Paradoxically he would first truly hear the black jazz of his native Harlem outside Harlem. He was especially taken with jazz not simply for its overt sensuality but also, strange as it may seem, for the liberating effects he had experienced at Negro Pentecostal church services. The improvising jazz soloist, he believed, was encouraged to express in sounds and rhythms the inmost depths of his being — his rage, his suffering, his joys and pleasures — along with the support of surrounding musicians who were in their own fashion "testifying." In one of Baldwin's best short stories, "Sonny's Blues," he writes of a pianist, Sonny, a recovering heroin addict, who returns after a year's absence to rejoin musicians he had once played with. At first the bass player and band leader, Creole, leans on his instrument with eyes half closed, listening to Sonny: "He was having a dialogue with Sonny." He wanted Sonny to "leave the shoreline and strike out for deep water...." Sonny struggles to find himself "like someone in torment." But after a few halting starts, the piano begins to articulate Sonny's despair. Creole understands. He makes the "little black man on the drums know it, and the bright brown man on the horn. Creole wasn't trying any longer to get Sonny in the water. He was wishing him Godspeed." Together with Creole and the other musicians Sonny succeeds in transforming his private hell into art, into something beautiful: "And he was giving it back, as everything must be given back, so that passing through death, it can live forever."

Baldwin describes other such moments in his third novel, *Another Country* (1962). A saxophonist, "wide-legged, humping the air, filling his barrel chest, shivering in the rage of his twenty-odd years, and screaming through the horn," cries out for love. "The men on the stand stayed with him, cool and at a little distance, adding and questioning and corroborating, holding it down as well as they could with an ironical self-mockery; but each man knew that the boy was blowing for every one of them." Besides discovering black jazz in the Village, Baldwin now began awakening more and more to his homo-erotic proclivities. One would not ordinarily make too much of this but for Baldwin in several of his writings the presence of homosexual love tempers some of the City's horrors. The homosexual, he believed, is represented in American culture as a figure as despised as the Negro. Indeed he may be the surrogate Negro. Still more significantly for Baldwin, the homosexual is just as likely a fulfilled human being inasmuch as he gives expression to the bi-gendered character of his nature. He is capable of giving comfort and compassion to lovers, black and white, men and women, both because he identifies with their pain and because he liberates their passions and spiritual yearnings.

One's first impression is that the central character in *Another Country* is Rufus, a tormented black musician who cannot resolve his conflicted animus toward the white woman he loves. At the end of the first section of the novel he commits suicide. Thereafter Eric, a white expatriate and erstwhile lover of Rufus, returns from France to Greenwich Village and gives succor (that is sex) to Rufus's white friends, male and female. One of these is Vivaldo, whose mistress, Ida, is Rufus's sister. As a general rule, Ida hates whites although she may on occasion service depleted white men. The plot of this implausible novel is much too baroque to summarize further. Suffice it to say it deals with the relationships of people, white and black, who knew Rufus but could not fathom his agony. After Eric performs his good deeds — that is, replenishing people in need sexually and therefore psychically — he is to be rewarded by his longtime French lover, Yves, who flies the Atlantic to join him in hellishly hot Greenwich Village. One assumes their renewed cloistered love nest will protect them from the worst ravages of the threatening city. In his own life, however, Baldwin found New York, indeed America, barely tolerable judging from his subsequent several novels, few of which carry the power and convictions of his earlier writing. He spent as much time abroad as he could, coming back from time to time for family visits and speaking engagements. He died in France in 1987 at the age of sixty-three.

Baldwin was not the first African-American writer to relate the deleterious and stunting effects of New York on its black inhabitants. As far back as 1902 Paul Laurence Dunbar's *The Sport of the Gods* tells of the degenerating effects on a black Southern family that had migrated to the city. For Dunbar (better known for his dialect poems) the message is clear: Negroes would be far better off to remain in the South, despite its cruelties. Although Dunbar's vision looks to be no more than the traditional depiction of the wicked city, it should be noted that at the start of the century New York was as segregated as any city in the country. Racial tensions stood high and the city had only recently experienced its worst race riots in thirty years. Some forty-four years after *Sport of the Gods*, the heroine of Ann Petry's *The Street* (1946) does not quite go as far as Dunbar in advocating a black return to the South, but she does declare the Harlem ghetto the moral equivalent of a Southern lynching. For Petry, Southern racism is at least more honest than New York's pretended freedoms. The central issue, she insists, is a matter of space. In the novel, the upright Lutie Johnson tries to live a respectable middle-class life on 116th Street, but she is utterly defeated by an environment that hardly allows any escape. Her young son now begins a life of criminal behavior and at the novel's finish Lutie kills a man who tries to rape her. The novel opens with a three-paragraph description of a windstorm that metaphorically announces her theme. It bears comparison with Crane's Mrs. Kelcey and Baldwin's John Grimes as they try ceaselessly and fruitlessly to stand up to the ever-encroaching dirt in their apartments:

> [The November wind] found every scrap of paper along the street — theater throwaways, announcements of dances and lodge meetings, the heavy waxed paper that loaves of bread had been wrapped in, the thinner waxed paper that had enclosed sandwiches, old envelopes, newspapers. Fingering its way along the curb, the wind set the bits of paper to dancing high in the air, so that a barrage of paper swirled into the faces of the people on the street.... It did everything it could to discourage the people walking along the street. It found all the dirt and dust and grime on the sidewalk and lifted it up so that the dirt got into their noses, making it difficult to breathe....

Ann Petry had a happier fate than Lutie, her protagonist. After stints at journalism on the (Harlem) *Amsterdam News* and the *People's Voice*, advertising, and several other positions, she returned to her native Saybrook, Connecticut, where she continued writing other novels and short fiction. She died at the age of eighty-six in 1997.

It would seem inevitable that two of the twentieth-century city's most volatile ethnic groups would one day clash. Blacks and Jews had lived in the city since its Dutch beginnings, and as noted in chapter three, blacks may well have constituted 20 percent of New York's population during the early decades of eighteenth-century British rule. But thereafter proportions dropped precipitously and even more so especially after New York's 1862 antidraft and anti–Negro riots. Post–Civil War years presaged a slow but gradual rise in the African-American population as more and more former slaves departed the states of the old Confederacy. Where they would settle, however, became a critical issue. Early nineteenth-century African Americans tended to live in the southern tip of Manhattan, but their descendants would gradually move northwards as Irish and Italian immigrants came to displace their neighborhoods. In the last years of the century, the construction of rail lines north seemed to many to make Harlem an attractive possibility.

The Jews of New York remained a tiny minority for the greater part of the 1800s. The first arrivals, refugees from persistent and ongoing inquisitions, came from Brazil and the Caribbean and Hispanic areas of the Americas; by mid-century larger numbers, fleeing political upheavals, emigrated from

Germany, but by far the largest Jewish influx began arriving in the late 1880s, many of whom were escaping eastern European persecutions and pogroms. These later populations settled mainly in New York's Lower East Side, Brooklyn, and the emerging areas of Harlem. White Harlem at the turn of the century was by no means Jewish — there were settled clusters of German, English, and Dutch residents — but many immigrant Jews eschewing crowded areas in other city neighborhoods began pouring in, and by 1915 Harlem contained one of New York's largest concentrations of eastern European Jews. In many ways their dress, diction, and religious practices differed from those of older generations of assimilated Jews who, as we know, seemed somewhat embarrassed by their presence. Interestingly, long-established New York City Negroes, sometimes calling themselves Old Knickerbockers, felt much the same way about newly arrived Southern black emigrants for many of the same reasons. In both cases the Sephardic and German-American assimilated Jews and the better established Negro Old Knickerbockers feared their "outlandish" compatriots could only stir up further anti-ethnic sentiments. And in fact tighter immigration laws promulgated in the 1920s intended to limit eastern and southern European immigration did to a large degree succeed in doing so. In New York, meanwhile, efforts by whites to keep Harlem's black population down failed and by 1910 steep declines in real-estate values drew large numbers of African Americans into what at the time were regarded as desirable neighborhoods. Whites would depart in comparable numbers and ten years later Harlem was largely black. Many Jews, however, retained their businesses, shops, and real estate even after moving away — and this would become a source of friction for much of the remaining century. As early as 1933 there were overt anti–Semitic demonstrations and periodic protests against Jewish landlords as well as against commercial enterprises that refused to hire Negroes. Not all the culprits of course were Jews but nonetheless many Harlemites perceived Jews as controlling their community. Nor was this view confined to the uneducated classes. Ann Petry's *The Street* describes a sinister character — perhaps Jewish — who owns Harlem's prostitution rings, nightclubs, and varieties of other shady enterprises. And James Baldwin, in a 1948 essay called "The Harlem Ghetto" (published, incidentally, in the Jewish journal *Commentary*), writes that Jews in Harlem "operate in accordance with the American business tradition of exploiting Negroes and they are therefore identified with oppression and hated for it." In addition, black anti–Semitism and Jewish racism, he argued, derived as well from the desires of both groups to identify with what they believed inherent in American culture. Perhaps a major source of the animosity was that Negroes felt themselves imprisoned in a suffocating Harlem ghetto to which Jews (being white and present) seemed to have confined them and from which Jews presumably had escaped. In his essay Baldwin writes what might have served as a prologue to what later became his novel, *Go Tell It on the Mountain*:

> All of Harlem is pervaded by a sense of congestion, rather like the insistent, maddening, claustrophobic pounding in the skull that comes from trying to breathe in a very small room with all the windows shut.

Not all Harlem's black inhabitants, however, shared this view (as Baldwin himself later admitted) and there were countervailing truths. Both blacks and Jews share long histories of oppression — indeed twentieth-century New York was never itself entirely free of ethnic prejudices — and tended sometimes to identify with one another. Jews in disproportionate numbers to other white population groups took active roles in civil rights organizations as far back as the beginning decades of the twentieth century. Nor were these Jews unrepresentative of their communities. Yiddish newspapers very nearly from their birth screamed out at the horrors of black lynchings and race riots. Finally, and perhaps most importantly for American culture at large, there were cultural exchanges, crossovers in sports and especially in music between black and Jewish performers, composers and musicians. In the long run these may have accomplished more in shaping and transforming American attitudes and outlook than the exhortations of religious figures or politicians.

Thus the relationship between the two groups was bumpy at best. When in the 1950s and 1960s African Americans attained more and more of their civil rights some among their leadership resented the presence of whites (often Jews) in their organizations and called for their ouster. As blacks attained more and more political power they called for more authority over the public schools their children attended. Here they came up against the opposition of white city teachers, again mainly Jews. Tensions heightened and this was the atmosphere that engulfed Bernard Malamud's New York as he wrote one of his last novels, *The Tenants* (1971). Struggles for space were no longer confined to geographical Harlem and other city ghetto areas but to political, economic, and artistic spheres as well. Few writers were prepared to take on the touchy subject of Jewish–African American relationships but none could have been better equipped to do so than Malamud. For one thing many of his short stories set in the 1930s deal with poor or marginally poor Jews struggling to maintain their place in the sun, their shops and their trades and their tenement hovels, against persons or forces or institutions that threaten their very physical survival. They may be weak but not necessarily passive and their suffering is not so much pitiable as it is something that sustains them, a rite of passage as it were, while casting shadows on a callous world beyond. They cry out in their fashion for a moral universe or a just God, who often appears to have absented himself. Most important, the love they expend beyond themselves, Jew and gentile, white and black, renders them some kind of small victory. In Malamud's story "The Mourners," a landlord who has twice evicted an impoverished, disagreeable, recalcitrant tenant discovers to his dismay that the tenant has reestablished himself in the vacated flat. At the landlord's appearance, the tenant sinks to the floor in prayers for the dead, at which moment Gruber, the landlord, realizes in shock that the evictee is not mourning for himself but for his oppressor, whereupon Gruber pulls a sheet about him and joins his victim in prayer. In another story, "An Apology," an unlicensed peddler who had been arrested for selling items on the Manhattan streets, perches himself on a tree outside the arresting officer's house demanding an apology. It is not easy to categorize these stories. In some ways they look to be raw naturalism, in some ways magical realism, and in some ways parables and morality tales. But parables of what, what morality? Malamud never tells us outright. The answers are elusive.

In at least two of the stories, blacks as well as Jews figure prominently, and physical space functions as a spiritual barrier. In "The Angel Levine," an aging declining tailor who seems to be suffering all the afflictions of Job prays God for relief. Soon a black man appears in his tenement flat, attired in the cheap, shabby clothing of an immigrant Jew, and announces he is an angel named Levine. Manischevitz listens and dismisses him as an impostor with delusions. Levine, however, tells him that if he truly needs him, he can be found in Harlem. Levine's departure produces an afterglow of better health for Manischevitz and his ailing wife, but some time afterwards they relapse into their previous condition. The tailor wonders if the black man is really an angel, let alone Jewish, and after some difficulty locates him in a Harlem nightclub. They return downtown to Manischevitz's apartment house, and Levine suddenly flies off from the roof into the night air. When the tailor returns to his flat, he finds his wife reinvigorated. The angel has evidently redeemed Manischevitz, but more importantly, by believing in him, Manischevitz has redeemed the angel. "A wonderful thing, Fanny," Manischevitz tells his wife. "Believe me, there are Jews everywhere."

Malamud navigates the story as both raw realism and magic, but it also works as a morality tale. Manischevitz restores himself, we learn, by conflating the spatial divide between his lower Manhattan neighborhood and faraway Harlem. The oneness of Jews and blacks, indeed the common acceptance of a common humanity does not, however, apply in Malamud's "Black Is My Favorite Color." Here the geographical divide defines insurmountable differences. Nathan Lime, a Harlem liquor store proprietor, falls in love with a black woman customer. He wants to marry her but when he is mugged accompanying her on a Harlem street she evidently feels that the differences between Jews and blacks are too great and she flees the relationship. Nat remembers that as a youngster he tried reaching out to an African-American boy in another black neighborhood but the sullen youth he had been trying to befriend beat him up. And even now, Nat's African-American cleaning woman will not sit at the kitchen table with him while she eats her hard-boiled eggs. In his way, Nat is a naïf who cannot gauge the depths of black suspicions. He tell his story in a Candide-like voice but the conclusions readers draw are not unlike Baldwin's. Black-Jewish relations are thornier than we would wish.

Malamud is a master of economy. If crowded spaces are, as we have seen, a matter of New York contention, there is little clutter in Malamud's prose style. He can within a paragraph or two tell of a struggling wife, a litany of events, or the complications of interracial communications:

> Charity Sweetness sits in the toilet eating her two hard-boiled eggs while I'm having my ham sandwich and coffee in the kitchen. That's how it goes only don't get the idea of ghettoes. If there's a ghetto I'm the one that's in it. She's my cleaning woman from Father Divine and comes in once a week to my small three-room apartment on my day off from the liquor store. "Peace," she says to me.

There is never any question of the clarity of the prose even when he renders immigrant English. If the syntax sounds a bit off, the grammar is by and large correct. In "The Angel Levine" Manischevitz, the tailor, praying for release from endless sorrows, intones, "My dear God sweetheart, did I deserve that this should happen to me? ... Give Fanny back her health, and to me for myself that I shouldn't feel pain in every step. Help now or tomorrow is too late. This I don't have to tell you."

Malamud came by his literary voice by attuning himself to the ambience of his own upbringing. Born in 1917, the son of an immigrant grocer, he grew up in Brooklyn neighborhoods where marginally poor Jews like his parents saw their livelihood threatened daily during the Great Depression. He managed nonetheless to attend the tuitionless City College and afterwards Columbia University, where he received a master's degree in English. He taught English in high schools in Brooklyn and Harlem and during World War II worked for a while at the Census Bureau in Washington. His first short stories were published in 1943 and his first novel, *The Natural* (1952), a baseball tale with echoes of Parsifal, does not partake of the ethnic materials he would later come to employ so successfully. His life thereafter was not outwardly the stuff of high drama. He married (out of the faith), had children, and taught writing for many years in colleges in Oregon and Vermont. He produced several more novels — the most acclaimed being *The Assistant*—and short story collections. He was honored in his lifetime — with a Pulitzer Prize and a National Book Award — and spent a year in Rome on a fellowship. At other times he would travel to Europe and Russia. His last novel imagined a world devastated by nuclear war. He died in 1986 of a heart attack.

But if Malamud's life appears on its surface to be devoid of Sturm und Drang, his fiction tells of high passions, yearnings, endurance, and intense near-religious seeking of meaning. Leo Finkle, a theological student in one of his most celebrated stories, "The Magic Barrel," relates that he wants to become a rabbi not because he loves God but because he doesn't. But by his fourth novel, *The Tenants*, the two chief characters are unable to make moral or spiritual connections because each locks himself in his own delusory ideological space. Harry Lesser, the principal protagonist, a twice-published author, has never been able to give himself "generously" to any woman, and is writing a novel about an ideal love where he hopes the hero of his work, a writer, will create in his creator the capability he lacks. Put another way, Harry's creation would in a sense re-create Harry. (In this respect he is not unlike Malamud's theological student Finkle, who hopes that by becoming a rabbi he may come to love God.) Harry's opposite is a black man, Willie Spearmint, a desperate Harlem proletarian would-be author who believes he hates whites and regards Jews as responsible for the countless miseries of Harlem's poor. When Willie speaks he expresses himself in a kind of stylized African-American street lingo somewhat equivalent to the Yiddishized English of Malamud's immigrants. Although Lesser and Willie are the only occupants of a near-abandoned apartment house on Third Avenue, they both, as we shall see, oppose one another regarding the techniques and values of literature. The decaying building they live in suggests an allegorical New York or an allegorical America where each artist seeks his space at the expense of the other. Needless to say, the novel is itself a Malamudian mélange of hard-scrabble naturalism and fantasy that we have noted in his short stories. A plot complication is that Harry and Willie both vie for the same white Jewish girl, Irene, who first appears as Willie's mistress and afterwards becomes Lesser's lover. But Malamud also throws other ingredients into the stew. One of the most obvious is that the ownership of the house belongs neither to Willie nor Harry but to Levenspiel, an immigrant who wants to eject all its occupants, raze the building, and erect a new apartment house. Lesser, a legal tenant, adamantly refuses to leave, fearing that any change of environment would upset the pace and rhythm of the book he is writing. Willie, meanwhile, who is also writing a book, clandestinely occupies another flat and tries to hide away from the landlord. When Lesser very nearly collides with black nationalists because he had bedded a black woman, Willie on this occasion saves him from a severe beating.

The central conflicts of the book, however, center around Harry's and Willie's hot-cold racial perceptions and their opposing takes on the books they are writing. Lesser regards himself as a careful craftsman, a "formalist" who believes structure, transitions, and certain kinds of sentence elegance are essential elements of meaning. Conversely, Willie (who sometimes likes to call himself Bill Spear) believes expressions of rage and violence at the degradation and depredations of black life take precedence over prose style. He avers white people could never understand the black experience:

> Black ain't white and never can be. It is once and for only black. It ain't universal if that's what you are hintin up to. What I feel you feel different. You can't write about black because you don't have the least idea what we are or how we feel. Our feelin chemistry is different than yours. Dig that?

But Willie cannot altogether believe what he is saying because from time to time he asks Lesser to advise him on the efficacy of his writing. Indeed Willie himself seems to be constantly revising his work. And yet if what he writes looks at times awkward and undeveloped, Lesser has to admit — even when their relationship is most strained — his prose has a kind of driving force. Each yearns for what the other possesses. Is there no space in the house of literature for both kinds of writer? Or better still, cannot each assimilate the other's virtues?

Closely related to Lesser's differences with Willie are Lesser's confrontations with his landlord, Levenspiel. Levenspiel cannot force Harry to leave because as a legitimate renter he is protected by City regulations. Still, Levenspiel, over the course of time, offers Lesser all sorts of financial inducements. But perhaps more importantly he appeals to Lesser's conscience reciting a litany of woes:

Hab rachmones, Lesser, I have my own ambition to realize. I've got fifteen years on you, if not more, and I'm practically naked as the day I was born. Don't be fooled that I own a piece of property. You know already about my sick wife and knocked-up daughter, age sixteen. Also I religiously go one afternoon every week to see my crazy mother in Jackson Heights. All the time I'm with her she stares at the window. Who she thinks she sees I don't know but it's not me. She used to weigh ninety pounds, a skinny lady, now she's two-twenty and growing fatter. I sit there with tears.

Levenspiel, a semi-comic, semi-choral figure in the book, may or may not be exaggerating his miseries. But early on, when Lesser says he's writing a "minor masterpiece," Levenspiel offers his own opinion: "Art, my ass, in this world it's heart that counts."

There are suggestions here and there that both Lesser and Willie long for the consciousness, indeed, the color of the other. Harry has dreams of marriage ceremonies, black and white, officiated by a rabbi and a tribal chief in the heart of an African jungle village. At about the same time Willie is writing a story about a black man whom he names Harry. The fictional Harry's black friends suspect him of betraying them and they paint him white. In the main, however, *The Tenants* is told from the point of view and sensibilities of Lesser, and, because Lesser is a writer so possessed by writing, Malamud's novel seems almost as much about writing as it is about black–Jewish hostility. Where Willie and Lesser both agree is that their books are more important to them than anything else in life. As a consequence both live sadly depleted lives as well as losing Irene, the woman they both desire. Lesser wants his art to serve as a substitute for love, Willie his art to serve as a measure of his negritude. The greater failure is Lesser's, who cannot even allow himself pity for his peculiar landlord. But Willie fails, too, because he cannot discipline his passions and because literature demands something more than ideology. At the end of the novel the two men kill each other, and Levenspiel, on discovering their corpses, is left crying out for pity and mercy in New York's space-conflicted wilderness.

6

❧❧

The Big Picture

William Dean Howells, John Dos Passos, Tom Wolfe, Don DeLillo

A delusion many Americans share is that western expansion during the first centuries of the republic was begun by resentful and frustrated inhabitants of overcrowded cities. The presumed free lands of the West — so the story goes — fired them with dreams of beginning life anew. In point of fact the opposite appears to be true. When city dwellers departed cities, they tended to move not very far away — or, often enough, to other cities. Conversely, farmers and persons living in the rural or western parts of the states more frequently pioneered and settled the West. It would seem then that rural Americans were the more resentful and frustrated — or just possibly more enterprising and adventurous than their city counterparts.

When in the 1890s the frontier was declared officially closed (despite the fact that there remained a great deal of unsettled territory), reverse patterns of migration began to take place. Large populations shifted from rural areas to cities, mainly for economic reasons. Although some technological advances helped accelerate concentrations of banks, businesses, and industries in cities, some of these same technologies caused agricultural overproduction, depressing rural economies. As already noted, cities began to suggest some of the same attractions that lured earlier generations West. Certainly cities seemed to offer a greater number of trades, skills, and occupations benefiting women, who now enjoyed greater economic and sexual freedom — though clergy and much of the establishment press expressed fears for their morality. Men, on the other hand, deprived of their farms and village economies found themselves more and more at the mercies of an impersonal industrial capitalism. Moreover, the very proximity of distinct city neighborhoods bred social, racial and ethnic tensions.

New York City was by no stretch of the imagination immune to these problems — indeed, many existed prior to the Civil War — still, no city produced greater allure. One of its main attractions was clearly cultural. Art markets, concert halls, museums, theaters, and publishing houses proliferated in the late decades of the nineteenth century, drawing more and more artists, musicians, and writers to a city already noted for its diverse communities. Celebrated literary figures like Mark Twain and William Dean Howells came to live in the city, at least for a while, and significantly the city also drew young painters who saw New York as *their* frontier. This is not to say they all stayed or liked what they saw. But several among them banded together (loosely called the Ashcan School) aiming to counter traditional nature paintings by depicting a non-genteel city of working- and middle-class neighborhoods, backyards, shops, streets, and popular entertainments. Theirs was a heightened realism reflecting their own contrasting moods, at once wondrous, melancholy, and celebratory.

Not unlike the Ashcan artists, young writers who came to New York in the years surrounding the new century (among them Stephen Crane, O. Henry, Theodore Dreiser, and Eugene O'Neill) would also look at New York from a fresh perspective. They, too, would dwell on settings, subject matter, and classes of New Yorkers hitherto neglected in genteel literature. Doubtless many viewed the city as tolerating attitudes and behavior unthinkable in other American communities. But the city was not of course necessarily iconoclastic nor immoral (though lurid tales of wicked New York abounded in the popular literature), nor was the city opposed to what the rest of the country deemed acceptable. Surely New York knew its share of Comstocks and Savonarolas for more than a century. It would perhaps be more fair to say that the city was indifferent to aberrant ways so long as they did not seriously impinge upon the city's main business of making money. Nor were radicals and bohemians unwelcome, since they seldom posed anything more than a symbolic threat to the social order; indeed, in their own ways they were just as likely to enrich the city with intellectual and cultural contributions. As for fin de siècle artists, the attractions of New York lay in the challenges to adapt to urban landscapes and to re-create the "new." The paradox is that so many regarded one of the oldest cities in America as undiscovered country. Were they wrong? A few, of course, achieved their dreams. If, however, it was happiness they expected, judging from the literature the results were decidedly mixed.

Perhaps inspired by the visual arts, several authors have since imagined

New York as a vast Brueghel-like canvas on which they could project the city as it actually was and as a metaphor for underlying American truths, in other words, realism married to a kind of metaphysics. The "ordinary" as being fraught with symbolic value was not of course foreign to American writers. New England Puritan clerics sought God's messages in such everyday events as toothaches — but as we shall see, among latter-day nineteenth-century realist authors, William Dean Howells was the first to discover meaning in the scattered lives of city dwellers.

Born in 1837 and brought up in mainly small Ohio towns, Howells apprenticed first as a printer and later worked as writer and editor on several Ohio newspapers. The Civil War years saw him serving an American consulship in Venice, a reward apparently for having earlier written Abraham Lincoln's campaign biography. He afterwards resumed journalism in New York for a brief period and in 1866 departed for Boston, where he had been appointed subeditor and, later, editor of the prestigious *Atlantic Monthly*. During his Boston tenure he established himself as an authoritative though somewhat genteel literary critic liked and trusted by such disparate authors as the urbane Henry James and the less refined Missourian Mark Twain. More importantly he produced several "realistic" novels, a few of which deservedly enhanced his reputation. But after twenty years in Boston, Howells agreed to move to New York to help edit *Harper's Monthly Magazine*. His decision signaled New York's new cultural power. The raw city, Howells came to believe, encompassed all of America's converging social and economic strains. His publisher encouraged him to write about them.

The point of view, the sensibility of *A Hazard of New Fortune* (1889), is for the most part that of a middle-aged editor like Howells who attempts to embrace New York (then only Manhattan) as something inchoately organic into which cross sections of immigrants, native New Yorkers, and newcomers find themselves living uneasily together. In his "Introduction" Howells admits *Hazard* to being autobiographical. His protagonist–alter ego, Basil March, a Boston-based magazine editor, is lured to New York to edit an upstart rival. As much as one can speculate, Howells' wife — here called Isabel — was not delighted at the prospect. ("It's so big and hideous!") Their search for an apartment (apparently as exasperating in the 1880s as it is today) allows Howells/March to travel to different parts of the city, absorbing impressions as he goes along. In the course of time, his editorial responsibilities will take him to other sections of the city where he will have to deal with people who in one way or another are important to his job. They in turn will hazard their fortunes with others, thereby generating several subplots.

March notes that New Yorkers do not appear to be of any dominant ethnic type. On a downtown elevated train, he becomes something of an artist-observer himself as he describes some of the other passengers:

> The small eyes, the high cheeks, the broad noses, the puff lips, the bare, cue-filleted skulls, of Russians, Poles, Czechs, Chinese; the furtive glitter of Italians; the blond dullness of Germans; the cold quiet of Scandinavians — fire under ice....

In a later passage he invests the swirl of streets and street signs with a Darwinian universality:

> ... the vagaries of the lines that narrowed together or stretched apart according to the width of the avenue, but always in wanton disregard of the life that dwelt, and bought and sold, and rejoiced or sorrowed, and clattered or crawled, around, below, above — were features of the frantic panorama.... Accident and then exigency seemed the forces at work to this extraordinary effect; the play of energies as free and planless as those that force the forest from the soil to the sky; and then the fierce struggle for survival, with stronger life persisting over the deformity, the mutilation, the decay, of the weaker.

Long afterwards, March comes to realize he no longer merely contemplates the spectacle of the city but has become part of the picture, while the city itself encapsulates History. At one point, while walking along quiet streets at a time of labor strife, he imagines the western frontier absorbed into the city's ongoing present: "He interested himself in the apparent indifference of the mighty city, which kept on about its business as tranquilly as if the private war being fought out in its midst were a vague rumor of Indian troubles on the frontier; and he realized how there might once have been a street feud of forty years in Florence without interfering materially with the industry and prosperity of the city."

Inasmuch as Howells was the first to embrace the entire city as a subject, it is not surprising that many of his characters would become prototypes (and stereotypes) subsequent twentieth-century authors would draw on. Among others are the capitalist plutocrat, the immigrant, the radical, the go-getter, the self-sacrificing idealist, the impoverished widow, the unreconciled Southerner, the socially secure aristocratic women and socially insecure social climbers, and the artists with and without integrity. Jews and Negroes also make cameo appearances. And below the surface there are conflicts between capital and labor, art and commerce, youth and their elders — indeed, currents in American life that would become more pronounced in the twentieth century. A drawback is that Howells attempts to resolve these conflicts too late in the narrative. Near the end of the book, a bloody streetcar strike breaks out, to which each of the major figures responds in his or her own way. Although he tries to be fair to each of his characters, Howells' benign socialist sympathies lie somewhere beneath the surface. Yet *Hazard* does not prepare the reader for the sudden violence nor for the hasty resolutions the violence brings about. Still, granting as much, Howells has otherwise re-created a vibrant fin de siècle New York very much on the brink of even greater changes than he ever imagined.

For all its modernist techniques, the wider scope of John Dos Passos's *Manhattan Transfer* (1925) succeeds less than Howells' traditional approach. One reason may be that at heart Dos Passos yearned for a premodern, preindustrial America where individuals could claim, with some justification, control over their lives. Dos Passos, who was himself born of affluent parents four years before the end of the nineteenth century, enjoyed a privileged upbringing somewhat removed from the turmoil of the times. As a youth he had traveled about in Europe and Mexico and planned to become an architect. But by his undergraduate years at Harvard he was expressing alarm and revulsion at the deindividualizing effects of a huge mechanized society. The outsized modern world for Dos Passos was the constant enemy of life, and his wartime experience as an ambulance driver during World War I reinforced this fear. For the next forty years or so in plays, fiction, memoirs, and essays he portrays the military, big business, the media, labor unions, and government bureaucracies as dangers to the human spirit. While his politics during this same period shifted from the extreme left to the conservative right, his outlook remained much the same: mass society and mass institutions threaten the sanctity of the individual.

Manhattan Transfer, his third novel, imagines New York in much the same way: as an immense machine crushing, alienating, and isolating the humanity within its borders. In effect the novel conveys almost as much revulsion as compassion for the city's inhabitants, this despite the "objective," near journalistic tone of the prose. As composition, *Manhattan Transfer* is a gathering together of fragments and events in the lives of a kaleidoscope of persons living in Manhattan in the 1920s. Some come from the West or elsewhere seeking new lives or new wealth. Some cross one another's paths and carry forward whatever momentum the novel has. Others make infrequent appearances and vanish. Among the numbers are noble proletarians, sleazy politicians, union organizers, theatrical producers, bohemians, journalists, immigrants, restaurant workers, bootleggers, bankers, and lawyers — each tenuously connected to one another and to their city. Most episodes are bound by themes of frustration, emotional vacuity, and a vulgar materialism, while interspersed are brief lyrical passages (about which more later). Biographical sketches, newspaper accounts, snatches of popular songs, and swift cinematic changes of scene are also integrated into the narration. Dos Passos would, however, put such techniques to far better use in a portrayal of his country, in his extensive *U.S.A.* trilogy of the 1930s. Paradoxically he would become more successful in depicting an entire nation than in portraying its largest city.

The outstanding figure in *Manhattan Transfer* is Jimmy Herf, an idealistic, disillusioned reporter who marries and divorces Ellen, an actress, who herself experiences bitter love affairs and compromising professional experiences. Together their failed lives are typical of the unfulfilled possibilities of others. A debilitating materialism permeates the city, contaminating city dwellers who seek ways to survive (or flee as Jimmy Herf does at the close of the novel). But the main trouble is not so much ideology as Dos Passos's efforts to tilt his fiction in the direction of ideology. Too many *Manhattan Transfer* characters are without dimension and say unlikely things to one another. Nor is much room allowed for ambiguity or mystery. At its best *Manhattan Transfer,* for all its variety of situation, gives off the feeling of a documentary. On some level Dos Passos must have known this, for, in describing his New York world, he intrudes from time to time (often at the start of chapters) to marry his "realism" to a kind of pictorial poetic prose:

> Night crushes bright milk out of arclights, squeezes the sullen blocks until they drip red, yellow, green into streets resounding with feet. All the asphalt oozes light. Light spurts from lettering on roofs, mills dizzily among wheels, stains rolling tons of sky.

But passages such as the above are more artifice than art, and Dos Passos's paintings — despite experimental daubs — succumb to pre–Civil War traditional images of cities as sites of corruption and despair. And in the peculiarly American tradition, Dos Passos's hero-protagonist, Jimmy Herf, like Huck Finn and countless other nineteenth-century American fictional figures, moves on West in hopes of finding peace and purity.

More than a half century after Dos Passos, Tom Wolfe would undertake another large-scale cityscape. *Bonfire of the Vanities* (1987) revolves around three individuals who in the ordinary course of their lives would not have had anything to do with each other. A hotshot Wall Street bond salesman, a middle-class Bronx assistant district attorney, and a dissolute English journalist — each in his thirties — comprise the three principals. But because their destinies intersect, a whole gamut of other New Yorkers are introduced: lawyers, judges, blacks, Jews, Park Avenue doyennes, newspaper publishers, preachers, financiers, policemen, and an assortment of thugs. The setting, like that of *Manhattan Transfer*, is extensive embracing of, among other sites, dismal portions of the Bronx, Wall Street boardrooms, Park Avenue apartments, and upscale restaurants. But where Dos Passos's narrative is fragmented, Wolfe successfully brings all his multiple plotlines together.

At its core the novel relates the travails of an arrogant Wall Street millionaire, Sherman McCoy, who is unjustly accused of being the driver in a hit-and-run collision with a black youth. For reasons having little to do with the unfortunate victim, Sherman is relentlessly pursued by a Bronx assistant district attorney, the tabloid media, and a charismatic black preacher who exploits guilt-ridden Jews and Episcopalians as well as the resentments of his African-American followers. Very few of Wolfe's New Yorkers behave selflessly; most act cynically or delude themselves and others as regards their true motives. Put another way, none is truly likable although a few may win the reader's grudging admiration, among them a coarse but courageous judge, a couple of honest working-class cops, and, at the end of the novel, Sherman himself, who casts off his insular upper-class delusions about how the world works and fights bravely to survive.

Wolfe's view of New York is thus scarcely less sour than that of Dos Passos, but because he is a better storyteller his book is more alive. Unlike Dos Passos he also understands that money and status are often inextricably bound up with ethnic sensibilities. Blacks, Jews, Irish, and "old guard" Protestant New Yorkers figure in the novel's conflicts (though surprisingly few Italians and Hispanics) and Wolfe also understands the powerful role of the media in shaping the New York culture. Catalysts in Sherman's downfall are unscrupulous newspaper and television stories re-creating the hit-and-run accident as a racist incident. At its best, though, *Vanities* can be devastatingly sardonic. The scenes in a financial district trading room are not only vivid visually but audibly frenetic:

> The shouts, the imprecations, the gesticulations, the fucking fear and greed...
> "This Goldman order really fucked things up good!"
> "— step up to the fucking plate and —"
> "— bid 8½ —" ....
> "— a hundred million July-nineties at the buck —"

"— Naked short —"
"Jesus Christ, what's going on?"
"I don't fucking believe this!"
"Holy fucking shit!" shouted the Yale men and the Harvard men and the Stanford men. "Ho-lee fuc-king shit."
How these sons of the great universities, these legatees of Jefferson, Emerson, Thoreau, William James, Frederick Jackson Turner, William Lyons Phelps, Samuel Flagg Bemis, and the other three-name giants of American scholarship — how these inheritors of the *lux* and the *veritas* now flocked to Wall Street and to the bond trading room....

Barbs are also aimed at their women: "social X rays" (near anorexic in their endeavors to become thin) or "lemon tarts" (young blonde second, third, or fourth wives). Nor are lower social levels spared. Wolfe's phalanx of lawyers, politicos, judges, and technocrats seethes with frustration and envy. Then there are the lumpen proletarians — chiefly young African-American males who defiantly saunter about in what Wolfe calls a "pimp roll." Unlike other self-deluded characters, they are granted no motives for their behavior. Rather they are seen from the outside — threatening, manipulating or being manipulated. Their suspicions and hostility are simply reported as unaccountable social pathologies.

The author's insensitivity to African-American angst is perhaps understandable. Born in Virginia in 1931 and educated at Washington and Lee and Yale, he was farther removed socially from city blacks than from some of the other types he describes in the book. As a journalist-author he has had to relate his own basically conservative temperament to the pretensions of the cultural elite as well as to some of the grittier vulgarities of the counterculture. He may well have wanted to alleviate some of these latter irritants with books celebrating the heroism of American astronauts in *The Right Stuff* (1979), and traditional nineteenth-century American architecture in *From the Bauhaus to Our House* (1981). But on the whole his major emphasis in more than half a dozen works of nonfiction lay in sardonic representations of what he would regard as the unwholesome or aberrant or simply cuckoo aspects of American life.

Vanities is Wolfe's first novel. (He would subsequently publish two more.) But like each of his earlier American works, much of the effectiveness of the writing depends on slightly exaggerated description and swift pacing. Even when Wolfe dwells on the outlandish décor of a financier's office, or the squalid interior of a Bronx courthouse, or the cramped furnishings of a West Side middle-class apartment, he still manages to move his characters quickly through their caprices. By and large, the city mirrors its inhabitants; the law, the press, philanthropies, and churches operate mainly on principles of self-aggrandizement. Very little virtue or goodness exists against which to measure Wolfe's "vanities." On more than one occasion he acknowledges his indebtedness to nineteenth-century social novelists, especially Dickens, but the latter conjure up good honest souls to confront the general wickedness. Not so Wolfe. On the whole one feels there is a smirk on Wolfe's face — or is the reader expected to smirk? In the end Wolfe's large canvas is less a panorama than a ship of fools whose passengers look a bit smaller than life.

In nearly all Don DeLillo's novels, a vague brooding sense of disaster hangs somewhere over the action. *Underworld* (1997) in this regard is no different from his eight earlier works, although now menace is as much metaphysical as physical, with large segments of the narration taking place in New York City. Still, it would be as much a mistake to call *Underworld* a New York novel as to call *Moby Dick* a whaling story. What DeLillo attempts here is a disinterring of the American soul, or perhaps the universal soul, in the latter years of the twentieth century. One role New York plays is to serve up icons and symbols around which the action revolves. Indeed, the geography of New York from the Bronx to Harlem to Greenwich Village to Staten Island yields a variety of images transferable to the larger world.

Central to DeLillo's vision are conflicts of life and death — death being symbolized by literal underworlds of nuclear waste, detritus, and landfills of garbage, as well as metaphoric underworlds of crime, betrayals, and violence. Everywhere in the novel the underworlds, like memento mori, are becoming more and more visible, emerging, as it were, from the depths while humankind attempts more and more to disguise (or deny) their message. (Klara, a conceptual artist, paints and decorates B-2 aircraft that were once intended to carry nuclear bombs; another character builds a tower of garbage that would otherwise be buried, and Moonman, a homosexual graffiti artist, paints subway cars that issue to the surface in garish colors.) Despite naturalistic detail *Underworld* suggests something of a medieval woodcut depicting Everyman's long struggle with death. Life, conversely, depends on the fragile relationships between men and women and, perhaps more importantly, the cohesiveness of families and community.

Notes of both loss and triumph begin the novel. In a 1951 play-off game between the Brooklyn Dodgers and the New York Giants, Bobby Thomson hits his famous ninth-inning home run. An African-American high school truant, Cotter Martin, recovers the ball and flees, pursued by a crazed white fan. Meanwhile, Nick Shays, a Bronx youth and secret Dodger admirer, rues his team's defeat as he listens to the game on the radio. Attending the game in box seats are J. Edgar Hoover and his pals Jackie Gleason and Frank Sinatra. Hoover is quietly informed that the Soviet Union has detonated a nuclear bomb, and afterwards a *Life* magazine page reproducing Brueghel's *The Triumph of Death* floats down from the stands and lands on his lap. Soon much of the city will erupt in joy at the game's storybook ending, but the Giants will eventually lose the World Series to the Yankees, and Nick, over the course of years, will attempt to take possession of Thomson's home-run ball (which has passed through many hands) as a reminder of what has been lost. What was lost for Nick was of course not simply a game but an innocence, a time relatively free of fear, when families and neighborhoods were somehow imperfectly joined.

Insofar as there are main characters — in a cast of dozens — they are New Yorkers. In addition to Nick and his brother Matt, born of Irish and Italian parents, there are the aforementioned Klara and her first husband, Albert Bronzini, a high school science teacher, Cotter Martin and his father, Manx, around whom strands of plot and chronologies converge, and Sister Edgar, a flawed nun (and counterpart to J. Edgar), who endeavors to salvage the lives of the lost and homeless in Nick's old Bronx neighborhood. The varying outlooks of each derive from their New York lives, which together reflect the novel's melancholy but stoic tone. Some are pioneers, in their way — indeed a few go West in a kind of mock reversal of history. Klara, reborn as an artist in Greenwich Village, paints her planes in New Mexico while Matt works as a physicist and Nick as a waste management executive — both in the Southwest. But as the years pass, they lose their links to their communities, their families are fragmented, and their marriages become problematic.

DeLillo likes to think of his novel as modernist, which indeed it is, with narration rattling back and forth in time, and with such characters as nuns, derelicts, teachers, bohemians, schoolgirls, businessmen, and gangsters popping in and out along the way. It would be hard to pinpoint a central plot, but its several stories are united by curious coincidences, leitmotifs and images as disparate as packages of Lucky Strike cigarettes or a landfill on Staten Island or a baseball or a nuclear bomb the size of a baseball. To be sure, there are excesses, perhaps too many scenes of Lenny Bruce's nightclub act "We're all gonna die!" Still, the book is brilliantly realized, communicating its thematic memento mori even in street corner banter:

Giulio Belisario, Juju, had never seen a dead body, including at a wake, and he was interested in the experience.

"Who's gonna die," Nicky said, "just so you can satisfy your curiosity?"

"I missed my grandmother when I had the measles."

"I'm looking around. I don't see any volunteers. You hear about Allie's father?"

"What?"

"You don't know this?"

"What? He died?"

"He hit a number."

"I was gonna say."

"He's buying a Buick. One day he's a fishmonger. The next day."

"I was gonna say. I just saw him yesterday in the market. How could he be dead?"

"How long does it take?" Nicky said.

"I'm only saying."

"One day he's selling scungilli. The next day, hey, kiss my ass."

"Who's better than him?" Juju said.

"I'm driving a big-ass Buick. Stand clear, you peasants."

From time to time DeLillo writes of his city from the point of view of an artist. There are marvelous passages imagining Klara standing on the roofs of Manhattan apartment houses observing the architectural and decorative elaboration of adjoining buildings. She discovers fascinating and intriguing details the ordinary viewer might otherwise overlook. Perhaps because he is a New Yorker with a New Yorker's large degree of skepticism, DeLillo does not grasp too literally at any of the myths of the city, but they are all there: the corrupt city, the decadent city, the lawless frontier city, the city of reborn hope and civilization, and finally the city of death in life. America is New York City writ large.

7

The Magic, the Mystery, the Miseries

Thomas Wolfe, F. Scott Fitzgerald, Dawn Powell, E.L. Doctorow, Paule Marshall

Was it hard to imagine? The city of mean streets, steel and concrete could become the city of transcendent romance and metaphysical revelations. Why not? Was it not also the city of possibilities and transformed identities? The promises of New York would also become enhanced by movies. But moving images almost by definition cannot long plumb the depth of dreams, or for that matter their dark side. The moviegoer who may or may not identify with characters on the screen involves himself chiefly with plot and awaits its outcome. Lights and shadows flicker and depart — unlike written words.

Still, granting as much, films powerfully convey the city's contradictions. One movie (among hundreds) must serve here as illustrative. Ostensibly *Forty-Second Street* (1933) is a formulaic musical about an "out-of-town" aspiring dancer who comes to New York to fulfill her dreams. With much hard work, misunderstandings, heartbreak, and luck, she succeeds — and in the process finds love and romance and ultimately stardom. But interestingly her Broadway debut also features choreographed scenes of congested neighborhoods, tenements, mayhem and sudden death. The film appears to be saying sweet dreams and mean streets are all integral to the New York experience.

As noted elsewhere mean streets are not of course the exclusive province of American letters. Indeed, their ancestry extends nearly as far back as the beginning of the novel. Among their nineteenth-century European masters were Victor Hugo and Charles Dickens, and in America Herman Melville

(*Pierre*, 1852), not to mention hosts of popular sensationalist authors who would portray American cities in horrendous images. Yet, after the 1890s, a different vision of New York would emerge. Alongside the city as a kind of Nineveh came depictions of a magical city, a city of earthly and unearthly delights, an Araby — whose promises, unhappily, were seldom realized.

At this point it is important to caution that perceptions of New York, frequently twofold, are often related from the point of view of outsiders. Some come to the city with romantic preconceptions, and their first experiences may, temporarily at least, reinforce their dreams. But then there are others, with few high expectations, whose consciousness may reflect the darker side of their new environment. In the latter case, individual consciousness may well stand as a metaphor for some aspect or other of the city. For the present, we focus on the city as a projection, however illusory, of momentary hopes and dreams. A succeeding chapter portrays the city as a dark force in itself whose currents emerge in the psychology of inhabitants. Needless to say there is blurring and diversity in many works (including some to be discussed here), but for the moment we deal with the city as much imagined as real.

If ever there were a writer who encompassed the multifarious myths and perceptions of the city in very nearly all his works, that writer would be Thomas Wolfe (1900–1938). Or put another way, these are the views of Wolfe's fictional alter egos, Eugene Gant and George "Monk" Webber. (Gant's New York life is told in *Of Time and the River*, 1934, and Webber's in *The Web and the Rock*, 1939, and *You Can't Go Home Again*, 1940.) Moreover, on first, second, or third readings Wolfe's effusions do not always appear to be headed in any one direction — although in due course I shall argue that towards the end of his life Wolfe seems to be taking a much clearer stand on how he understands New York and, in fact, America as a whole.

One way to try to explain the confusion is to suggest that Wolfe projects onto the city his own volatile disposition as well as the momentary circumstances he finds himself in. But there are other considerations we must address. First and foremost is that Wolfe was a Southerner from a small North Carolina town who brought to New York many Southern cultural assumptions regarding race, foreigners, homosexuals, and Jews. But he brought with him as well a pre–Depression years Southern outlook — its romanticism, its sense of a coherent community, and pride of independence. Yet even these we must qualify, for Wolfe himself tells us in his novels that in his Southern youth he often saw himself as an outsider, a loner, and a questioner who did not or could not swallow the whole of Southern culture — and, one may note parenthetically, he did not see Southern culture as being all one homogenous blob. In addition, Wolfe regarded writing not only as a means of discovering himself (although it is sometimes surprising how little he seems to understand himself) but as a means of ingesting Whitman-like as much as he can of human experience, however naïve that may sound. Finally there is the question of the "authenticity" of Wolfe's New York views. To a small degree his relationship to his editors (Maxwell Perkins at Scribner's and Edward Aswell at Harper's) must be taken into account. It is well known that Wolfe transmitted to them huge chunks of manuscript, and trusted them to arrange, rearrange, and revise these materials into book form. Wolfe himself, via his fictional surrogates, pretty much agreed to any and all of Perkins's suggestions although afterwards he gave that as one of his excuses for changing publishers. But Wolfe's last two novels (*The Web and the Rock* and *You Can't Go Home Again*) were published posthumously, and in shaping them into novels Aswell interpolated short stories and some material omitted from Wolfe's *Of Time and the River*. As a consequence there have been allegations that both Perkins and Aswell themselves wrote portions of Wolfe's books. Yet, if true, these could not have been very significant and Wolfe's style and spirit, especially as regards the city, strike one as being consistent with his character.

Inasmuch as this book is about New York myths, we may as well start with the ways Wolfe dealt with them. To begin with, despite their different names, Wolfe's two autobiographical protagonists are for the most part interchangeable. (In Wolfe's first novel, *Look Homeward Angel*, 1930, detailing his pre–New York City life, he is also called Eugene Gant.) Their stories in the main adhere to the same general outline. Both Eugene and George come from small North Carolina towns and both as youths had dreamt of New York as "the shining city." And, unhappily, both in the course of their New York lives discover the city not quite as they had imagined it. On his arrival at Pennsylvania Station, Eugene, the first of Wolfe's alter egos, had visited the city before and is again appalled at its swarming "mongrel" masses, "the brutal stupefaction of the street, the immense and arrogant blaze and sweep of the great buildings." He is once more repelled and fascinated by the multiethnic character of faces, "dark, dingy, driven, harried and corrupt," and he specifically cites the "cruel, arrogant and knowing beak-nosed Jews" and the "red beefy" faces of Irish cops replete with "stupid, swift and choleric" menace. Nor does he find the voices of the city any more appealing but rather one extended "strident snarl."

During Eugene's first year in the city, he finds employment as an English instructor at a university near Washington Square and lives in a dismally sterile residential hotel nearby. (Wolfe, who had attended the University of North Carolina and Harvard, did in fact teach for several years at New York University and lived apparently at the Albert Hotel on University Place where he had begun writing his Southern novel, *Look Homeward Angel*. In *The Web and the Rock,* he condescendingly calls the institution "an education factory" and names it the University of Utility Cultures, Inc.) He pictures his students as near Bosch-like demons swarming about the university's "brawling and ugly corridors," and even in the refuge of the classroom feels near drowned in its smaller hordes of "Jews and Jewesses, all laughing, shouting, screaming, thick with their hot and swarthy body smells, their strong female odors of rut and crotch and arm-pit and cheap perfume, and their hard male smells that were rancid, stale, and sour...." Only one among them responds to the glories of English literature and the great poets, whom they reproduce in their papers as Wadsworth and Keiths. Nor does Eugene find any respite among his colleagues. Their humanity is affected, he believes, by the cruelty and cowardice of the engulfing city. They fear for their jobs and the professors who hired them, they envy one another's promotions and stand obsequious before the Dean.

Eugene begins to move apart from his mass impressions of New Yorkers — especially his curious mix of revulsion and attraction to Jews — when, reluctantly and against his better judgment, he befriends an intellectually oriented student, Abe, and comes to admire the endurance and courage of Abe's Lower East Side family. Oddly, despite Eugene's Jewish phobias and anxieties, Abe seems to be the only New York City friend he makes in this novel. Still, by and large, Eugene deplores the mass mindless energy of the city that deprives New Yorkers of their individuality. He notes especially its effects on the alienated youths who slink along the city streets looking to fight others or to fight one another. Nor does he feel himself immune from being swept up in the swarms of people dreaming of escape. But escape *from* what, *to* what? Prowling the streets each night he experiences "the huge and quickening desire to which all life in the city moved ... past hope and past belief to the huge glare, the swarming avenues of night, with their great tides of livid night-time faces."

And yet from time to time he does escape, occasionally visiting friends beyond the city's boundaries, occasionally going off on his own. Still, on his return there are always the faces of city people with dead and dull lusterless eyes, "who had been hurled ten thousand times through the roaring darkness of a subway tunnel, who had breathed foul air, and been assailed by smashing roar and grinding vibrance ... until their ears were deafened, their tongues rasped and their voices made metallic." At the start of the summer university holidays, Eugene manages to get away to Europe, and oddly, while in France, begins to think fondly of his adopted city. He writes in his journal that the opportunities for learning and acquiring a culture are greater in the city than anywhere else in the world. Books are plentiful, and music and theater in New York are the best in the world. But there is, he avers, something we can learn from the French: "We have had niggers for three hundred years living all over the place — but all we did about it was to write minstrel shows and coon stories until two or three years ago when the French discovered for us how interesting they are."

The Web and the Rock was published five years after *River*, but in a general sort of way it tells much the same story, especially as regards the protagonist's pre–New York years. Eugene Gant is now George Webber and his New York City life is central to his evolving sense of self. What strikes the reader most, perhaps, is Wolfe's far kinder vision of the city. Indeed, he tells of the romantic transformative powers of the city for the young who are escaping the prejudices and provinciality of their small towns and rural communities. At the start of George's New York life, he has taken a room with four other Southern boys in the upper portion of the "fabulous Island of Manhattan" — and their first year together was "in many ways a good one." There were girls, romances, parties, and "cheap gin," as well as the city's cultural highlights — the Public Library, Carnegie Hall, and the Metropolitan Museum. To be sure, the city may for the most part appear "hideously ugly," yet one remembers it as a place of "proud and passionate beauty" where people seek to fulfill the hunger in their lives. He observes that Southerners cling together as proud regional "patriots" far more than other nonnative New Yorkers, often out of fears of rejection or defeat. But it is precisely because of their fears and their defensiveness that they prevail, and when they choose to stay on they contribute "a warmth of earth, an exultant joy of youth, and a burst of living laughter and living energy...."

In the end, of course, each of Eugene's Southern friends has to go his own way — each responding to the city's complicated designs in accord with his own needs; some return home decrying the city's monstrousness, others may be swallowed up in the city's fashionable opinions as regards the arts and very nearly everything else — and others, like George himself, may move away to small single rooms, desperate to absorb experience and penetrate the "surfaces of life."

In contrast to his first happy year in the city, George now undergoes a desperate loneliness: "Alone, he tried to hold all the hunger and madness of the earth within the limits of a little room, and beat his fists against the walls, only to hurl his body savagely into the streets again, those terrible streets that had neither pause nor curve, nor any door that he could enter." Once on the streets, however, he is repelled by the coarse proletarian voices he hears along the way: "Oh, to hurl that stony growl of their barren tongues forever, forever with a million million repetitions into the barren ears of their fellow dead men." There are, however, other moments when his mood changes and he discovers in the crowds and streets "nothing but delight, the promise of some glorious adventure. At such a time he would sink himself wholly and exultantly into the City's life." On these occasions he seems to approximate the anticipation of the joys of the city he had once imagined in his Southern youth.

In this novel George still has a little money left over from an inheritance and he travels for the first time in his life to Europe. On his return journey, he is introduced aboard ship to Esther Jack, who will become the chief focus of the rest of the book. Esther, a wealthy "Jewess," is an older married woman and a supremely successful stage designer who is about to become George's paramour for the next several years. She truly loves George and George is himself immediately smitten. (In *Of Time and the River* Eugene Gant sees this same Esther as he prepares to board ship at Cherbourg for his return trip to New York. One look at her and he knows that he will be forever "impaled on the knife of love.") George's feelings for Esther appear now to produce a less ambivalent view of New York. As he debarks, he speaks of the city as his home, "the most homeless home in all the world. It is the gigantic tenement of Here Comes Everybody and that is what makes it so strange, so cruel, so tender and so beautiful." Indeed, it is the haven of people escaping small-town meanness, offering instead "the bounty of its passionate life, the mercy of its refuge and the thrilling inspiration of all its million promises." But it is also the immortal city of oblivion. Our presences and our toil and sufferings inevitably vanish as we vanish. We shall all be forgotten.

As George's intensely sensual love affair with Esther grows, his emotions continue to reflect the ways he sees New York. New York at night is supreme among the cities of the world. It is the "city of the night," but despite its cruelty overwhelming and "tender" in its loveliness. George, however, also gets to see the New York world in more down-to-earth ways. Because of Esther's connections, he will meet important figures in established New York literary and theatrical circles, most of whom he comes to believe are superficial and affected. He becomes angry and depressed when publishers turn down his manuscript and worries that he's being pulled more and more into Esther's orbit. They quarrel often and as the book ends George severs the relationship and leaves for Europe.

Heretofore we have seen in Wolfe's novels more or less self-absorbed protagonists; that is to say, figures whose hopes, dreams, reactions, hates, and loves constitute their main concern. In *You Can't Go Home Again* we see Wolfe (via George Webber) moving more and more out of himself, trying to imagine the lives, thoughts, and feelings of other persons. And as the novel progresses, we view George also endeavoring to maintain his sharp eye for detail as well as identifying himself with the great mass of poor and dispossessed Americans suffering through the worst years of the Depression. He surrenders his youthful hopes for fame and glory — and looks forward to his writings as being somehow engaged in the struggles to restore dignity and decency to American lives. The time span of this somewhat sprawling book is roughly eight years, from 1929 to 1937.

This last novel of Wolfe's begins sometime in 1928 with George's return to New York from his European sojourn. He takes an apartment in Greenwich Village and resumes his love affair with Esther. He seems now more reportorially (and less metaphysically) inclined to describe his surrounding neighborhood, another tenant in the building, the activities he views from his window, and several street scenes. He even now projects himself into what Esther may be doing and thinking as she goes about her daily life. One senses he begins to enjoy the ordinariness and the small dramas and color of New York life while simultaneously resigning himself to its vulgarity. When George learns that the manuscript about his Southern years has finally been accepted he is both exhilarated and anxious about its New York reception. (As things turn out it will be the residents of the town he had grown up in who become very upset.) But George's evolving philosophical awakening probably really comes about when he travels to his small North Carolina community, Libya Hill — in reality Wolfe's Asheville — to attend the funeral of the aunt who had brought him up. Here he views the deleterious effects of rapacious business practices and varieties of excessive speculation (that he had assumed mainly inherent to New York culture) on the lives, and web-like cohesiveness of the community. Indeed, here he learns that one reason he "can't go home again" is that the home he knew in his youth no longer exists.

Yet, even before he leaves for Libya Hill, the city again begins to loom in his mind as something larger than itself, as an existential metaphor that he had not considered in quite the way he now considers it, a marriage, as it were, of time and humanity. Fittingly, his new insight comes to him at New York's Pennsylvania Station and stands in stark contrast to Eugene Gant's revulsion of the city's throngs on his arrival there:

> For here, as nowhere else on earth, men were brought together for a moment at the beginning or end of their innumerable journeys, here one saw their greetings and farewells, here, in a single instant, one got the entire picture of the human destiny.

Wolfe's efforts to stand outside himself, to put himself into other lives, resume in Book Two of the novel. Wolfe/George calls this "The World That Jack Built," and in the chapters that follow the narrator tries again to imagine Esther's, and now also her husband's, thoughts and musings as they go about their day. Esther deals with her servants, her friends, and her daughter, while Frederick Jack directs his thoughts to family and business. But now Wolfe also descends to lower strata of city life as he tells of the squabbles, resentments, and perspectives of the various employees who work in the Jacks' apartment building. However strained or exaggerated some of these portrayals may appear to be, they reveal at the very least Wolfe's endeavors to individualize his New Yorkers rather than to depict them en masse.

The principal chapters of this section of Book Two focus on the preparations for a lavish, and somewhat tasteless, party Esther gives for her upscale friends and professional colleagues. She manages to induce a very recalcitrant George to attend but when he does arrive his reactions to all he sees, hears, and feels persuade him to finally break up with Esther. The Jacks' insular world is not his, it could not be; it is in its own way petty, snobbish, and artificial, and removed from the authentic heart and experiences of most Americans. When, after the party, two of the workmen in the building die in a fire, their deaths seem only perfunctorily acknowledged.

George moves away to a dingy South Brooklyn apartment, quits his teaching position, and for the next four lonely years works on a new book. We are in the depths of the Depression years and George lives among the poor working classes. Paradoxically his small and pinched Brooklyn neighborhood gives him an expanded sense of America. His neighbors, Wolfe writes, "are for the most part Armenian, Italians, Irish and Jews — in short, American." Afterwards he will speak of South Brooklyn as a "universe." He admires the character and courage of the common man who, however desperate, deprived or inarticulate, expresses in his own way an innate love of life and "unquenchable hope." Some of Wolfe's most affecting passages are given over to the dispossessed. On cold bitter nights he sees homeless men huddled together at a downtown Manhattan subway station. Among them, "shambling hulks ... old men, all rags and bags and long white hair and bushy beards stained dirty yellow, wearing tattered overcoats in the cavernous pockets of which they carefully stored away ... crusts of bread, old bones with rancid shreds of beef still clinging to them and dozens of cigarette butts." Others are "wanderers from town to town, the riders of freight trains, the thumbers of rides on highways, the uprooted, unwanted male population of America." At an adjacent underground latrine a kind of "devil's comedy" plays out as derelicts squat in open doorless stalls and argue savagely about their possession, "which all of them wanted more for rest than for necessity." On the street above, the "giant hackles of Manhattan shone coldly in the cruel brightness in the winter night." The Woolworth Building is not far away and "farther down were the silvery spires and needles of Wall Street...."

The latter part of the book deals with George's journey once more to Europe. It is 1936 and he is in Germany, a country he had loved since his first visit in the twenties. He becomes aware of the terrors and brutalities of the new Nazi regime and will surely write about it. He returns to New York more convinced than ever to engage in struggles to reinvigorate American dignity and democracy. Despite the times, he believes it possible. His beloved friend and editor, Foxhall Edwards (Maxwell Perkins), does not share his urgency, and they part ways.

As we know, Wolfe never saw the publication of his last two novels, but during his New York City years their predecessors were often lauded for their poetic power and openness of soul. But he would also be criticized for excessive self-regard, prolixity, and adolescent attitudes. Both points of view have their validity, although it should be remembered that all his writings were in a sense a work in progress, as was Wolfe himself. Despite his zigzags, we see an emerging maturity as Wolfe encapsulates mythic mixed city dreams into a fused vision of the American experience. He was embarked on a speaking tour when he was stricken with miliary tuberculosis of the brain. He died, one month before his thirty-eighth birthday, in the Johns Hopkins Hospital in Baltimore. He did, however, finally get to go home again — buried among his family in Asheville, North Carolina.

Some two decades into the twentieth century, F. Scott Fitzgerald would begin to revise the usual vision of New York. Rather than engage in gritty struggles for survival, his heroes look to the city as a means of romantic transcendence. Here requited and unrequited lovers bask in its seeming splendor and promise of adventure, its dimmed speakeasies and glowing night windows, and most especially Fifth Avenue and Central Park — and of course the celebrated hotels the Ritz, the Plaza, the Commodore. Innocents in their fashion, Fitzgeraldian young men blind themselves willfully to their naiveté and the dark side of their dreams. Long after he departed New York, Fitzgerald would remember his first impressions: the city as gloriously "glittering and white with all the iridescence of the beginning of the world." He had come to New York from Princeton imagining triumph and sophistication, but these he ultimately discovers were delusions. In reality, of course, Fitzgerald never really "knew" the city. Despite occasional earlier visits, he had lived in New York only in short spurts (from 1919 to 1923) and yet his finest writings convey the city with an aura and a sorrow few other writers have achieved.

Fitzgerald's ambivalence was characteristic of his general outlook. Toward the end of his life he remarked that the test of a first-rate mind was the ability to contain opposing ideas at the same time. The observation was certainly applicable to what he felt about New York. He was both attracted and repelled by the city's display of riches. A Minnesotan (and a Catholic), he felt himself an outsider. Money, he believed, would ease the way to acceptance. But, judging from his own experiences, he also knew wealth gives license to wasted energy and talent. The city with its sybarite culture offered testing grounds for both views. At twenty-five, Fitzgerald's first and immensely popular novel, *This Side of Paradise* (1920), made him *feel* rich, and to celebrate he and his wife, Zelda, engaged in well publicized bacchanalian exploits that looked to corroborate his fictional protagonist's excesses.

Paradise is a poorly constructed autobiographical novel whose hero, an unfocussed budding author-university student, undergoes much Sturm und Drang as he relates to his several "flapper" girlfriends. The self-indulgent Amory Blaine undoubtedly struck a responsive chord for many post–World War I readers long subject to the moral tones and strictures of the war years. New York is Amory's playground as well as the locale of his extended drinking bouts in Prohibition speakeasies. His debaucheries notwithstanding, he finally consoles himself that at least he has been "indispensable" to some people. Fitzgerald published several short stories and a second novel the following year. *The Beautiful and the Damned* (set mainly in New York) plays again on the dilemmas and disillusionment of youth. Anthony Patch, the very rich central character, behaves and drinks irresponsibly, believing his money allows him the freedom to discover his artistic soul. At the novel's conclusion, however, he learns that he has had to expend much of his spirit simply to salvage his fortune. The irony of *Beautiful* is a bit heavy-handed; still, one feels that even in his weakest fiction Fitzgerald's young men's worldly immersions are not ends in themselves but rather aimed at something beyond themselves — transcendent love or beauty or Nirvana. They are mistaken. The consequences are often the same: failure, sorrow, heartbreak, and even, in Fitzgerald's fine story "May Day," suicide.

Much of Fitzgerald's best New York novel takes place paradoxically outside New York City. Jay Gatsby, the western gangster of *The Great Gatsby* (1925), has long dreamt of running away with Daisy, the wife of Tom Buchanan, a rich Midwestern scion. The greater part of the action is set in Long Island communities Fitzgerald calls West Egg and East Egg, and journeys to the city from either place suggest a mix of evil and romance. To get there, the motor road passes through a "valley of ashes," a portent of failed dreams. Tom has occasional sordid trysts in the city with his mistress, and New York also serves as the home base of Gatsby's mentor, a Jewish gambler who had undermined American innocence by bribing World Series players.

Still, however dark the city's heart, Nick Carroway, *Gatsby's* fictional narrator, remembers her in other ways. He tells of "enchanted" evening streets with their lovely young women and lonely yearning young men. He tells of the "pastoral" feeling of Fifth Avenue on soft warm Sunday afternoons and the city's thrilling vista on crossing the Queensboro Bridge:

> Over the great bridge, with the sunlight through the girders making a constant flicker upon the moving cars, with the city rising up across the river in white heaps and sugar lumps all built with a wish out of non-olfactory money. The city seen from the Queensboro Bridge is always the city seen for the first time, in its first wild promise of all the mystery and the beauty in the world.

It is unlikely that Gatsby, who has by now reinvented himself as a parvenu socialite, would have noticed any of the above, so obsessed is he with Daisy. For him Daisy embodies pristine elegance and wonder, and as in medieval romances a lover's longings lead to inevitable death. Daisy, "careless" and coarsened by Tom's inherited wealth, reveals herself incapable of understanding or reciprocating her lover's passion. Nick, who has himself been having an uneasy affair with a slightly "dishonest," New York–tainted woman, determines to abandon the East and return to his Midwest home. His illusions regarding the city's wonders correspond in their way to Gatsby's dream of Daisy. The money that has created the gorgeous and powerful city corrupts its inhabitants, whoever they are, wherever they're from, wherever they choose to live.

Decades afterwards, authors such as Truman Capote (*Breakfast at Tiffany's*, 1958) and Jay McInerny (*Bright Lights, Big City*, 1984) would portray their young protagonists as seeking city pleasures, but unlike the Fitzgerald figures they are far too knowing or cynical to suffer utter demoralization. At length Fitzgerald came to realize his love affair with New York had long passed and he wrote in the Depression years of his "lost City" as "bloated glutted [and] stupid with cakes and circuses." Perhaps. But as a young man some of his most exquisite prose describes the intensity of another vision. Fitzgerald would publish one more novel in his lifetime. *Tender Is the Night* (1934), set on the French Riviera, displaces in its way romantic bittersweet New York. But his last years, ironically, were passed in Hollywood manufacturing screenplays for Hollywood studios. At the time of his death in 1941, he had very nearly completed drafts of a novel (*The Love of the Last Tycoon*) about an idealistic creative film producer crushed by New York financial moguls. Not only was Fitzgerald's city no longer a New West of bright promise, it had reverted to its older image as a fount of evil whose poisons spread across a continent.

Dawn Powell (1897–1965), another Midwesterner, would not have agreed with Fitzgerald's post–Jazz Age pessimism. For her the magic of New York lay less in Fitzgerald's "bright promise" than in the city's offerings of individual freedom and its amazing diversity which feeds the imagination and fantasy life of writers and artists. No less sanguine than Fitzgerald about the likelihood of happy endings (her characters are far more fallible, less innocent), Powell's city abounds nonetheless in thrilling energies. To be sure, notes of melancholy enter her writing during the war years of the 1940s, and her late novels contain more than a mordant strain regarding the city's future. Among other things, she feared for the survival of the arts and worried about bourgeois encroachments on the haunts of the city's artists — their studios, cafes and bars. Still, if Powell believed New York City was becoming less and less hospitable, she continued to the end singing paeans to the city's indomitable bohemian spirit.

She arrived in New York, a twenty-one-year-old, a few weeks before the end of World War I. At this time, a young woman coming alone to the city, without family or friends and very little money, looked to be audacious. But she was inured to hardships, having grown up in a dysfunctional family in several Ohio farm communities and hard-hit industrial towns. As a consequence her works about Ohio reflect the traumas of her Midwestern upbringing in contrast to her writings about New York which, despite some large reservations, portray the city as a haven of tolerance and transformation. Two years after taking up residence in the city, she was married, writing freelance specialty articles for trade papers, and working off and on at small New York–based magazines. By 1925 she had begun publishing some of her own fiction and thereafter appeared to move easily in literary circles. Among her great friends were John Howard Lawson, John Dos Passos, Gore Vidal, and Edmund Wilson — and yet, despite these associations, her considerable output of fiction, plays, and screenwriting seldom achieved sustained attention. Powell's life in New York was not without drama. She had given birth to an autistic son in 1921 and during her lifetime she tried valiantly to care for him. Her husband, Joseph Gousha, an advertising executive, became an alcoholic, and Powell herself seems to have taken several lovers. She nonetheless stayed married and in her fashion remained loyal to Gousha until his death in 1962. Three years later she died, impoverished and stricken with cancer. She had donated her body parts to the Cornell Medical Center, but since no one claimed her remains she was buried anonymously in one of the city's potter's fields.

Powell's New York fiction may best be termed social comedy. She laughs at and with the follies of her protagonists, who are usually artists and writers of one sort or another, and feels for them in their difficult love affairs. But as in all social comedy, there is the enemy — in Powell's novels the self-indulgent and hypocritical rich, and the self-righteous, intellectually dishonest coterie of patrons and hangers-on whom artists and writers often depend upon for survival. Worse still are the Babbits and commercial forces intent on undermining the presence of the arts in the city.

Of Powell's fifteen published novels, seven have New York settings, a few of which Powell notes in her diary are *about* New York. It is not, however, the all-embracing New York of Dos Passos or Tom Wolfe or Don DeLillo, but rather a much smaller New York whose major ground is Manhattan and especially Greenwich Village, and whose cast of characters, as noted, are largely artists, literati, and the persons they deal with. Still, given this small fraction, some of the chief figures respond to the city as something magically organic. Indeed, for them the city becomes another being, a marvel, even in its decay. One spokesman for Powell is her fictional author, Dennis Orphen, who appears as a central character in the best of her New York novels, *Turn, Magic Wheel* (1936), as well as in slighter cameo roles in other books. Orphen's city instincts are Powell's, but she does not create him as someone of noble nature. In *Wheel* he is the constant companion of Effie Callingham, the discarded first wife of a famous Hemingwayesque author who lives mainly abroad. Unknown to Effie, Dennis is secretly chronicling her life for what he hopes to be a thinly disguised best-selling novel. The pathos in *Wheel* lies not only in Effie's dependence on Orphen but also in her fantasies that one day the erring philandering Callingham, whom she hasn't seen in twenty years, will return to her. Though Effie and Orphen are not lovers, Orphen does have a mistress, the wife of a rather smug businessman whose house he occasionally visits as a dinner guest. But Orphen is not a complete cad. He does, in his fashion, love both women and makes the surprising self-discovery that even his novel about Effie is less a betrayal than an effort to free her from her fantasies. These fantasies, as we shall see, are further nourished by the abundant allure of goods in Fifth Avenue shops.

To sketch *Wheel*'s plot is to do it less than justice. The prose is terse and witty, especially where Powell-Orphen's deadpan observations skewer New York's literati — self-serving publishers, editors, authors, book reviewers, society matrons, communist intellectuals, and the like. The novel also movingly captures Effie's tortured psyche as she struggles to extricate herself from fantasies that Callingham will one day return to her. To be sure, *Wheel* belongs to Effie and Dennis, but the city acts almost as a character in their lives. For Dennis, its constant, diverse, surging humanity serves not only his lifework as a writer but also his need to lose himself in the lives of others:

> Some fine day I'll have to pay, Dennis thought, you can't sacrifice everything in life to curiosity. For that was the demon behind his every deed, the reason for his kindness to beggars, organ-grinders, old ladies, and little children, his urgent need to know what they were knowing, see, hear, feel what they were sensing, for a brief moment to *be* them.

The book opens with Dennis on Second Avenue following a young woman as she pauses at shop windows, food stalls, street signs and banners. Dennis imagines her job, her tastes, her social life, her ambitions — and speculates how at some point his own life could intersect with hers. When he loses sight of her, the city suddenly engorges him and he becomes at one with its energized mass:

> Magically the five o'clock people came to life, bounced out of their subways, jumped out of their elevators, bells rang, elevator bells, street-car bells, ambulance bells; the five o'clock people swept through the city hungrily, they covered the sun, drowned the city noises with their million tiny bells, their

five o'clock faces looked eagerly toward Brooklyn, Astoria, the Bronx, Big Date Tonight. They enveloped Dennis, danced about him ... whirred off into night and were gone....

For Effie the city is something different — a magic country that would bring back what she likes to think about as her romantic past. When she learns Callingham is returning to New York after so long an absence, she shops Fifth Avenue frantically for items that will return her to a romantic past — lingerie, shoes, dresses, curtains, furniture, all inappropriate to her present circumstances: "Reason had fled before this sudden urgency, years of discretion and economy were wiped out. Let other women of her years prepare for age, here was one who was building for youth." In her wild imaginings Fifth Avenue's endless array of shops could not only erase the present, but also create a new magical time. In the end, of course, Effie is jolted back to reality. Callingham dismisses her almost casually, but on seeing him again she realizes he had always been too fond of himself to love anyone. Her Fifth Avenue accumulations are now detritus, but the reader may safely assume Dennis will continue to immerse himself in the city's wonders.

Powell's other writings view New York as a haven of freedoms unimaginable elsewhere in America. Tim Page, her biographer, quotes from a letter she wrote to a cousin in Ohio in 1931: "New York City [is] the only place where people with nothing behind them but their wits can be and do everything.... What I mean, friend, is that you can be yourself here and it's the only place where being genuine will absolutely get you anything you want." The freedom to be one's true self extends especially to sexual freedom. No stigma in Powell's novels is ever attached to lovers, adulterers, or homosexuals; see the protagonists of *The Locusts Have No King* (1948), and *The Happy Island* (1938). In one of her darker wartime novels, *A Time to Be Born* (1942), the leading figure, Amanda, a character based loosely on Clare Boothe Luce, commits herself to having a secret abortion. The atmosphere is somewhat sordid and Amanda is herself unscrupulous and manipulative. Still, one never gets the feeling she suffers because she has violated her marriage vows, but rather because she uses sex as a means of self-promotion.

The most pessimistic of Powell's New York novels is the postwar *The Wicked Pavilion* (1954). At its start, a middle-aged Dennis Orphen sits in the Cafe Julian, soon to be demolished, writing in his notebook:

> There was nothing unusual about that New York winter of 1948 for the unusual was now the usual. Elderly ladies died of starvation in shabby hotels leaving boxes full of rags and hundred-dollar bills; bands of children robbed

and raped through the city streets, lovers could find no beds, hamburgers
were forty cents at lunch counters, truck drivers demanded double wages to
properly educate their young in the starving high-class professions; aged
spinsters, brides and mothers were shot by demented youths, frightened girls
screamed for help in the night while police, in pairs for safety's sake, pinned
tickets on parked automobiles....

In the city the elements themselves were money: air was money, fire was
money, water was money, the need of, the quest for, the greed for. Love was
money. There was money or death.

Despite this opening note, the novel unfolds as a New York love story where
young lovers, despite themselves and the numerous obstacles put in their
paths, come together at last. The cafe that frames their romance (in reality
the old Cafe Lafayette in the now-defunct Hotel Lafayette) also serves as a
gathering place for writers and artists. Its imminent destruction by "develop-
ers" represents a grave blow to the city of art and love. Yet, in the last of Powell's novels (*The Golden Spur*, 1962), besieged lovers, writers, intellectuals,
artists, confined now in the main to Greenwich Village, still appear to be
hanging on, if only by the skin of their teeth.

We have thus far observed the city of wonders and magic, the sparkling
city, less a reality than the product of the wishes and imagination of others.
Powell and Fitzgerald were Midwesterners whose protagonists come to New
York anticipating triumph. Disillusionments and disappointments are
inevitable given the baggage of their own pasts, not to mention the city's own
ever-shifting messages. In their own way, they are romantics, blessed if only
momentarily by some ideal or vision of beauty beyond themselves. Their dis-
enchantments, whatever they may have been, seldom match the fervor of their
dreams which in the end make the dreams so memorable.

Not surprisingly, New York–raised children acquire more balanced views,
unconsciously assimilating the city's contradictions. Still, like all children,
they cannot help but fix their imagination on the ordinary and obvious and
create these into objects of wonder and magic. Two novels about children of
the 1930s from opposite sides of the city, who on the face of it could not be
more different from one another, illustrate the city's catalyzing capacities.

To date, E.L. Doctorow has written eight novels, most of which take
place in New York during the first half of the twentieth century. Though some
deal with true-life prominent public figures, none can be properly called "historical." What Doctorow aims for is the spirit of the "times" and how the
times affect *all* persons. And yet, while he does his best not to sentimental-

ize, underlying tones of nostalgia persist. Whether or not this is inevitable in all such writing is moot, but even if one were to grant as much Doctorow's most movingly effective novel, *World's Fair* (1983), tells of the Depression during his own growing-up years in the Bronx.

For most of the novel, Edgar, the child, lives in a two-family house with his father, mother, older brother, and for periods of various lengths an unemployed uncle, a grandmother, and a distraught aunt. In the course of years, his father loses his small business and the immediate family moves to smaller quarters in a less desirable neighborhood. The larger part of the novel relates Edgar's first nine years in the first person, but from time to time he lets his mother, aunt, and his brother tell their stories as well. In sum they speak of not unfamiliar moments of marital strains, sibling rivalries, school experiences, and neighborhood friends, bullies, and hoodlums. Surely nothing very "exciting" happens in the novel, its climax being reached when the nine-year-old Edgar realizes his dream of attending (not once but twice!) the 1939 World's Fair. Nonetheless the novel appeals partially because of its artfully unaffected style — at once a child's point of view and that of an adult looking back — as Edgar shifts consciousness from the day-to-day to the curious, to fears and disappointments, panic and amazements, back and forth. Indeed the city is itself his world's fair long before he attends the real thing. The amazements are of course what the child sees, what the city offers up, however prosaic. A skimpy backyard in the winter serves as the North Pole where Edgar and his brother build an igloo, the envy of neighborhood children. The bed of a coal truck rises up tilting back on hydraulic lifts "with such grinding protest" that it transforms itself in his mind "into a screeching rearing dinosaur." He also learns the world through its "dark signs" — a found slingshot whose "powerful magic ... had some animating force of its own" well beyond his own strength. Meanwhile, the workings of a street-cleaning water wagon may be as astonishing to him as another's first sighting of Niagara or the Grand Canyon:

> An enormous cylindrical tank was mounted on the flatbed of a Mack truck.... As it turned into our street two fanlike jets of water shot out of the nozzles suspended under the tank. Oh what a sight! An iridescent rainbow moved like a phantom light through the air, disintegrating into millions of liquid drops of sun and forming an instant torrent in the gutters at the curbstones.

The New York World's Fair which Edgar visits first with his young friend Meg and her slightly disreputable mother (she apparently has no husband!), comes as a revelation. For Edgar, the immense Trylon and Perisphere signal a utopian future for a world beyond the Bronx. Certainly much of the fair is kitschy and cockeyed but even the razzle-dazzle translates Edgar into another consciousness. At times he loses all sense of himself and becomes one with its crowd and music. The fair becomes the only reality: "I didn't think of my mother or my father or my brother or of school or the Bronx or even of keeping my wits about me...." He and Meg visit exhibits, pavilions, freak shows, amusements, and of course General Motors' astounding "World of Tomorrow"—which in several respects looks like the New York of today. It was "the most fantastic sight I had ever seen, an entire city of the future, with skyscrapers and fourteen-lane highways, [and] real little cars moving on them at different speeds...."

Significantly, Edgar also experiences inchoate sexual stirrings and terrors. Meg's mother, Norma, works in a sideshow as one of five or six women who wrestle with Oscar, the Amorous Octopus, in a tank of water. Edgar is aware that Oscar is someone disguised as an octopus with threatening tentacles, yet he stands transfixed as Oscar tugs away at the women's bathing suits and afterwards slides a tentacle between Norma's legs: "I couldn't breathe. I felt a thrumming kind of heat between my legs but I felt sick too, as if I were going to faint...." When Edgar attends the fair again, with his parents and brother, Norma's troupe no longer performs. But, like the city itself, the fair remains emblazoned in Edgar's mind, a "secret amazement" thrusting its needle into the sky and "whitening" his future.

Across New York at about the same time that Edgar is attempting to puzzle out the wonders of the New York World's Fair, ten-year-old Selina Boyce, a child of Bahamian parents, explores her own world feelings in Brooklyn's shifting neighborhoods. The central figure in Paule Marshall's *Brown Girl, Brownstones* (1959), Selina, is a stand-in for the author, who grew up in Brooklyn during the Depression years and graduated from Brooklyn College in 1953. *Brownstone* is Marshall's first novel and though her several other works of fiction, stories and novels, take place for the most part outside New York, each returns in one fashion or another to *Brownstone*'s main themes of cultural-psychological conflicts. A bildungsroman of sorts, the novel takes Selina into young womanhood and describes her efforts to find within herself a balance between the complications of New York life and the older easier traditions of West Indian immigrants. Selina's unfolding understandings are related in third-person prose by an omniscient author looking back at an earlier time.

At the beginning Selina's New York is a mix of magic delights, fantasies, and incomprehension. She is aware that the houses "Bajans" now live in served previous generations of whites whose histories and outlook were far different from those of the present inhabitants. (Selina, as we shall see, still feels their presence.) She is aware, too, that her immediate Brooklyn neighborhood — its buildings, parks, streets — announce different lifestyles, different messages. Which will be hers? Which would she adopt? She is vaguely cognizant of the antagonisms between Bajans and American-born Negroes, and of the hostility and resentments of blacks and whites in the worlds beyond her neighborhood. More than anything else she is painfully aware that her parents embrace contrasting goals and dreams. Deighton, her father, longs for the joys and beauty of the Bahamas; Silla, her mother, reaches for upward mobility, property ownership, and money. In Selina's childhood the city environment may be muted or haunting or terrifying or exhilarating, but as she grows older, racial, social, and cultural strife will force her to take sides and make cruel decisions whose outcomes are far from clear. Sadly, she will begin to see her New York world in terms of black and white.

Unlike Doctorow's *World's Fair*, which is more or less episodic, Marshall builds on these conflicts to develop her novel. In the main, most issues converge on the struggle of her parents: her father, charming, ineffectual, and poetic; her mother, fiercely ambitious and acquisitive. When Deighton learns quite unexpectedly that he has inherited land in the Bahamas, Silla manages to steal the inheritance and sell it. Deighton thereafter declines, spending all their money, and afterwards falls victim to a religious charlatan, modeled presumably on Harlem's Father Divine. His outraged wife has him deported as an illegal alien and the family later learns that he has mysteriously disappeared while at sea. Selina has much of her father's romantic nature but also much of her mother's angry determination. If she rejects her mother's bourgeois aspirations, she possesses something of her mother's guile, and she schemes to leave home and discover for herself her father's Caribbean paradise.

The novel is not without its flaws. Selina's decision to depart New York after experiencing her first overt confrontation with racism appears too forced, as are the contrived means by which she manages her escape. But these are small reservations in a New York novel which otherwise effectively uncovers Selina's awe and revulsion and ambivalence. The seeds of much of the drama lie in Selina's childhood, and Marshall describes the Bedford Stuyvesant neighborhood West Indians now occupy in terms Selina may well have conceived. On Chauncey Street an unbroken line of brownstones are transformed in her mind to an "army massed at attention." Though squat (they are only three or four stories high), they give the impression of formidable height. Out-wardly monotonous, they manifest considerable difference in detail and design — Gothic, Romanesque, Greek, among others — that give off feelings of confused and doomed worlds. Selina also fantasizes about earlier genera-tions of Dutch, English, Scots, and Irish who lived on her street. In her own home there had once been afternoon teas and long skirts rustling along the parquet floors. Imagining past years she metamorphoses herself into an ele-gant white lady, raising slightly her gown as she descends the stairs. A retinue of others follow, "their white hands [trailing] the banister, their mild voices [imploring] her to give them a little life. And as they crowded around, fus-ing with her, she was no longer a dark girl ... but one of them, invested with their beauty and gentility.... The floor-to-ceiling parlor mirror retained their faces as the silence did their voices." But abruptly she realizes that white and genteel traditions must always exclude people like her: "Glancing up at the frieze of cherubs and angels on the ceiling," she knows that it will always belong "to the ghost shapes hovering in the shadows."

Chauncey Street may belong to white genteel history, but not far away is Fulton Street, where Saturday nights are a whirling surreal microcosm of black life — bustling crowds, neon lights, crowded fire escapes, and shops and bars issuing smells of fish sandwiches, barbecue, and chitterlings. "Wailing blues" emanate from juke boxes while police cars shriek into the night, their lights "stabbing nervously at faces and windows. Fulton Street on Saturday night was all beauty and desperation and sadness." Deighton loves it, Selina is ambivalent. Perhaps as a counterpart to Fulton Street, the second section of the novel is called "Pastorale" where Selina, now age eleven, and her friend Beryl take a Sunday afternoon trolley ride along Tompkins Avenue to Prospect Park. Each claims a window seat, observing passing groups of well-dressed boys and girls, men and women in their Sunday finery, and church sisters garbed in black as if "mourning their own imminent deaths," followed again by groups of children. For Selina the passing generations transmogrify into a metaphor of life's cyclical constancy, its possibilities, its freedoms, "change and return." Afterwards in the park, Beryl tells her she has lately begun to menstruate, and now Selina cannot help seeing young lovers embracing amid the greenery. Brooklyn streets, parks and neighborhoods have awakened her to the mysteries of sex, regeneration, and new life.

If the city's houses and parks and streets send metaphysical messages, Selina has yet another New York experience that will permanently affect her consciousness. At the outbreak of World War II, she calls on her mother, who at this time works in a war factory. She enters a room where she is met by visions of relentless intimidating power — whirling, clanking networks of pipes, pulleys, and machines, large and small. The mature author's prose meshes with the not quite articulate reactions of an eleven-year-old: "This machine-mass, this machine-force was ugly, yet it had grandeur. It was a creative force, the heart of another, larger, form of life that had submerged all others, and the roar was its heartbeat — not the ordered systole and the diastole of the human heart but a frenetic lifebeat all its own." Workers who had built this machine-mass seem now like "small insignificant shapes" whose "movements mimicked its mechanical gestures." As Selina grows into young womanhood she will assume more and more the bleak dehumanizing machine-shop view of her home city — and in Marshall's several subsequent novels and stories, New York (and by extension America) is characterized in much the same way. In reverse fashion, sadly her disaffected protagonists — mainly women — no longer seek the wonders of renewal in New York but rather look for spiritual strength to the Caribbean their ancestors once fled.

8

Darker Visions —
Death and the City

THEODORE DREISER, NATHANAEL WEST,
PAULA FOX, SAUL BELLOW, PAUL AUSTER

In New York novels, the interactions between city on mind, mind on city are necessarily reciprocal. When does author or subject project his own fantasies on the city? When does the city alter one's consciousness? Are Fitzgerald's characters misled by the marvels they see, or do they see only their deepest feelings? Where does one begin, one end, or, as Yeats might have phrased it, how does one tell the dancer from the dance? In the previous chapter we have observed fictional figures imagining a city of their dreams and desires. New York, enormous, diverse and amorphous, would appear to accommodate anyone's vision.

But when dreams truly turn sour, the city may transform itself into variations of Edith Wharton's City of Dis, or convolutions of nightmarish images. We have already alluded to such visions in di Donato's immigrant perceptions of New York skyscrapers, or Don DeLillo's garish painted subway cars and rising garbage landfills, or Ellison's flaring Harlem race uprising, or Paule Marshall's roaring, clattering factory works overwhelming human life while reducing people to machines. Put another way, twentieth-century New York fiction never totally discards ancient perceptions of cities as unalloyed, festering evil — although most mix their antiurbanism with some elements of frontier optimism.

Still other works convey more of a sustained view of New York as a kind of hell, and we now turn our attention to some of these. Suffice to say that although they all portray New York in darker colors, each does so in different

ways. There were foreshadowings. Herman Melville's *Pierre* (1852) describes
the plight of two people who arrive from the west (Albany!) to begin new
lives in New York City. They are overcome by their inner nature as well as
by their urban environment, but implicit at the very least is the city's illusion of false promise. A far gloomier view is the same author's short fiction
"Bartleby the Scrivener." Here the unstated metaphor is (capitalist) New York
as a kind of prison inducing several varieties of mental and spiritual aberra-
tion. In this "Tale of Wall Street" the little scrivener-copyist sits in his
employer's office literally facing a wall where he walls himself off, or is perhaps himself walled off from others. So alienated is he that he assumes a
passive-aggressive stance, refusing to do any work he would ordinarily be
expected to perform. Nor will he voluntarily leave the premises. Bartleby's
behavior, however bizarre, is in its way a response to an atrophied existence.
Even his fellow clerks are rendered as eccentrics. Finally his "reasonable"
decent employer, Bartleby's fictional narrator, moves away from his place of
business rather than forcibly evict Bartleby, which, when one thinks about
it, is also a bit mad. Bartleby ends his last days in the city's walled prison,
aptly called the Tombs, suggesting itself as a starker truth about the larger
New York world beyond.

One of the earliest post-frontier works is Theodore Dreiser's *Sister Carrie* (1900), a good portion of which takes place in Chicago. But when the
middle-aged married George Hurstwood and his young working-class mistress, Carrie Meeber, flee to New York anticipating new identities, their experiences radically diverge. Carrie, who is at first dazzled by the city's glitter
and wealth, will eventually succeed as a celebrated stage actress. Hurstwood,
meanwhile, gradually descends step by step into the city's lower depths, unable
to withstand the city's rigors, and it is Dreiser's fine detailed portrayal of the
despairing Hurstwood's decline into abject poverty that constitutes the novel's
most moving passages. To be sure, Dreiser's twist on the myth of renewal is
that its achievement yields only further desire (Carrie at the pinnacle of her
fame still yearns for the ineffable), and that survival in America depends less
on morality than on blind luck and impersonal social forces.

Hurstwood's defeat gives New York the aura of a Darwinian jungle or
untamed West as he struggles to find a footing. A moderately successful
businessman in Chicago, he is ultimately reduced to begging in New York
for his survival. Although Dreiser believed he was writing a novel of dispas-
sionate objectivity — life as it is rather than as one would wish it to be — it
is clear he extends his compassion to Hurstwood and men like him at

New York's bottom rung. Here they queue up nights on cold city streets for shelter:

> They fell into a sort of broken, ragged line.... There was a wooden leg in the line. Hats were all drooping, a group that would ill become a second-hand Hester Street basement collection. Trousers were all warped and frayed at the bottom and coats worn and faded. In the glare of the store light, some of the faces looked dry and chalky; others were red with blotches and puffed in the cheeks and under the eyes; one or two were rawboned and reminded one of railroad hands.

Ruthless, amoral laws of the universe condemn them all and nowhere are these more apparent than in New York. At the end, while a melancholy Carrie sits isolated in lavish Waldorf quarters, Hurstwood's sadly depleted spirits converge with his dreary surroundings. In a seedy Bowery room he kills himself, uttering heartbreaking words: "What's the use?"

At publication, *Carrie* undoubtedly would have reinforced readers' perceptions of New York as the wicked city. That the great world yawns at Carrie's and Hurstwood's behavior, past or present, outraged the wife of Dreiser's first publisher and she prevailed upon her husband, Frank Doubleday, to vastly curtail the number of books he printed. She denounced the work as blatantly immoral and by the genteel standards of her day she was right. Neither cohabitation nor adultery appeared to hinder Carrie's ascent. (She had even lived with another lover before coming to New York with Hurstwood.) Equally shocking was Carrie's failure to feel any guilt or shame about her former attachments. Even Hurstwood's sorry fate had less to do with bigamy than with his declining energies in a fiercely competitive environment. But if the contemporary reader may no longer feel shock at their behavior, the power of the novel remains in the cruel disparity of their New York destinies.

Dreiser, for his part, never felt he was telling less than the truth. Carrie's story was in part inspired by Dreiser's sister's history; she years before had run away from Chicago to New York with a married man who, like Hurstwood in the novel, had stolen money from his employer. At seventy-five Dreiser died, forty-five years after *Carrie*'s first printing, but very little had changed his mind about the inchoate forces that govern the universe. Nor did he feel less compassion for life's losers, and toward the end of his life he came to believe that Communism might mitigate their suffering. His output was prodigious — novels, short fiction, journalism, magazine features, even travel pieces about New York — but *Carrie* was his one fiction where New York almost becomes a character in his narration. He would not simply tell the fate of his protagonists but how the city affects their souls and how their souls reflect back again on the city.

An equally terrible vision of New York is Nathanael West's *Miss Lonelyhearts* (1933). Written in the depths of the Depression, the novel depicts most characters as mad products of city life whose protagonist, Miss Lonelyhearts, a newspaperman, observes them not in the "detached" manner of a journalist but rather as one who appropriates their passions and terrors. The anguish of West's New Yorkers does not, however, seem so much related to the hard times of the 1930s as to an overall disintegration of shared aspirations. Believers and idealists are mocked, but the mockers, cynics, and "sophisticates" are themselves sufferers. What West discerned perhaps better than any other New York writer was how the city's — and by extension, the country's — popular culture erodes both mind and heart. "People always fight their misery with dreams," Miss Lonelyhearts muses, but dreams "once powerful ... have been made puerile by the movies, radio and newspapers."

The story is deceptively simple, the style stark and terse, and the structure somewhat episodic. Miss Lonelyhearts is the pseudonym of a male "advice" columnist who begins to take seriously the naive, barely literate letters he receives from unhappy readers. The solemn platitudes he ordinarily dispenses now mock him as much as they were once intended to amuse his newsmen colleagues. He assimilates the vast pain of his letter writers and attempts, Christ-like, to assume their suffering. Along the way, he witnesses the emptiness, cruelty, and guilt of his fellow journalists as they try to engage him in their worldliness. Even his well-meaning fiancée appears incapable of penetrating to the despair he feels all about him. In the end he is shot by the jealous husband of a woman he has been trying to help. The message is unmistakable. In an absurd world, even the imitation of Christ is fruitless.

Each of West's New York inhabitants dwells in an urban wasteland — and the city's very physicality is permeated by a kind of latent violence. Skyscrapers are built of "forced rock and tortured steel" and nature displays "no signs of spring":

> The decay that covered the mottled [park] ground was not the kind in which life generates. Last year ... it had taken all the brutality of July to torture a few green spikes through the exhausted dirt.

Citizens, too, mirror the violence of their environment: a kiss seems like the "blade of a hatchet," and Miss Lonelyhearts' editor, Shrike (note the name), constantly taunts him about nostrums of redemption. Beauty, art, science, religion, hedonism, and nature are jokes, he jeers, and indeed, in the novel, they are. In effect, West's city is a graveyard of hopes, the very antithesis of frontier optimism. For all their intensity, his characters might just as well wear death masks. Was it an intended irony that Miss Lonelyhearts' newspaper is called the New York *Post-Dispatch*?

Miss Lonelyhearts' violent early death foreshadowed West's in 1940. He was thirty-seven when he was killed with his wife in an automobile collision on a return vacation trip from Mexico. On the whole his works were not taken very seriously during his lifetime, and like Fitzgerald (they died within a few days of each other) he had been working in Hollywood as a screenwriter. One wonders whether he savored the irony that he had become a producer of the popular culture he had once savaged. Still, unlike Fitzgerald, he skewered Hollywood and its culture in a 1939 novel, *The Day of the Locust*. Other earlier satires, *The Dream Life of Balso Snell* (1931) and *A Cool Million* (1934), do not stand up nearly as well. Yet it is hard to imagine how he could have gone much beyond the black pessimism of *Miss Lonelyhearts*.

Very closely approximating that pessimism are two near apocalyptic novels, *Desperate Characters* (1970) and *The Widow's Children* (1976), by Paula Fox, an author whose prior publishing successes had been chiefly children's books.* Fox's New York novels are as fiercely succinct as West's but contain less violent surface realism. Another major difference is that West in *Lonelyhearts* describes a more disparate array of unhappy New Yorkers. Miss Lonelyhearts' many supplicants are often lumpen proletarian: poor or ignorant, vulgar or cruel, bewildered or stupid. In the end Lonelyhearts' compassion embraces them all, extending well beyond his own suffering or the suffering of his sophisticated professional colleagues. By contrast Fox's despairing characters may have known poverty at one time or other but all are fairly intelligent, articulate, educated, and to one degree or other cultured. More to the point, they tend to view the very kind of characters Lonelyhearts has come to love as portents of a degraded New York.

And yet, despite her subject matter, Fox never reaches for hyperbole or strained metaphor. Indeed, she writes a kind of compressed prose that moves invisibly from one character to the next while almost simultaneously render-

---

*Her first novel, *Poor George*, was published in 1967, *Desperate Characters* was her second, *The Widow's Children* her fourth.

ing their memories, their inner thoughts, and outer voices. Interstices of these passages also introduce enough description and exposition so that readers know as much as they need to know about a character's present or past relationships. The challenges of this kind of writing are especially daunting in *The Widow's Children*, where from time to time Fox shuttles among four or five people at close quarters. I dwell here as much as I do on Fox's interior-exterior prose style because it so successfully conveys structure to her characters' anarchic perceptions of self and City. Whether or not their author shares their views one cannot tell — but in a loose sense all of Fox's books are autobiographical.* She was born in 1923 in New York of a volatile Cuban-American mother and an alcoholic screenwriter father who promptly deposited her in a home for foundlings. For her next fifteen or sixteen years she appears to have been passed along from one guardian to the next. She lived for a while with an upstate New York Congregational minister, with her Spanish-Cuban grandmother in Queens and in Cuba, with her parents for short periods in Florida and California, and with her father's heiress fiancée in New Hampshire. As for her formal education, it was obviously spotty, though she tells of a happy year in a finishing school in Montreal. Many years later she would study French literature at Columbia University. At seventeen she married, but gave up her first child for adoption; there would be two more children by a second husband, and a third marriage which has lasted more than forty years. Before becoming a professional author she held a variety of jobs — among them as a dance studio instructor, as a machinist for Bethlehem Steel during World War II, as a reader of Latin-American books for Warner Brothers' Studio, as a newspaper stringer in Europe, and as a private-school teacher in New York. Not surprisingly the instability of her life translates itself into the instability of her characters. Their uneasiness projects itself outward in images of a troubled city.

New York in the 1960s. A malingering infection serves as the opening metaphor of *Desperate Characters*. Sophie Bentwood, who lives with her "high income" lawyer husband, Otto, in an upwardly struggling Brooklyn neighborhood, is suddenly bitten by a stray cat she had been trying to feed. At first she denies to herself and others any danger, but when the cut begins to ache and fester she fears rabies. Her first attempts to get emergency treatment are temporarily frustrated by unavailable doctors and bureaucratic hospital procedures. But Sophie knows that her anxieties could be considerably allayed if

*See for example her memoir, *Borrowed Finery* (2000), or an interview in the March 4, 2001, *New York Times Magazine*.

the cat were captured and tested for disease. Some time passes before Otto can catch the cat, whereupon Sophie realizes that the cat will be euthanized. Humane intentions lead to death. The cat's terror, fury, and brute volatility are emblematic of a world the Bentwoods cannot escape. Sophie's wound hovers ghostlike over the rest of the novel.

Each of the principal figures in the novel is himself or herself spiritually wounded. Otto finds it difficult to acknowledge disorder and likes to imagine law is a bulwark of reason. He stifles his emotions and suffers accordingly. His marriage is tenuous and all but loveless. At one point he expresses momentary hatred of Sophie by raping her. A long-time friendship with his law partner, Charlie Russel, crumbles as each accuses the other of moral blindness. Charlie is often given to feeling sorry for himself and blames bourgeois values for the collapse of society, not to mention his own deteriorating family life. It is Charlie, however, who underlines a passage from Thoreau (which accounts for the book's title) that the mass of men live lives of quiet desperation. Sophie is the most sensitive and intuitive of the lot. In the past she had immersed herself in the high culture of French and German letters — perhaps as self-protection — but now finds the present barely tolerable. Her lackluster years with Otto had once given way to an adulterous adventure but that has petered out and she is left with sad memories.

One of the pleasures of *Desperate Characters* is that it does not confine itself to the angst of an educated bourgeoisie. Nor does it abase itself to the fashionable left radicalism of the times, or for that matter to simplistic reactions. The wounds of the 1960s suppurate on all levels. Race, tensions, and class hatred lurk everywhere. Professors despise and fear their students; parents cannot connect with their children. At the same time the young self-righteously proclaim anti-intellectualism as a virtue; and a middle-aged serious artist, at the end of his tether, produces nihilistic paintings which the public eagerly seeks out. When Sophie and Otto flee to Long Island for a weekend, they drive across a countryside wasteland denuded of birds and trees only to discover their country home vandalized. They suspect their mendacious caretaker and his semi-impoverished family.

But it is the city finally that assumes the novel's most coruscating imagery. From its very first pages, pictures of city streets, houses, and institutions carry messages of filth, sloth, and decay. The Bentwoods' efforts to improve their community are met by a kind of silent resistance from long-time residents who resent the encroachments of rich newcomers:

> An Italian family that had lived on the block during its worst days, finally moving out the day after all the street lamps had been smashed, was held responsible for this breach of taste.... There was still refuse everywhere, a tide that rose but barely ebbed. Beer bottles and beer cans, liquor bottles, candy wrappers, crushed cigarette packs, caved-in boxes that held detergents, rags, newspapers, curlers, string, plastic bottles, a shoe here and there, dog feces. Otto had once said, staring disgustedly at the curb in front of their house, that no dog had deposited *that*.

Signs and symptoms of the sick, poor, and demoralized are everywhere. A hospital waiting room is "a dead hole smelling of synthetic leather and disinfectant." Municipal buildings look like "large threatening carnivorous animals momentarily asleep." A stone is thrown through the bedroom window of a Brooklyn Heights psychiatrist. A Central Park West apartment feels like a "rain of ashes." A half-naked black man reels along the sidewalk, gripping his "bunched up" trousers, and suddenly collapses in a sea of vomit. Sophie's backyard neighbor urinates out the window. Graffiti on a subway platform reads, "Fuck everybody but Linda." Another message reads, "Kiss me someone." Queens sidewalks are "brutal slabs of cement" behind which "cries of boredom and rage are scrawled on the sides of buildings." Little wonder Sophie and Otto cling to one another. Their world is in shambles.

If *Desperate Characters* tells of a wounded people in a lacerated city, death as an uninvited ghost haunts the consciousness of the major figures in *The Widow's Children*. But here, despite its presence, Fox leaves the reader with faint glimmers of hope for at least two of the characters. Moreover, menacing streets play less of a thematic role since much of its narrative takes place indoors, as for example in a stuffy hotel room and corridor, or in a congested fashionable midtown restaurant, or in small, spare Manhattan apartment dwellings. Of course one need not call this "typical" New York, but they do in Fox's prose convey a New York sense of heightened intimacy where suppressed antagonisms cannot be wholly contained. To add to whatever else these settings may impart, Fox provides her characters with plenty to drink so that underlying emotions expose themselves more easily.

The plot of *The Widow's Children* does not on its face look to be especially dramatic, and yet the psychological relationships that emerge are complicated. Each of the characters has a sense of a semi-lived life, and each from time to time admits to an awareness of his or her own mortality. Laura Clapper, the imperious fifty-five-year-old wife of Desmond, has arrived in New York about to embark with her husband on a trip to Africa. One of the first things they do is arrange for drinks in their hotel room and a bon voyage restaurant dinner afterwards. Invited are Clara, Laura's twenty-nine-year-old daughter by an earlier marriage, Laura's brother Carlos (there is another New York brother, Eugenio, a dysfunctional failed travel agent who has apparently not been invited), and Peter Rice, Laura's long-time friend of twenty or more years. Before her guests arrive, Laura learns that her widowed mother, Alma, had just died alone in a New York nursing home. Laura determines not to tell anyone until after dinner. They all drink copiously before heading for a restaurant, where more drinks make them irritable, hostile, and on occasion oddly introspective. Tensions mount and the dinner ends disastrously as Laura, angry and envious of her daughter's youthful personas, flees before telling anyone about Alma. Later on she will telephone Peter and ask him to call on each of her brothers personally to inform them that their mother has died and that a cemetery burial is being planned for the following day. She expressly forbids Peter to inform Clara, but Peter believes it immoral not to do so and decides he will call on her as well. As a consequence, he manages to persuade a reluctant Clara to attend her grandmother's funeral with him.

Alma's death inevitably affects them all. Within each member of the family there are levels of self-reproach and changing perceptions. Laura and her brothers had communicated rarely with their mother and doubtless feel guilty. Clara, too, had been neglectful. (She was brought up by Alma when Laura abandoned her at birth.) Everyone in the Clappers' gathering in one way or another is in psychological thrall to Laura, and the drama revolves around how each — so different from one another — will respond not only to the news of Alma's death but also to Laura's demands.

Clara lives with her knowledge of Laura's rejection; Laura had probably intended her to be aborted. Desmond, Laura's rich and weary alcoholic husband, has long submitted himself to Laura's erratic impulses, and like Laura's first husband appears to be drinking himself to death. Carlos, Laura's bored and self-loathing homosexual brother, sporadically challenges her will, but in the end he usually submits. Peter, a restrained celibate book editor, remains devoted to Laura, whose allure had long ago enticed him as a young man. He now thinks of himself as having become like his deceased grandmother, "an armful of dry twigs." And Laura, ostensibly free of constraints, ultimately reveals herself to the reader as perhaps as vulnerable as her retinue. Her casual anti–Semitism belies her Sephardic ancestral identity, and she views her daughter's younger years as a diminishment of her own life. Thus Peter and Clara's defiance not only strikes a blow but incidentally liberates them, if only temporarily, from her deathlike grip over their lives.

Fox does not of course rule out New York's sinister night streets, with all sorts of people walking about with murder in their hearts. Even the mild-mannered Peter sometimes harbors fantasies of killing off all the arrogant mediocre authors he must deal with. But Fox also takes us to Eugenio's and Carlos's apartments, whose squalor reflects as much their moral sloth as their circumstances. She takes us also to Clara's apartment, whose décor and Spartan rooms suggest something both generous and bottled up in her nature. All the while, night in the city gives off impressions of an ambivalent threatening morality: "At night in the city, things were never invisible, always somewhat visible as though lurking. There was no utter black night in the city. Day drained away; darkness came diluted by a pale but ruthless artificial light."

But just as night follows day, day follows night, and with daylight there lie hints of redemption. On a rainy day among the headstones of the dead, Peter and Clara glimpse possibilities of new life.

As may be imagined, authors whose characters respond badly to New York do not much like the city. One such author is Saul Bellow, who on more than one occasion stated his aversion. Still, not all Bellow's narrations appear biased at the outset, but as they evolve, Bellovian New Yorkers' pathologies begin to reflect something of their city. In contrast, with only few exceptions, his fictional Chicagoans flourish, from *The Adventures of Augie March* (1953) to the flamboyant sybarite *Ravelstein* (2000). Indeed, the reader is led to believe that their Chicago surroundings endow them with positive vitality. The eighty-nine-year-old Montreal-born Bellow died in Boston in 2005.

Bellow's New York dwellers are not portrayed as monsters, but rather as deeply injured individuals whose spiritual and psychological aberrations are linked or aggravated by their anarchic turbulent New York environment. To be fair, all Bellow's creatures, New Yorkers and non–New Yorkers alike, struggle with their identity (usually Jewish-American), with ideas, with their personal history or History, and what they owe to themselves and the great world beyond. If they are, however, New Yorkers, they are far more likely to disintegrate like the unhappy pseudonymous Humboldt of *Humboldt's Gift* (1975), Bellow's fictional treatment of his erstwhile friend, the poet-critic-writer Delmore Schwartz.

One of Bellow's first published works is *The Victim* (1947), whose protagonist, Asa Leventhal, may have inadvertently caused a gentile, Kirby Allbee, to lose his job. Asa is himself racked with guilt and self doubts about his own responsibility toward family, wife, and friends, and not a little troubled by his own internalized anti–Semitism. The novel's opening sentences announce both the atmosphere and the city's character:

> On some nights, New York is as hot as Bankok. The whole continent seems to have moved from its place and slid nearer the equator, the bitter gray Atlantic to have become green and tropical, and the people, thronging the streets, barbaric fellahin....

The principal action centers around the semi-obsessed (and suicidal) Allbee, who emerges from the past and accuses Asa of destroying his career. Intense and ambiguous relations spring up between the two as Allbee's parasitic presence constantly penetrates Asa's consciousness. What does Asa owe Allbee? Who is the victim and who the victimizer? A park in their city describes a strangling, oppressive New York symbiosis which reminds Asa of a story he once read of "hell cracking open":

> The trees were swathed in stifling dust, and the stars were faint and sparse through the pall. The benches formed a dense, double human wheel; the paths were thronged. There was an overwhelming human closeness and thickness, and Leventhal was penetrated by a sense not merely of the crowd in this park but of innumerable millions, crossing, touching, pressing. What was that story he had once read about Hell cracking open on account of the rage of the god of the sea and all the souls, crammed together, looking out?

Years later Bellow's 1956 novella *Seize the Day* depicts a city given over to the worship of money. And, as we shall see, he equates greed with the anti-life. The plot, such as it is, tells of Tommy Wilhelm, a failed husband, actor, and businessman on the verge of financial ruin, who comes to New York to ask his wealthy father, a retired doctor, for help. The old man rejects Tommy as one of life's losers, and Tommy discovers practically everyone else he comes in contact with too obsessed with money to regard him with any respect. From their point of view, he might as well be dead: "How they love money, thought Wilhelm. They adore money! Holy money! Beautiful money! ... While if you didn't have it, you were a dummy, a dummy! You had to excuse yourself from the face of the earth."

In despair, he allows himself to be swindled of his remaining dollars by a charlatan-comic-sage, Dr. Tamkin, who promises him returns on a surefire investment.

Like so many of Bellow's other works, the novella is really a confrontation between life and death. The relentless pounding pace of the city transforms everyone Tommy meets (mainly old men) into near-death figures — and lust for money becomes a kind of violent death. "*M*oney and *M*urder," says

Dr. Tamkin, "both begin with *M.*... People come to the market to kill. They say 'I'm going to make a killing'.... They make a killing by a fantasy."

Tommy is revived finally by Tamkin's counsel to seize the day, to seize life at its fullest most intense present. Paradoxically Tommy's epiphany comes not in the hurly burly of New York streets but in the quiet hush of a funeral parlor.

Dreams of the West — freedom, individualism, and reinvention — run amok in *Mr. Sammler's Planet* (1970), Bellow's novel of the New York counterculture during the Vietnam War years. What was once deemed the unconscious is now flaunted as the authentic. Reason, discipline, and restraint have given way to license. The libido reigns in its broadest sense. Carried to their extremes, dreams of new frontiers of sexual freedom now threaten civilized behavior. The point of view in *Sammler* is mainly that of a highly cultured Anglophile Polish Jew who has experienced the worst of the Holocaust. But, unlike Bellow's other more or less passive-impulsive protagonists, Mr. Sammler is capable of taking action — as when in his European past he killed a Nazi soldier. Elderly and blinded in one eye (like the seer Tiresias?), he sees better than others the city's entropy. People flounder all about him seeking fulfillment — some aggressively, some desperately, some frantically, some mindlessly, among them his daughter, his niece, grandniece, and grandnephew, a sex-tormented fellow refugee, even loutish university students. Still Bellow's New Yorkers differ considerably from Tom Wolfe's near caricatures or Dos Passos's stick figures.

Oddly, Bellow's sad souls seem closer to the small-town obsessives of Sherwood Anderson's 1919 *Winesburg, Ohio*. Anderson called his characters *grotesques* because some aspect or other of their psychology was out of kilter. Much the same can be said of Bellow's people, but the comparison ends there. Anderson's figures were misfits in an otherwise stifling insular community while Bellow's New Yorkers are representative of a city very near anarchy. Early on Mr. Sammler ruminates:

> You had to be strong enough not to be terrified by local effects of metamorphosis, to live with disintegration, with crazy streets, filthy nightmares, monstrosities come to life, addicts, drunkards, and perverts celebrating their despair openly in midtown. You had to be patient with the stupidities of power, with the fraudulence of business.

At more than one point in the novel, Sammler appears to take seriously, or at least respectfully, an Indian scientist's proposals to depart the earth and permanently establish settlements on the moon. Another of Bellow's kinder portraits is that of Dr. Elya Gruner, Sammler's nephew, who had rescued him from a displaced persons' camp in Europe and brought him to New York. Gruner is warmhearted and generous although perhaps a bit too sentimental for Sammler's taste. But even Gruner has a shady past performing illegal abortions for Mafia bosses. The most fearsome figure Sammler faces is a gigantic, gorgeously clad Negro pickpocket who exposes his genitals as a threat should Sammler attempt to report his activities to the police. For Mr. Sammler, given the "sex ideology" of the times, the black man's organ might just as well have been a "symbol of superlegitimacy or sovereignty."

Bellow's forte was never narrative suspense but rather skeptical observations of character and ideas, and a mix of eloquent literary prose, the demotic, the colloquial and swinging street smarts. The flimsy plot hinges largely on Mr. Sammler's attempts to return a manuscript his daughter has foolishly stolen from the moon scientist, and afterwards reach a hospital in time to comfort the dying Dr. Gruner. As the novel approaches its conclusion Mr. Sammler appears to be adopting a more compassionate outlook. Despite reservations, he will grant the others in his life their humanity, commiserate in their sorrows, and share in their common obligations to serve and to love:

> Remember, God, the soul of Elya Gruner, who, as willingly as possible and as well as he was able ... was eager ... to do what was required of him.... The terms which, in his inmost heart, each man knows. As I know mine. As all know. For that is the truth of it — that we all know, God, that we know....

Even the Negro who menaced him had something "princely" about him, and an oversexed grandniece doubtless dreams in her own way of the ineffable. Nonetheless, Bellow's novel remains a severe indictment although Sammler somewhere concedes that the city's debased culture may be not so unlike that of other large cities on the planet. If so, so much the worse for the planet.

While not always explicitly spelled out, events in Bellow's lifetime hover over the atmosphere of his novels: the Holocaust, student and racial unrest, and the so-called counterculture with its reliance on drugs and sex. Echoes of these times similarly inform Paul Auster's post-modernist novels of the eighties and nineties. The kind of city Auster writes about is a New York where the darkly unpredictable may overtake ordinary events, and human beings move about in a half-light of what only seems true. Along the edges of these stories hangs a sense of the preternatural and characters discover reason and will may count for little.

Auster came to his outlook not entirely in the city. He was born in

Newark in 1947 and in a long autobiographical essay writes of a childhood attempting to get through to Sam, his mysterious uncommunicative father. Much later Auster learned that Sam's mother had killed her husband (Sam's father), which might account at least in part for Sam's stifled emotions. In several of Auster's New York tales the narrative revolves around a character in search or pursuit of another whose secret life remains elusive. Suspense in these stories is often enhanced by ever-changing city surroundings. As a young man, Auster attended Columbia University, whose neighborhood he uses in more than one novel. He never completed his studies and afterwards worked as a seaman on oil tankers. In a later period he spent several years in Paris writing and translating poems and literary essays. Near poverty in Paris and subsequent hand-to-mouth years during the 1970s in Manhattan figure strongly in his works. He was thirty-four when his first fiction was published, but since then novels, essays, radio talks, and screenplays have followed. While at the start Auster did not exactly become a household name, he had enjoyed some critical successes in France and England. Perhaps Auster's characteristic preoccupation with the inexplicable is more attuned to European sensibilities. Since 1980 he has lived in Brooklyn, which also serves as a setting for his works.

The best known of Auster's New York works, *City of Glass,* was published in 1985, succeeded the following year by *Ghosts* and *The Locked Room.* The three were collected in one volume by Penguin Books in 1990 under the title *The New York Trilogy.* To sketch their plots is to render them a disservice. They are "absurdist" without being absurd and Auster may also have been affected, consciously or otherwise, by French deconstructionist theory. But if some of his influences are European, they enhance rather than detract from the New York–Americanness of his themes. To reinforce such impressions, he may allude in his writings to Hawthorne or Melville and, as with these predecessors, the issues he deals with are rebirth or assumption of a new identity. Ordinarily in New York writings, to adopt a new identity is to suggest the positive possibilities of an alternate life. But in Auster, identity is so fragile a concept that any transference of personae may endanger one's very existence. This is especially true of Auster's protagonists, so obsessed with themselves or with an idea that they isolate themselves from the rest of humanity.

Ostensibly, in Auster's New York, gridded numbered streets and avenues appear constructed on rigorous mathematic principles. At first these seem to bear little resemblance to Auster's aimless peripatetic heroes. Yet as the tales unravel, differences turn out to be largely illusory. The city, for all its extended symmetries, is as mysterious and improbable as any western wilderness.

Conversely, Auster's fictional third and first person narrators like those of Poe (another author whom Auster from time to time invokes), tell their mad tales in ordered, rational voices as if in deference to stolid listeners. Indeed, the chief characters of Auster's first two novellas are private detectives who apply inductive and deductive methods to the problems they face, and the title of Auster's third novella, *The Locked Room*, summons associations of countless detective mysteries. Needless to say, none of these writings conforms to expectations.

In an earlier novel, *Moon Palace* (1982), a homeless destitute Columbia University student, Marco Stanley Fogg, reasons that, since he truly has no prospects, he will allow fate to take its course by simply following the city's numbered streets south. He will accept without complaint, he says, whatever happens to him. But after some days, the streets and parks and avenues yield no coherent meaning. Surprises, sheer luck, faint kindnesses, unexplained cruelties, indifference, and near starvation come in nearly equal parts; hence there is nothing to be learned from the great world of New York other than that design only serves to conceal underlying disorder. From time to time his consciousness registers allusions to the moon — the name of a Chinese restaurant (Moon Palace), for example, or astronaut landings — which seem to suggest some mysterious signals, but even these are indecipherable. Later, in a kind of ironic reversal, Fogg abandons his wife and travels West to seek his true self. There are strange coincidences, unlikely connections, peculiar portents, and varieties of adventures not unlike the kind one sees in "western" movies, but in the end what he experiences makes no more sense in the larger America than in New York. If somewhere there exists a note of hope it is that Fogg as a kind of Everyman will stumble along undaunted in a bewildering universe.

Incoherent worlds also underlie Auster's subsequent novellas in *The New York Trilogy*. In *City of Glass*, a private detective named Quinn writes first-person detective novels under the pseudonym William Wilson about a fictional detective named Max Work, who pretends to be a private detective named Paul Auster. His mission is to track down Stillman, a presumed lunatic-scholar who may or may not be bent on murdering his own son. In the course of his investigation Quinn-Auster learns Stillman aspires to invent a new language more in accord with what he believes the real world to be. Meanwhile, Quinn-Auster speculates that Stillman's son Peter and Peter's wife, Virginia, who hired him, may or may not be who they say they are. No identity is certain and Quinn-Auster is not certain that the man he has been trailing along

Manhattan's streets is the Stillman he has been hired to pursue. Quinn-Auster sketches street maps (reproduced in the book) of Stillman's meanderings, but though several intriguing patterns emerge each implies multiple or contradictory interpretations. *City of Glass* is not simply a send-up of traditional "whodunit" fiction, but also calls to mind the mathematician Charles Dodgson–Lewis Carroll's *Alice Through the Looking Glass*, where all logic and reason and language are Humpty Dumptyishly turned upside down.

Ghosts, the second book of the trilogy, is set for the most part in Brooklyn not far from the Brooklyn Bridge where Blue, a private investigator, is hired to spy on the movements and behavior of a stranger. Blue does not know why he has been hired or who his employer is, but so obsessed does he become with his task that gradually he dehumanizes himself, unconsciously severing all links to his friends and lovers, past or present. Eventually he kills the person he has been investigating only to discover his victim has all along been spying on him. At the start each of the characters is named for a color, thereby appearing as something of an abstraction. Thus when Blue kills Black he loses whatever little self he still possesses. Indeed Blue and Black are versions of each other. Nightmarishly, new identities are much like the old — and reality remains elusive. The consequence is death.

The Locked Room, Auster's third work in *The New York Trilogy*, contains much the same message. Some of the action takes place in Paris and some in Boston. The hero assumes the matrimonial and literary roles of a disappeared writer whom everyone assumes is dead. Their symbolic exchange of identities very nearly destroys the protagonist's consciousness, not to mention his marriage. When his predecessor does turn up in Boston in a locked room, he refuses to let anyone enter. His reasons for self-abnegation are unclear. The notes he leaves behind are gibberish.

After *The New York Trilogy* Auster's vision darkens further. *In the Country of Last Things,* published in 1987, describes an unnamed city in shambles where destruction, hunger, betrayals, and suicide are commonplace, and where the saving graces of civilization, rarely remembered, are even more rarely practiced. On this occasion the protagonist is a woman who searches for her lost brother. But in Auster's next novel, he repairs somewhat to the mystery mode. *Leviathan* (1992) extends the New York metaphor to the country at large, and like Melville's enigmatic whale, Moby Dick, Auster's leviathan is an America whose "meanings" appear unfathomable. In this work, the FBI and the narrator seek out Benjamin Sachs, a onetime brilliant New York writer who now travels about the country blowing up small-scale models of the Statue of Liberty. In addition to Melville, the allusion to Thomas Hobbes' seventeenth-century *Leviathan* is unmistakable. Hobbes, who opposed republican liberties, argued that the common good demands absolute submission to the power of the state to curb the selfish and antisocial tendencies inherent in human nature. But Auster's epigraph at the start of the novel quotes Emerson: "Every actual state is corrupt." Could both authors be right? Auster's "benign" reborn terrorist doubtless believes he protests not only the state's impingement on individual liberties but also its authority to make war and take human lives.* (Though not made explicit, the aura of anti–Vietnam War activism hangs over the novel.) Yet Sachs' activism also causes at least one inadvertent death — not to mention his own. In Auster's works, imperfect individuals like Sachs cannot help but mirror their tainted worlds. City and State are after all human constructs. Whoever one is, wherever one is, his "New York" sits on the edge of his consciousness.

Thus, in their fashion, Auster and postmodernist writers like him embrace and elaborate myths of New York, albeit unconsciously, as a kind of new West where, for better or worse, identities are born and shed and reborn. Death and defeat are never finalities. The restiveness of the city reaches out beyond the covers of these books — and New York plays itself out as a kind of concentrated metaphor of the swirling undercurrents of American life. When we fail to recognize the signs, it may be that they are so New Yorkishly outsized that we dismiss them out of hand. As for what lies ahead, we may be certain that despite, or perhaps because of, her ever-changing ethnic populations, great fortunes and terrible misfortunes, the city will continue to furnish American letters with its astonishments.

---

*Needless to say, the term "terrorist" did not contain the associations it does today after the September 11, 2001, attacks on New York and Washington.

PART THREE:
A CENTURY OF THEATER

9

Mirrors of the City

Eugene O'Neill, Arthur Miller, Edward Albee, Herb Gardner, and Others

By 1890 the twenty-six theaters on New York's Broadway far exceeded those of any other city — even Boston, which still liked to think of itself as America's cultural capital. To be sure, New York's most popular entertainment was vaudeville, which was being performed not only on Broadway but also in other parts of the city. Boisterous and rowdy, vaudeville's appeal lay largely with New York's toiling classes, especially immigrants and first-generation Americans despite and probably because of its wide-ranging caricatures of ethnic street types. But vaudeville now also attracted large segments of respectable bourgeois audiences, women as well as men, since performances containing especially rude sexual content were now being diverted to what became known as burlesque houses. Of course other major cities drew large vaudeville audiences as well, but vaudeville performers viewed "playing" New York — especially its Palace Theater — as the epitome of success. Everywhere else was simply "camping out."

Now, even African-American variety shows saw their New York beginnings. In his autobiography, *Along This Way* (1933), James Weldon Johnson, one of several pioneer writers and composers, relates their birth throes. White audiences as well as black might attend their performances, he writes, despite the city's sporadic race violence. (When Johnson came for a summer visit in 1900, he witnessed one of New York's worst race riots.) From time to time black musical theater was banned on Broadway, though by the 1920s several Negro shows had begun returning. Meanwhile, black performers, singers, and comedians might occasionally appear as specialty acts in white vaudeville.

165

Too often, they were required to further blacken their faces and undergo hosts of other indignities. Still, granting as much, it may not be too far-fetched to say that America's first faint pusillanimous forays at integration took place in New York's popular theater.

More than a decade earlier, in 1887, the southern portions of Manhattan saw the emergence of what would become a flourishing non–English-speaking Yiddish theater. In the main, Yiddish plays dealt with matters of assimilation, intermarriage, and generational differences. But they did so in such a sentimentalized and bombastic manner that one can only conclude they aimed to exploit anxieties rather than enlighten their audiences. Yet, despite their stylized shortcomings, Yiddish plays, like African-American theater, could not help but contribute bits and pieces of realism, colloquial diction, and perhaps even a wry sense of New York humor to mainstream American drama.

Notwithstanding, first-rate American theater was slow in coming. When one considers that at the start of the century Ibsen, Shaw, Strindberg, Molnar, and Schnitzler were making giant strides in Europe, the New York stage for the most part was still mired in melodrama and contrived sentimentalities. What one does discover, however, is that in the first decades the portrayals of New York as the wicked city were becoming more nuanced. The great shifts of American population from rural areas to cities were beginning to reflect themselves in drama. That is to say, the countryside and the West do not always necessarily represent unalloyed virtue, nor were cities, with emphasis on New York City, always utterly immoral. In several works the West is often pitted against New York, with each now claiming the positive values of the other. For instance, in Clyde Fitch's *The City* (1909) an idealistic young man comes to New York and in the course of time becomes a corrupt politician. At one point he will say that the only thing one needs to know about New York is "where your interest lies." The city is nothing more than a "rush for success," and success, like the horizon, seems forever beyond one's reach. Yet, later on in the play the contrite protagonist cries out: "Don't blame the City. It's not her fault! It's our own. What the City does is bring out the strongest in us.... If the bad is strongest, God help us! Don't blame the City! She gives the man the opportunity; it is up to him what he makes of it!"

A more conventional view of wicked New York is conveyed in Eugene Walters' *The Easiest Way* (1909). A difference now is that the West is also portrayed as no less sinful. In the play, the former mistress of a rich man makes her way East from the Rockies to attempt a new life as an actress in New York. She has left behind a suitor who has forgiven her past, and promises to marry her as soon as he makes his fortune. But after refusing to compromise herself with New York predatory theatrical types, the heroine finds herself impoverished and succumbs once again to the blandishments of her wealthy former lover. When her western hero at last comes to New York and discovers her shocking lapses, he abandons all plans to marry her. Although New York here is clearly fraught with sad disappointments and perils, the western milieu is also depicted as morally questionable, and western men emerge as sanctimonious, condescending, and priggish. Doubtless, audiences in 1909 held women to higher sexual standards than they would expect of men (at least on Broadway), but the heroine's journey East also suggests New York has nonetheless become for her a symbolic land of new hopes.

One characteristic about New York plays is that they announce social cultural themes that transcend strictly local concerns. This is not to say that non–New York plays do not search for deeper meanings, but for better or worse New York's special place in the American imagination draws more attention. Saul Bellow once wrote that what is "barely hinted at in American cities is condensed and enlarged in New York." The observation could well be extended to the whole country's gradual shifting of cultural attitudes. But needless to say, these especially manifest themselves in plays set in New York where social changes are so conspicuously exposed. In general, American discomfort revolved around three themes: the rising independence of women, a growing race consciousness in both whites and blacks, and the dilemmas of individual choice in a changing urbanized and industrial world. The last of these has spawned a variety of dramatic personae, some lost and bewildered, others alienated or defiant. If the plays to be discussed appear to be arbitrarily chosen, I can only plead they are not necessarily intended as "major" or "best," but as works typically illustrative of twentieth-century America's restless consciousness.

One source of dismay was a new ambivalence about the status of women, which at the start of the century coincided with growing migration from rural to urban areas. Now fewer women had to depend for their survival on patriarchal largesse, since cities offered jobs as well as a limited degree of privacy. At the same time, countless church sermons, newspaper editorials, and popular novels reacted to women's changed status as threatening the bedrocks of American society: family stability and sexual morality. Sociological writings also took up as a constant theme "the home in peril."* Nor was the popular theater far behind with melodramas galore exploiting those fears with shifty-eyed, mustachio-twirling city villains endeavoring to lure innocent country maidens into lives of endless shame. On a more artistic level, there stood the sexually amoral heroine of Dreiser's *Sister Carrie* (1900), but as we have seen, that book's circulation was severely limited for the first ten years of its life. Finally, as proof positive of crisis, divorce rates rose rapidly, especially in western cities among persons whom the British social historian James Bryce called "the humbler classes."†

Thus on the face of things the sophisticated, literate, upper-strata characters of Langdon Mitchell's comedy *The New York Idea* (1906) are a far cry from simple country girls and big city villains. And yet the real villain (tongue somewhat in cheek) is the city — New York City. The New York "idea" is divorce and what Mitchell has done here is transfer what was widely perceived as a nationwide dilemma to New York's upper classes. Of course, by today's standards divorce is not regarded as much of a scandal, but the play does reveal in its way how in 1906 much of the country looked at New York, as sophisticated but destructive, frivolous but serious, behind and ahead in its views about the sanctity of marriage.

The play tells chiefly about two divorced couples. In both instances the women initiated their divorces for apparently "whimsical" reasons. Cynthia Karslake comes to realize that she is really in love with her former husband and she will presumably remarry him. The ex-wife of the man Cynthia had planned to marry will next marry an English aristocrat and live in England, where marriage and family are taken far more seriously than in the city. The Englishman remarks that "New York is bounded on the North, South, East, and West by the state of divorce," but then later opines that the New York phenomenon is really representative of "American marriage." The play is intended to amuse, which it does; indeed, theater historian Alan S. Downer regarded it as superior to any other American play of the twentieth century's beginning decades. But its underlying warnings about the precarious relationship of the sexes are also present. The women in the play divorced their husbands as adventures, because it would give them opportunities to select new mates or do really whatever they wanted to do. So much New York free-

*See James R. McGivern, "The American Woman's Pre–World War I Freedom in Morals and Manners," *Journal of American History* (September 1968), pp. 315-33.

†See James Bryce, *The American Commonweal*, 1891 ii, p. 724. Also Harvey Wish, *Society and Thought in Modern America*, 1952, pp. 132-33, p. 446.

dom, so much American freedom, indeed so much freedom for women can be unsettling.

Theatrical treatment of race as a cultural or social issue was scarcely touched upon during the first twenty years of the century. Despite rising racial tensions, the consequence, in part, of confrontations between Negro migrants fleeing Southern racism (as well as economic deprivation) and Northern urban whites seeking work, was that neither black nor white playwrights saw these events as conversionable material. Nor did they endeavor to portray the ordeals of Southern blacks seeking to adjust to city life. In the main, these and related themes would have to wait until the start of the Federal Theater projects in the 1930s. Indeed, Broadway's only approach to race during its early years was Edward Sheldon's *The Nigger* (1903), which tells of a Southern gubernatorial candidate who, at the last moment, learns of remote strains of Negro blood coursing through his veins. He, of course, "honorably" steps down. The play, however, stresses the nobility of his sacrifice (he also surrenders his plan to marry a white woman) rather than the absurdities of racism. If Negroes were to be depicted at all sympathetically it would be only as poor, humble, and loyal figures, like Uncle Tom in the numerous ever-popular Uncle Tom melodramas dating as far back as the 1860s, or as good-natured simpleton buffoons in vaudeville specialty acts.

It would not be until 1923 that the thirty-five-year-old playwright Eugene O'Neill undertook serious portrayals of relationships of blacks to whites. He set his play in "lower New York," where black and white lives both intersect and divide and where deeply ingrained racial perceptions penetrate layers of consciousness. As a premise, he would marry a black man to a white woman and observe the deterioration of their lives over the course of years. *All God's Chillun Got Wings* may not be O'Neill's best play, but given the temper of the times, it is surely his boldest. Most of the action in the first act takes place on a geometric convergence of three narrow streets — one of the streets being wholly inhabited by blacks, another by whites, while on the third, white and black interact. As the curtain rises, melancholy songs, Negro and white, are heard from afar, subsequently superseded by sounds of the city: "a clatter of the Elevated ... the ruminative lazy sound of a horse car." But if the setting appears to be symbolic, we shall see O'Neill also reaching back for a hard realism, with characters literally parroting street talk, black and white (not, however, always convincingly). For example, white: "It won't be de odder guy. It'll be youse dames he kidded — and de ones what's kidded him." Or black: "Listen to me nigger: I got a heap to whisper in yo'ear! Who is you, anyhow?" The jarring juxtaposition of realism and symbolism suggests O'Neill had not quite worked out his style, reflecting perhaps unconsciously the author's own unresolved racial feelings. What he does communicate is the essential incommunicability of both blacks and whites, especially the incapacity of the lovers to get beyond their culturally induced racial images.

At its start the audience sees white and black children playing together apparently unconscious of race. As evening approaches most of the children scatter and Ella Downey (white) and Jim Harris (a Negro) are seen alone expressing fondness for one another. Jim tells Ella he has been drinking "lots of chalk and water" in a wish to become white. In scene two nine years have passed. They are now adolescents and it is clear that although Jim has remained devoted, Ella dismisses him contemptuously, preferring Mickey, a white street tough who is about to become a prize fighter. The following scene takes place five years later. Ella has been abandoned by the womanizing Mickey, who had impregnated her (the baby had died), whereupon she turns to Jim, who still loves her. In the interim, neighborhood blacks and whites have berated them both for race disloyalty. But Ella tells Jim, "You've always been white to me" and Jim responds that all love is white. Act one ends as Jim and Ella, who have just married in a Negro church, are seen rushing off to Europe for their honeymoon.

Whereas the first act spans fourteen years, act two concentrates twelve months in three scenes, chronicling the doomed couple's descent. They have returned to New York to live in the house Jim's mother and sister have bequeathed them. Their two-year sojourn in "race-free" France has left each uneasy. Underneath, one feels they need the oppression of race to come to terms with their own inner nature. Put another way, each has been so conditioned by color prejudice that racism of one sort or another is integral to the ways they can deal with reality. Here O'Neill is quite perceptive in depicting levels of African-American reaction to a dominant white culture. Jim's mother believes blacks and whites should live apart and have as little to do with each other as they can. Jim's sister is defiantly proud of her blackness and her African heritage, while Jim, as we shall see, has so ingested a sense of defeatism that he is unable to cope with a self-destructive wife.

For her part, Ella descends into madness, a bundle of contradictory visions. She loves Jim, she hates him, she hates and fears Negroes but she depends childlike on Jim and calls him Uncle Joe, she pretends to herself she is a little black girl, she needs Jim's love but then again she wants him to fail his exams as evidence of the superiority of whiteness. At one point she stabs a decorative Congo mask. O'Neill directs that, in the last scenes, the walls of the house appear to be shrinking, signaling presumably the obsessed couple's self-suffocation.

O'Neill's New York house is thus a cauldron of the entire nation's racial confusions. Ella's anguish has so consumed her it becomes obvious she will soon die, but a broken Jim believes his suffering is ordained by God. Weeping at the end of the play, he cries out: "Forgive me God, for blaspheming You! Let this fire of burning suffering purify me of selfishness and make me worthy of the child You send me for the woman You take away!"

Whether or not Jim's suffering is God-ordained or socially enforced, it is clear that like so many other O'Neill protagonists he is also driven by inner psychic demons. A seemingly inexplicable self-destructiveness dooms him to put up with a woman who will torment him his entire life. In an earlier work, *The Emperor Jones* (1920), O'Neill's Brutus Jones, another American Negro, succumbs to atavistic terrors on the jungle floor of a Caribbean island. White protagonists in O'Neill's New York settings are not much better off. There is some faint hope of a new life for the waterfront former prostitute heroine in *Anna Christie* (1921), but none at all for Yank (the name is perhaps significant), the central figure of *The Hairy Ape* (1922). Yank is so locked in to his tooth-and-claw physical nature that he cannot cope above the bowels of a ship where he had worked happily as a stoker. Rejected both by Fifth Avenue bloodless society types and IWW union chiefs, he chooses in despair to identify himself with beasts in the zoo. For Yank, the city — and by extension the country — is jungle. On opening a cage to join other animals, he is crushed to death by a hairy ape. To a degree the theatricalism is effective, but the play leans so heavily and deliberately on symbolism that it threatens to become what it deplores — an abstraction too far removed from ordinary flesh-and-blood lives.

Few theater historians would, however, dispute that O'Neill is America's first major playwright, who, after the country's initial twenty years of largely theatrical pablum, established high standards for contemporaries and successors alike. While nearly all O'Neill's works still deserve serious attention, his masterpiece remains arguably *The Iceman Cometh* (1940). Here the setting is Harry Hope's downtown "last resort" tavern-rooming house, and Harry's customers are not so much a crossroads of the world as they are a crossroads of New York's shattered humanity. Among their number are former newspapermen, professors, lawyers, anarchists, a Negro gambling house proprietor, bartenders, and streetwalkers. All drink endlessly to delude themselves that their tomorrows will be better, that they will reach out into the world someday and realize their ambitions. In due course their old companion, the seemingly successful salesman Hickey, arrives and eloquently exhorts them all to face up to the dismal realities of their lives and truly begin to renew and reassert themselves. He very nearly succeeds in shaking them free of their delusions, but when it is discovered that Hickey is in his way as deranged as they are themselves, they revert once more to the stupor of their dreams. The play is pessimistic, perhaps partially as a reflection of the 1930s mood of the Depression years. As one character sadly puts it, "The lie of the pipe dream is what gives us life." O'Neill's New York (America?), once a refuge of hope for so many, is instead a graveyard of unrealized dreams.

Long before O'Neill's *Iceman*, Elmer Rice employed a large cast of characters whose main business was to portray the day-to-day lives of ordinary New Yorkers. Much of *Street Scene* (1929) takes place on the front steps of an apartment building whose lower-middle-class occupants include Jews, Irish, Italians, and Swedes, among others — a microcosm of ethnicities, but not quite yet a melting pot. That they are so diverse may also hint to audiences that they constitute cross sections of the American nation. Be that as it may, the emphasis lies in their individuality, their humanity, their tensions and conflicts, and the variety of views they exchange with one another on matters as far-ranging as marital fidelity and politics. Implied as well, not very subtly, is a vision of an unjust American dog-eat-dog world that would deny them the possibilities of fulfillment.

Although the play is intended as a large slice of life, much of the drama centers on the unconsummated love affair between a sensitive Jewish youth (Sam) and a courageous pragmatic Irish girl (Rose), and culminates in the murder of Rose's mother by her raging father, who suspects his wife of adultery. Rose then determines to leave New York for a more benign environment. Sam wants to join her but Rose demurs. On a microscopic scale, the differences between them unwittingly reveal the competing and self-contradictory strains in American culture. Ironically, almost paradoxically, Sam, the son of a radical Communist father, takes a traditional "possessive" view of love and family. Rose, the daughter of a patriarchal father, assumes a more "modern" independent stance. A New York–like Emersonian self-reliance now extends to women. Earlier in the play she tells her father, "Things are different nowadays, Pop.... Girls ain't the way they used to be — sort of soft and helpless. A girl nowadays knows how to look out for herself." When Sam later proposes he and Rose run away together "because we love and belong to each other," she answers, "I don't think people ought to belong to anybody but themselves. That's why I don't want to belong to anybody and why I don't want anybody to belong to me." Below the surface of their lovers' quarrel the ideological message is mixed. Does the skewed society that has nurtured them require more interdependence as Sam believes or more independence as Rose avers? Who is the traditionalist and who the modernist — and why?

Whatever the answers, it is clear that most playwrights of the twenties and thirties regarded the business society as a scourge of happiness. And where were its ravages more manifest than in the city? It's a far cry from O'Neill's lumpen proletarian *Hairy Ape* to the figures in the high society comedies of Philip Barry, but both authors do apparently share a hostile view of an American autocracy. On the eve of the Depression, Barry's *Holiday* (1929) tells of an exceedingly promising young broker who decides to get away from it all, to break his engagement to be married to a tycoon's daughter, and flee to Europe where he will be free of all the deadly onerous responsibilities of money — and be free as well "to find out who I am and what I am and what goes on." As things turn out, his fiancée's rebellious sister secretly sympathizes with him and rushes off to join him. Yet, as the Depression deepened, the plays of the 1930s did not much reconcile corporate capitalism and self-reliance. In general, artists and intellectuals divided pretty much along left-right lines, but even those on the right tended to equate capitalism with materialist greed and mass mediocrity. The latter, however, constituted a distinct minority, and alternatives they proposed — ranging from libertarianism, to something resembling elitist rule, to racial and ethnic purity, to homegrown fascism — did not carry much weight with the majority of New Yorkers, who, as we know, had always been a rather mixed lot to begin with. On the whole, the arts in New York, and especially theater, leaned steadily to the left, reflecting some of the more class-conscious and liberal sentiments of much of the rest of America. Indeed, most Americans could now enjoy serious theatrical works beyond New York, many subsidized by New Deal federal arts programs. Still, as in early vaudeville days at the start of the century, to produce or create a show *in* New York drew far more prestige and attention than anywhere else.

Two New York plays that reflected some of the cultural-political ferment of the times are Clifford Odets' *Waiting for Lefty* and *Awake and Sing*, both produced within a few weeks of each other in 1935. In *Lefty* there is not much doubt who the bad guys are. The curtain rises as Mr. Fatt, a labor boss, or more likely an agent for the owners of a fleet of taxis, tries to dissuade a gathering of drivers from calling a strike. He is not to be trusted. There follow scenes depicting the sufferings of various cabbies exploited more and more by the "system." A strike is finally called when the cabbies learn that their leader, Lefty, has been murdered. We can pretty much guess who ordered him killed. The play is closer perhaps to agitprop than naturalism, although from the start Odets places actors in the audience in order that spectators and players alike feel they are part of the community. Beyond its anticapitalist message, the play appears to be saying that upward mobility must now depend on group or class effort rather than on individuals. But Americans could never altogether abandon the individualism inherent in their culture — nor could Odets, whose *Awake and Sing* provided unlikely heroes.

Awake and Sing, a family drama set in the Bronx, may be truer to the country's Depression moods than the superheated *Lefty*. Several unhappy members of the family include a father who appears baffled and defeated by the times, an elderly grandfather who "understands" the times, reads Marx and Engels (and later kills himself), and an unmarried pregnant daughter who will marry a sad and lost German Jewish refugee. Constant visitors are an embittered World War I veteran and a rather oily businessman uncle — self-congratulatory and successful — who believes that everyone is responsible for his own economic well-being.

But there are heroic figures who rise above the general gloom, among them a twenty-two-year-old son who refuses to surrender to the torpor of lower-middle-class life. He will fight "Till we don't look out on an airshaft. Till we can take the world in two hands and polish off the dirt." The most striking member of the family, however, is Bessie, the mother, not just a survivor but an individualist, strong and capable, who manages to keep her disparate family together. It would be a mistake to say that each of the characters represents a specific type of American, but it might be fair to say that their range of attitudes during America's Depression years was not untypical.

After World War II, New York's role as a symbol of America's unresolved cultural conflicts diminished somewhat — while several new, nationally recognized playwrights (Tennessee Williams, William Inge, Lorraine Hansberry, David Mamet, for example) probed for America's soul in other parts of the country. Perhaps one reason lies in the great popularity of radio and movies, which as early as the twenties and thirties began focusing American attention on regions hitherto neglected. Surely the advent of postwar television furthered even more diverse images. Then, too, the war itself changed perceptions. New

York was no longer viewed simply as a central city but as an international one — indeed the world headquarters of the United Nations would be located in the city. Finally, enhanced technologies so extended communications that whatever happened anywhere in the world would now be instantly known — which meant, among other things, that the city need no longer be the principal harbinger or predictor of changing cultural attitudes.

Still, granting all the foregoing, playwrights using New York settings produced provocative and often disturbing works detailing the crises and dilemmas of American individualism. That is to say, an individualism nurtured by Puritan introspection and pioneer ingenuity seemed to transmogrify into a sour subjectivity as the new century unfolded. A preponderance of dramatic works tells us that nineteenth-century dreams of self-fulfillment and self-reliance were no longer realizable in a new era of impersonal cities where wealth and power seemed to be concentrating in fewer and fewer hands. Doubtless, too, dramatists were also influenced by intellectual fashions — the determinism of social Darwinists or Marxists or Freudians. New York City, which, as we have observed, represented in the minds of many an abundance of choices once associated with the West, could itself disappoint. The consequences were an individualism turned inward — morbid, asocial, or antisocial — which neither organized religion, nor national pride, nor ideologies seemed able to arrest.

In nearly all his works, Eugene O'Neill may have been the first major playwright to portray the self-obsessed on-stage. Among the pieces discussed, we have noted that the principals of *All God's Chillun* talk past each other and seldom to each other, so locked are they in their private thoughts. Worse off is O'Neill's Hairy Ape, who is unable to communicate with anyone, not even beasts in their cages. As for the lost souls of *Iceman*, each is so immersed in his own dreams that only the Iceman can momentarily arouse them. (Paradoxically, mainly left wing Depression writers like Odets revert to nineteenth-century models of romantic heroes, who would rise above the masses to liberate them.) Still, on the whole, O'Neill's unhappy neurotics are more characteristic of twentieth-century portrayals.

Transitions between the fiercely individualistic vision of the frontier and the stark realities of the present have rarely been better illustrated than in Arthur Miller's *Death of a Salesman* (1949). As anyone familiar with the play knows, the tensions revolve around Willy Loman, a luckless traveling salesman who can no longer connect effectively with his own sons, let alone the business world or his own boss. From time to time, Willy invokes images and memories of his older brother, Ben, who years before ruthlessly exploited natural resources in the wilds of Africa and Alaska. Willy never had the courage or the will to follow in Ben's footsteps. Still, he admires the single-minded frontiersman-like passion of his brother and attempts to imbue in his own sons something of Ben's ardor. He fails, and fails as well to endow them with his notions of success: that is, to be well liked and envied. Indeed, one son, Biff, has occasionally escaped his father to work on "real" land, western ranches and farms about which he speaks glowingly.

Here, Miller conveys a dual picture of nature: first in the person of Ben, who views nature as a means to personal wealth, and second in the person of Biff, who sees nature as a conductor of transcending authenticity. In the main, however, the play focuses on Willy's growing hopelessness — ostensibly because he can no longer sell successfully (it is never made clear what it is Willy sells). But Miller's audience gleans that the real reasons lie in Willy's values, which not only separate him from others but also obviate self-understanding. Ironically, Willy is unable to see that the dog-eat-dog zeal he so reveres in his brother is not unlike the relentless capitalist competitiveness that will lose him his self-respect. The feral business world is as raw as that of any frontier jungle. In his own way Willy despises himself as less than a man, and like O'Neill's Hairy Ape he eventually invites his own death.

The despair that drives Willy to suicide suggests an inner violence capable of turning outwards. In Edward Albee's *The Zoo Story* (1959), two men confront one another on neighboring park benches. Peter, in his forties, is revealed as a solid member of the bourgeoisie. A family man, he lives in a fashionable East Side neighborhood and doubtless regards himself as decent and responsible. Jerry, about the same age, is restless and edgy. He lives in a West Side rooming house whose sad, lonely, and obsessed inhabitants are obviously worlds apart from the sort of people Peter knows. The vaguely uneasy tone below their beginning cordial exchange portends a kind of menace. Jerry resents "orderly" people like Peter who try to "make sense of things." Jerry tells Peter he'd been to the zoo "to find out about the way people exist with animals and the way animals exist with each other and with people too." But it probably wasn't a fair test "what with everyone separated by bars from everyone else...." The analogy is clear. Life is itself a zoo where everyone is isolated in his own frantic cage. In the end Jerry goads Peter into killing him — a kind of suicide — and the smug Peter will now presumably acknowledge the chaos of his own animal nature and the darkness that lies beyond.

The violence of self-loathing takes a nuanced twist in LeRoi Jones' 1964 one-act play, *Dutchman*. (Jones would afterwards rename himself Amiri Baraka.) The play's title alludes to the legendary ancient spectral ship doomed never to come to port, thematically linked here to the African American's seemingly endless quest for haven. *Dutchman* was once intended to be included in the same bill as Albee's *Zoo Story* and there is, as we shall see, a subtext of self-destruction as in Albee's work. Prior to its production, Jones' writing — poems, speeches, and essays — inveighed against the black bourgeoisie who accommodate themselves to the humiliations of the white world. *Dutchman* would prove Jones' most powerful vehicle. The near surreal allegory depicts a white woman, Lula, who approaches a conservatively dressed young black man, Clay, in a speeding subway car. She is at first flattering and seductive but then suddenly taunts him as vile and revolting, a creature whose attempts to approximate white respectability are ludicrous. Lula has undoubtedly struck a chord; Clay secretly hates himself for submitting to white condescension. After something of a delayed response, he spews out his hatred of whites which in his heart he must know will destroy him. Lula stabs him, and white passengers throw him off the train. Jones' underground passage serves as his metaphor for America's racial truths. At the play's end, Lula approaches another black man.

Israel Horovitz in *The Indian Wants the Bronx* (1968) uses race in yet another way. Implied in this play is that rootlessness, an absence of the links to family, church, or community, produces unacknowledged shame and self-hatred. These in turn convert to hostility directed at others who are seen as even more vulnerable. At the start, the curtain rises on a darkened stage where a middle-aged East Indian man is seen standing alone between a bus stop and a telephone booth. To his right are several city-owned litter baskets, "the latter signaling an atmosphere of the City's abandoned refuse, extending to anyone who will occupy this space." In the distance two adolescent voices are heard trying to harmonize, their song beginning with the words, "I walk the lonely streets at night / a looking for you," and ending, "But baby no one cares." The song announces one of the themes of the play. When no one cares, life is dross.

At length two boys appear "playfully" punching and insulting one another while their conversation exposes them as all but homeless and seemingly forgotten by their social worker. When the Indian tries to tell them in his own tongue that he is trying to reach his son in the Bronx, they mock him, slash him, and afterwards cut the telephone wire to make it impossible for him to call for help. Before departing, they remark on the inferiority and the hopelessness of foreigners like the Indian. But the audience gathers that, on deeper levels, the boys identify themselves with the gasping lonely prey they have left behind. The violence visited on the Indian is self-violence deflected. As they abandon the Indian, so they have been abandoned. As the song goes, "no one cares."

The main characters in Mart Crowley's *The Boys in the Band* (1968) talk about their plight as homosexuals in a homophobic world. The play may well be the first of its kind to portray homosexuals with some compassion. Subsequent plays by other authors dealing with similar subject matter would be more defiant, militant, even celebratory, but *Boys* is important because it signals a beginning willingness to confront uncomfortable questions of sexuality. Beyond that, however, the play suggests another train of thought; the figures Crowley depicts are persons whom the sociologist David Riesman could have called "the lonely crowd," although surely he wasn't thinking of a homosexual subculture. According to Riesman, much of the American character is no longer driven by deeply ingrained moral and social values embedded in one's private conscience, but rather by externals — notions of prestige promulgated by the mass media, for example, and the need or desire to be liked and admired, especially by others. (Think of Willy Loman.) The term "conformist" as a pejorative became fashionably employed at this time. In Riesman's words such people are "other directed." In Crowley's play his homosexuals are a thrice-cursed lonely crowd: first because as a group they are generally regarded as undesirable; second because they have internalized this view of themselves; and finally because they practice among themselves a kind of tyranny of conformity which leaves each feeling as lonely as before.

The action takes place in a fashionable East Side apartment. Michael, aged thirty, is making preparations for a surprise party for one of his friends. The guests — all "screaming fairies," among whom he numbers himself— arrive one by one, and the audience immediately gleans the uneasy relationship each has to the others. In vino veritas. They drink, expressing anxieties and self-derision in acid exchanges. One of the guests, Cowboy (an ironic allusion to the iconic western hero), is a not very bright male prostitute intended as a gift to the birthday celebrant. An uninvited caller is Michael's former "straight" college roommate, who may or may not be what he seems to be. But the turning point of the play comes when each is expected to reveal a long-held hidden love — a love which might well be ridiculed were it known. Solitude, alienation, and shame now come to a head. The party ends on a melancholy note.

Quite the opposite sense of New York may be found in William Alfred's verse play *Hogan's Goat* (1965). But now the setting is the city of Brooklyn in 1890 before that community integrated itself as a borough of the larger city across the East River. The drama revolves around a fierce political struggle among Irish immigrant factions for mayoral control. The Elizabethan-like plot links impassioned lovers, secret marriages, and the hubris of overweening politicians to the health and governance of the larger community. The players are diverse in the powers they possess. Besides politicos of all sorts, their henchmen and hangers-on, there are their constituents, police, priests, prostitutes, mistresses, and guilt-ridden wives. Indeed this is a Brooklyn more akin to a Wild West frontier town than a City of the Lonely. Still, for all its unsavory goings-on, late nineteenth-century Brooklyn remains singularly cohesive, bound together by the authority of the church and a sense of its own Irishness, which is perhaps the play's unspoken message. Here, as opposed to the city it would soon become part of, an individual's actions have community-wide reverberations.

Among John Guare's works, two of his New York plays stand out. The first, *The House of Blue Leaves* (1971), is a dark farce with something of the frenetic energy of a Marx Brothers comedy. But then again it may be indirectly suggesting something about a country at odds with itself about the Vietnam War while its citizens spin out for themselves narcissistic fantasies. All the action takes place in a Queens apartment at the time of the Pope's first visit to New York. To relate the plot would be to give structure to what is intended to be a portrayal of anarchy. Very nearly all of the characters are to one degree or another so focused on their own inner imaginings that they commonly talk past each other. Indeed, some speaking parts are addressed to the audience. The main members of the cast include Artie, a song-writing zoo keeper; his certifiably nutty wife, aptly named Bananas (at times she believes she is Artie's pet dog); Artie's mistress, Bunny, self-admittedly rotten in bed but good in the kitchen; and Ronnie, Artie's AWOL son, who plans to assassinate the Pope to compensate for his failure to get a movie role as Huckleberry Finn. There are also lesser parts for a deaf film actress, three zany nuns, and a Hollywood producer.

In the play, the House of Blue Leaves is a lunatic asylum, but Artie's apartment could serve just as well. At one point Bunny says, "Sometimes I think the whole world has gone cuckoo, don't you?" The answer is *yes*— not only cuckoo but cuckoo-violent. A climactic moment arrives when a bomb explodes, killing off several of the characters, not long after which Artie prepares to throttle his wife. Implicit here, too, is that their deaths mean very little in an American culture so besotted that it gives as much weight to Hollywood celebrity worship as it does to the Pope, viewing him as a kind of pop star. In Artie's entourage, religion itself is cheapened, reduced to magic as Bunny and others believe their luck would change if only the Pope were to glance at them. At the close of the play, the Pope's voice is heard on television uttering homilies and banalities from Yankee Stadium.

If the lower-middle classes are satirized in *Leaves*, so too is the upper bourgeoisie in *Six Degrees of Separation* (1990). And like their counterparts in *Leaves*, the main characters so deceive themselves in their smugly "enlightened" class attitudes that when a transformative experience comes, only one of them awakens to its possibilities. The experience comes in the person of a young Negro confidence man, Paul, who intrudes himself into several of their homes, representing himself as the son of the film actor Sidney Poitier. His tale is always the same: he has unaccountably lost all his savings and is awaiting his father's arrival at a New York hotel. The principals, who undoubtedly like to think of themselves as being generously liberal, invite him into their homes but later discover he has violated their hospitality by stealing small objects — or, in one case, taking a male hustler to bed with him.

Very nearly all the young people in the play — students at elite colleges — are depicted less sympathetically than one might expect. They are spoiled, querulous, self-righteous, and of course insecurely alienated from their parents, whom they regard as hopelessly out of touch with the real world. Nonetheless, Paul's deceptions have genuinely injured several people, some far worse than others (there is even a reported suicide), and everyone's outrage is understandable. Yet what nearly all lack is an imaginative empathy for Paul, a capacity to reach beyond their own privileged selves to discover other lives, which after all is what Paul has done.

At the curtain's rise, a Kandinsky painting revolves high above the stage. On one side the forms are geometric, suggesting reason and somber analytic consciousness. The other side is "wild and vivid." As the play progresses, we are given to understand that, like the painting, human nature consists of both reason and in its most comprehensive sense the structureless libido or unconscious. Paul has perhaps indulged too much of the latter at the expense of the former, but he has at least penetrated to other worlds. Only one character, Ouisa, comes to realize what Paul has really been up to — and in the course of her understanding comes to better know herself. At one point her husband, an art dealer, tells the audience, "Cezanne would leave blank spaces in his canvases if he couldn't account for the brush stroke, give a reason for the color." To which Ouisa replies, "Then I am a collage of unaccounted-for brush strokes. I am all random." Ouisa's awakened self-knowledge may now allow her to extend herself beyond herself, to touch others, indeed to touch the entire world. Earlier in the play, she ruminates: "I read somewhere that everybody on this planet is separated by only six other people. Six degrees of separation. Between us and everybody else on the planet ... It's a profound thought ... how every person is a new door opening up into another world. Six degrees of separation between me and everyone else on this planet."

Both Guare's plays ring with disparate fragments of New York life. What they convey is that no man or woman is an island, that extremes of individualism deemed so essential to American freedoms may also in the end isolate us from our fellow human beings and our humanity. Guare's themes are not, of course, spelled out overtly but instead are rather effectively played as farce (*Leaves*) or in a kind of dreamlike mode (*Separation*) where time is collapsed and expanded at will and characters step in and out of confrontations with one another to address the audience directly.

Perhaps none of the plays we have considered thus far are so flagrantly New York as those of Herb Gardner. Gardner's works, so popular with New York audiences, have not always met with critical success. Are they simply middlebrow, sentimental, and too obvious? Do they make New Yorkers "feel good"? So much depends on what one is looking for. To be sure, on the whole they are well made plays (accessible, no tricks or stage illusions, nothing experimental to speak of) which in their transparency may bruise sophisticated sensibilities. In reality they are not as optimistic as some critics tend to believe — and yet they are not without hope, which may best describe New Yorkers' attitudes during the latter years of the century. As in so many of the plays we have looked at, they take up issues of individualism in an atmosphere of social pressures to conform. They breathe at least the wish to trust and act on one's best instincts despite consequences. In that sense Gardner's New York plays have come nearly full circle in embracing frontier dreams of freedom and renewal.

The first of Gardner's Broadway successes, *A Thousand Clowns* (1962), was produced when he was only twenty-three. A comedic *cri de coeur* for the old individualism, its central character is a child-hating children's television writer who has quit his job because he can no longer abide the mindless drivel he had been daily spewing out (his show is called "Chuckles the Chipmunk"). Unfortunately for Murray, the social worker bureaucracy descends on his apartment, pressing him to return to his job or give up his twelve-year-old ward, Nick, his orphaned nephew. Murray's untidy and unconventional living quarters and his defiance of the bureaucracy's notions of a proper adolescent upbringing aggravate the case against him. Eventually Murray surrenders — he will resume his television career — but not before he seduces Sandra, one of the social workers who had called on him. He may even marry her although it is not altogether clear that young Nick will in the future enjoy the fruits of a "wholesome" family life. One hopes not.

Murray, Nick, and several of the protagonists of Gardner's other comedies like to imagine themselves as persons they are not. As role players they free themselves from any fixed characterizations the world would otherwise impose on them. Although the plethora of New York personae may become an existential nightmare for others, especially African Americans (see chapter 3, "Black Manhattan"), for Gardner a variety of identities is devoutly to be wished. If Gardner and Guare have anything in common, it is the celebration of the liberating imagination as a means of entering other lives.

A case in point is Gardner's popular Broadway comedy *I'm Not Rappaport* (1985), successfully revived sixteen years later. The action, such as it is, centers mainly on the verbal exchanges of two elderly men who sit on Central Park benches. One is Midge, a near-blind black man, fearful of losing his job as superintendent of a nearby apartment building. His new companion, Nat, a Jewish ex-communist, is still feisty and garrulous, and, above all, given to pretending to fantasy identities and past romantic heroics. Midge more than once expresses exasperation at what he calls Nat's "lies," but Nat's lies serve, temporarily at least, to stave off intruders — among them the landlord who wants to fire Midge; Nat's daughter who wants to put him in a safe retirement home; a young thug who extorts protection money; and a dangerous drug dealer named Cowboy (again the fallen western hero!) who threatens violence. Although Midge and Nat are not always successful, they nonetheless emerge from these encounters as unbowed survivors.

The theme of the play lies in its title, an old Willy Howard vaudeville routine extolling flowing identities that segue into laughter and absurdities. Nat and Midge act out the skit. Theirs is a playful independence of spirit freed from the dismal realities of their circumstances:

NAT: Hello Rappaport!

MIDGE: I'm not Rappaport.

NAT: Hey, Rappaport, what happened to you? You used to be a tall fat guy; now you're a short skinny guy.

MIDGE: I'm not Rappaport.

NAT: You used to be young fellah with a beard; now you're an old guy without a beard! What happened to you?

MIDGE: I'm not Rappaport.

NAT: What happened, Rappaport? You used to dress up nice; now you got old dirty clothes.

MIDGE: I'm not Rappaport.

NAT: And you changed your name too!

An earlier play, *The Goodbye People* (1968, revised version 1979), may be Gardner's most imaginative. The play's two acts are set on a part of the board-walk and beach on Coney Island. Other props consist of a stairway leading down to the beach, two battered phone booths, and an ancient boarded up refreshment stand. Each of the acts opens around dawn on cold February mornings and the audience sits on an imagined shoreline facing a sloping beach. The bareness of the stage suggests both a Beckett-like wasteland and paradoxically the beginnings of creation, which in fact is what the play is about. *The Goodbye People* is aptly named because it tells of three people who meet accidentally to say goodbye to their past sterile lives and start anew to build for themselves the lives they had always dreamed of having. Everybody in the busy worlds they have left behind tells them that what they are about to undertake is crazily impractical — and two of the principals are indeed fearful of what lies ahead.

The strongest of the three is Max Silverman, a seventy-four-year-old man on the brink of a second heart attack, intent on reconstructing the beach-front refreshment store, "Max's Hawaiian Ecstasies," he had abandoned years before. His principal financial backer will turn out to be Arthur Korman, another early morning visitor to the beach, who longs to give up his well-paying job sculpting elves in a Santa Claus factory. Arthur has been coming to Coney Island for several days to observe the sunrise but always falls asleep moments before dawn. The birth of a new day has been eluding him both literally and figuratively. The third character is Max's unhappy promiscuous actress daughter, Nancy, who despite dependence upon a psychiatrist remains unmoored and angst-ridden.

Max is the most unrelenting in recovering his lost paradise. His bound-less energy and earthy Jewish humor ultimately persuade the other two to join him in literally putting together a new wood structure for reopening his business. By so committing themselves, they liberate themselves. Work is well under way when Max is stricken with what looks to be a mortal heart attack:

ARTHUR: *(Kneels next to him on step)* Max, what should I do, I —
MAX: I don't know. I never died before.
ARTHUR: *(His arm around* Max*)* Oh, my God ...
MAX: Look at you. If I don't hurry, you'll beat me to it.

In the distance a rousing Dixieland band is heard. Max had hired them to celebrate the rebirth of Hawaiian Ecstasies — and at the curtain's fall, Nancy and Arthur are left to carry out Max's mad and "hopeless" dream.

Here is the paradox. Max is as much a model of the romanticized western hero as he is a peculiar idiosyncratic New Yorker. He is courageous, unconventional, and an individualist, a reborn lone ranger on the sands of Coney Island staving off the deadening forces of conformity and dreary good sense. Elaine May, who had once directed the play, would agree. In an "Introduction" she writes that she first reacted to it as "an intensely Jewish play about New Yorkers on Coney Island," but afterwards changed her mind. It is "a quintessential play about America, about discounting the odds, about having hope without evidence ... about thumbing your nose at death with dignity, and in fact thumbing your nose at dignity. It is about the tough, unregenerate, screw-you exhilaration of the Old West, still alive and doing business in Coney Island."

Well, yes — but we know that the long-ago expansive western spirit was long ago realized. The West was won. With Gardner we cannot be quite sure. His heroic old men, Max, Midge, Nat, may resemble less America's fearless frontiersmen than their noble mythic Indian counterparts. Like the last of the Mohicans, they may be the last of a dying breed.

Epilogue:
September 11, 2001

A few of these chapters were written around the time of the terrorist attacks on New York City's World Trade Center, and although today's hindsight cannot alter the past it does perhaps reveal our present strengths and weaknesses. As already noted, myths are ahistorical. If they arise as a projection of our anxieties, needs, and desires at historic moments, they nonetheless persist generation after generation long after the conditions that created them have passed. Put another way, they remain a part of how we identify ourselves and understand our experiences. Thus, like it or not, New York myths and dreams linger as the stuff of American realities. Despite the calamities of September 11, myths of the city live on as immortal, much like rays from the sun, impervious to the destruction below.

But what do they tell us? Writers interpret and reinterpret city myths in accordance with their own orientation, their own experiences. None speak of utter triumph, some of near defeat. A few (though not discussed in this book), like Hugh Selby, Jr., Richard Price, or Bret Easton Ellis, return the city to a nineteenth-century version of urban hell. A case could be made, of course, that some of the works included in this book also reach for lower depths. Regardless of that fact, wherever we look, we find gradations of shadow. Immigrants, as we have seen, even while basking in the exhilaration of new liberties, express now and then a hollowness of heart, a sort of melancholy for the loss of old customs that had helped sustain them in other places, harsher times. For African Americans, New York's bewildering array of seemingly new identities (often devoid of underlying authenticity) may feel as oppressive as a caste system they had hoped they escaped. But for all her tiers of darkness, New York has always retained a kind of hypnotic allure. Even turn-of-the-century aristocrats, like Henry James and Edith Wharton, who fled the city's "barbaric yawp" would themselves seek an illusory New York free of crass materialism, aesthetic degradation, and moral decay in the atrophying traditions of European high culture.

Some of the writers we have looked at speak as well of a quasi-metaphysical New York: a New York of stoicism and suffering; a New York as a microcosm of a divided America; a New York as absurd, random, and directionless as that of its enveloping universe. Still, even here, as authors draw on their worst fears, they tell of survivors. Indeed, as creations, whatever their outlook, they are themselves affirmations of life. Hope and endeavor and dreams of renewal also sit at the heart of the New York soul. The Swiss architect Le Corbusier may well have caught something of its spirit. By no means a wholehearted admirer, he wrote of a New York that had "such courage and enthusiasm that everything can be begun again, sent back to the building yard and made something still greater." To be sure, he went on, there were "hours of despair in the violence of the city" but also "hours of enthusiasm, confidence, optimism, in the fairy splendor...." And now, today, the very real physical city — literally built on rock and stone — still draws thousands of artists, writers, the young and aspiring, as well as persons and immigrants from very different parts of the world. Each partakes in his or her own way of the city's aura. Each in no time at all thinks himself a New Yorker. A city of myths has become in its own fashion a myth of itself, a myth of the larger America.

Selected Bibliography

Citations comprise alphabetical listings of novels, and collections of authors' shorter works discussed or alluded to in this study. In many instances other editions are available. First publication dates are usually found in chapters dealing with the authors. The complete writings of some of the better known authors may also be found in Library of America volumes.

Fiction

AUCHINCLOSS, LOUIS

Honorable Men. Boston: Houghton Mifflin, 1967.

Portrait in Brownstone. Boston: Houghton Mifflin, 1962.

The Rector of Justin. Boston: Houghton Mifflin, 1964.

Tales of Manhattan. Boston: Houghton Mifflin, 1967.

Venus in Sparta. Boston: Houghton Mifflin, 1958.

AUSTER, PAUL

The Country of Last Things. New York: Penguin Books, 1988.

Leviathan. New York: Penguin Books, 1993.

The Moon Palace. New York: Viking Press, 1989.

The New York Trilogy. (Contains the novellas *City of Glass, Ghosts,* and *The Locked Room*). New York: Penguin Books, 1999.

BALDWIN, JAMES

Another Country. New York: Dial Press, 1962.

Go Tell It on the Mountain. New York: Knopf, 1953.

Going to Meet the Man. New York: Dial Press, 1965.

Notes of a Native Son. Boston: Beacon Press, 1955.

BELLOW, SAUL

Humboldt's Gift. New York: Viking Press, 1975.

Mr. Sammler's Planet. New York: Viking Press, 1970.

Seize the Day. New York: Viking Press, 1965.

The Victim. New York: Vanguard, 1947.

CAHAN, ABRAHAM

The Imported Bride and Other Stories. New York: Penguin Books, 1966.

The Rise of David Levinsky. New York: Harper & Row, 1960.

CRANE, STEPHEN

Maggie: A Girl of the Streets and Other Tales of New York. (Contains *George's Mother*). New York: Penguin Books, 2000.

The Red Badge of Courage. New York: New American Library, 1960.

DeLillo, Don

Underworld. New York: Scribner's, 1997.

Di Donato, Pietro

Christ in Concrete. New York: New American Library, 1993.

Doctorow, E.L.

World's Fair. New York: Random House, 1985.

Dos Passos, John

Manhattan Transfer. Boston: Houghton Mifflin, 1925.

Dreiser, Theodore

Sister Carrie. New York: New American Library, 1961.

Ellison, Ralph

Invisible Man. New York: Random House, 1952.

Fitzgerald, F. Scott

The Beautiful and Damned. New York: Scribner's, 1922.
The Crack-Up. New York: New Directions, 1945.
The Love of the Last Tycoon. New York: Cambridge University Press, 1993.
Tender Is the Night. New York: Scribner's, 1934.
This Side of Paradise. New York: Scribner's, 1920.
The Stories of F. Scott Fitzgerald. New York: Scribner's, 1956.

Fox, Paula

Desperate Characters. New York: W.W. Norton, 1970.
The Widow's Children. New York: W.W. Norton, 1976.

Fuchs, Daniel

Three Novels by Daniel Fuchs. (Contains *Homage to Blenholt, Low Company,* and *Summer in Williamsburg*). Garden City, New York: Basic Books, 1961.

Gold, Michael

Jews Without Money. New York: Sun Dial Press, 1941.

Hijuelos, Oscar

The Empress of the Splendid Season. New York: HarperCollins, 1999.
The Mambo Kings Play Songs of Love. New York: Harper & Row, 1990.
Our House in the Last World. New York: Persea Books, 1989.

Howells, William Dean

A Hazard of New Fortunes. New York: New American Library, 1965.

James, Henry

The American Scene. New York: Horizon Press, 1961.
The Bostonians. New York: Random House, 1956.
The New York Stories of Henry James. New York: New York Review of Books, 2005.

Johnson, James Weldon

The Autobiography of an Ex-Colored Man (a novel). New York: Hill and Wang, 1960.

Larsen, Nella

Quicksand and *Passing.* New Brunswick, New Jersey: Rutgers University Press, 1986.

Malamud, Bernard

The Complete Stories of Bernard Malamud. New York: Farrar, Straus and Giroux, 1997.
The Tenants. New York: Farrar, Straus and Giroux, 1971.

Marshall, Paule

Brown Girl, Brownstones. New York: The Feminist Press of the City University of New York, 1981.

Ornitz, Samuel

Haunch, Paunch and Jowl. Garden City, New York: Garden City Publishing, 1923.

PETRY, ANN

The Street. Boston: Houghton Mifflin, 1946.

POWELL, DAWN

Dawn Powell at Her Best. (Includes *Turn, Magic Wheel*). South Royalton, VT: Steerforth Press, 1994.
The Golden Spur. South Royalton, VT: Steerforth Press, 1997.
The Happy Island. New York: Farrar and Rinehart, 1938.
The Locusts Have No King. South Royalton, VT: Steerforth Press, 1995.
A Time to Be Born. New York: Scribner's, 1942.
Turn, Magic Wheel. New York: Farrar and Rinehart, 1936.

PUZO, MARIO

The Fortunate Pilgrim. New York: Lancer Books, 1973.

ROTH, HENRY

Call It Sleep. New York: Avon Books, 1964.
A Diving Rock on the Hudson. New York: St. Martin's Press, 1995.
From Bondage. New York: St. Martin's Press, 1996.
A Star Shines Over Mount Morris Park. New York: St. Martin's Press, 1994.

SCHWARTZ, DELMORE

In Dreams Begin Responsibilities and Other Stories. New York: New Directions, 1978.

WEST, NATHANAEL

Miss Lonelyhearts & TheDay of the Locust. New York: New Directions, 1962.

WHARTON, EDITH

The Age of Innocence. New York: D. Appleton, 1920.
Collected Stories, 1891–1915. New York: Library of America, 1998.
The Custom of the Country. New York: Scribner's, 1923.

The House of Mirth. New York: New American Library, 1980.
Novellas and Other Writings. New York: Library of America, 1990.

WOLFE, THOMAS

Look Homeward, Angel. New York: Simon and Schuster, 1995.
Of Time and the River. New York: Scribner's, 1935.
The Web and the Rock. New York: Scribner's, 1939.
You Can't Go Home Again. New York: HarperCollins, 1998.

WOLFE, TOM

The Bonfire of the Vanities. New York: Farrar, Straus and Giroux, 1987.

WRIGHT, RICHARD

The Outsider. New York: Harper and Brothers, 1953.

YEZIERSKA, ANZIA

The Bread Givers. New York: Persea Books, 2003.
Hungry Hearts and Other Stories. New York: Persea Books, 1985.
Salome of the Tenements. Urbana and Chicago: University of Illinois Press, 1995.
Red Ribbon on a White Horse: My Story. New York: Persea Books, 1981.

Theater

In large part the most accessible play scripts may be found in individual playwrights' collections or period anthologies. Play titles are listed alphabetically.

ALBEE, EDWARD

The Zoo Story. In *Famous American Plays of the 1950s.* Selected and introduced by Lee Strasberg. New York: Dell Publishing, 1962.

ALFRED, WILLIAM

Hogan's Goat. In *Famous American Plays of the 1960s.* Selected and introduced by Harold Clurman. New York: Dell Publishing, 1972.

BARRY, PHILIP

Holiday. In *Famous American Plays of the 1920s.* Selected and introduced by Kenneth Macgowan. New York: Dell Publishing, 1959.

CROWLEY, MATT

The Boys in the Band. In *Famous American Plays of the 1960s.* Selected and introduced by Harold Clurman. New York: Dell Publishing, 1972.

FITCH, CLYDE

The City. In *Plays by Clyde Fitch.* Vol. 4. Edited by M.J. Moses and V. Gerson. Boston: Little, Brown, 1930.

GARDNER, HERB

The Collected Plays. (Includes *A Thousand Clowns, The Goodbye People,* and *I'm Not Rappaport*). New York: Applause Books, 2000.

GUARE, JOHN

The House of Blue Leaves. New York: Samuel French, 1968.
Six Degrees of Separation. New York: Dramatists Play Service, 1972.

HOROWITZ, ISRAEL

The Indian Wants the Bronx. In *Famous American Plays of the 1960s.* Selected and introduced by Harold Clurman. New York: Dell Publishing, 1972.

JONES, LEROI

Dutchman and *The Slave.* New York: William Morrow, 1964.

MILLER, ARTHUR

Death of a Salesman. New York: Dramatists Play Service, 1982.

MITCHELL, LANGDON

The New York Idea. In *Representative Plays by American Dramatists.* Vol. 3. Edited by Montrose J. Moses. New York: Benjamin Blom, 1964.

ODETS, CLIFFORD

Awake and Sing. In *Waiting for Lefty and Other Plays.* New York: Grove/Atlantic, 1994.

O'NEILL, EUGENE

All God's Chillun Got Wings. In *Nine Plays by Eugene O'Neill.* (Includes *The Hairy Ape.*) New York: Random House, 1932.
Anna Christie. In *Complete Plays 1913–1921.* New York: Library of America, 1988.
The Iceman Cometh. New York: Random House, 1999.

RICE, ELMER

Street Scene. In *Seven Plays.* New York: Viking Press, 1950.

SHELDON, EDWARD

The Nigger: An American Play in Three Acts. New York: Macmillan, 1915.

WALTER, EUGENE

The Easiest Way. In *Representative Plays by American Dramatists.* Vol. 3. Edited by Montrose J. Moses. New York: Benjamin Blom, 1964.

Biographies

In treating authors' New York City experiences, several biographies are useful. The following are among the best of these.

On JAMES BALDWIN:

Campbell, James. *Talking at the Gates: A Life of James Baldwin.* New York: Viking Press, 1991.

Selected Bibliography

On SAUL BELLOW:

Atlas, James. *Bellow: A Biography.* New York: Modern Library, 2002.

On STEPHEN CRANE:

Stallman, R.W. *Stephen Crane: A Biography.* New York: George Braziller, 1968.

On THEODORE DREISER:

Lingeman, Richard. *Theodore Dreiser: At the Gates of the City, 1871–1907.* Vol. 1. New York: Putnam's, 1986.

On F. SCOTT FITZGERALD:

Mizener, Arthur. *The Far Side of Paradise: A Biography of F. Scott Fitzgerald.* New York: Avon Books, 1974.

On HENRY JAMES:

Kaplan, Fred. *Henry James: The Imagination of Genius.* New York: William Morrow, 1992.

On JAMES WELDON JOHNSON:

Johnson, James Weldon. *Along This Way* (autobiography). New York: Viking, 1968.

On EUGENE O'NEILL:

Alexander, Doris. *Eugene O'Neill's Last Plays: Separating Art from Autobiography.* Athens: The University of Georgia Press, 2005.

On DAWN POWELL:

Page, Tim. *Dawn Powell: A Biography.* New York: Henry Holt, 1995.

On HENRY ROTH:

Kellman, Steven G. *Redemption: The Life of Henry Roth.* New York: W.W. Norton, 2005.

On DELMORE SCHWARTZ:

Atlas, James. *Delmore Schwartz: The Life of an American Poet.* New York: Farrar, Straus and Giroux, 1997.

On NATHANAEL WEST:

Martin, Jay. *Nathanael West: The Art of His Life.* New York: Farrar, Straus and Giroux, 1970.

On EDITH WHARTON:

Lewis, R.W.B. *Edith Wharton: A Biography.* New York: Harper & Row, 1975.

On RICHARD WRIGHT:

Rowley, Hazel. *Richard Wright: The Life and Times.* Henry Holt, 2001.

Index

193

Index

Index

Index